The ABCs of Classic Hollywood

The **A** **B** **C** **s** of Classic Hollywood

Robert B. Ray

UNIVERSITY PRESS

2008

OXFORD
UNIVERSITY PRESS

Oxford University Press, Inc., publishes works that further
Oxford University's objective of excellence
in research, scholarship, and education.

Oxford   New York
Auckland   Cape Town   Dar es Salaam   Hong Kong   Karachi
Kuala Lumpur   Madrid   Melbourne   Mexico City   Nairobi
New Delhi   Shanghai   Taipei   Toronto

With offices in
Argentina   Austria   Brazil   Chile   Czech Republic   France   Greece
Guatemala   Hungary   Italy   Japan   Poland   Portugal   Singapore
South Korea   Switzerland   Thailand   Turkey   Ukraine   Vietnam

Published by Oxford University Press, Inc.
198 Madison Avenue, New York, New York 10016

www.oup.com

Oxford is a registered trademark of Oxford University Press

Library of Congress Cataloging-in-Publication Data
Ray, Robert B. (Robert Beverley), 1943–
The ABCs of classic Hollywood / by Robert B. Ray.
p. cm.
ISBN 978-0-19-532291-0; 978-0-19-532292-7 (pbk.)
1. Motion pictures—United States.   I. Title.
PN1993.5.U6R377 2007
791.430973—dc22   2006038592

9 8 7 6 5 4 3 2 1

Printed in the United States of America
on acid-free paper

In memory of

William D. Evans, Jr.

and

John D. Martin III

Acknowledgments

Walter Benjamin's *Arcades Project* notebook contains the following entry:

> These notes, which deal with the Paris arcades, were begun under the open sky—a cloudless blue which arced over the foliage—and yet are covered with centuries of dust from millions of leaves; through them blew the fresh breeze of diligence, the measured breath of the researcher, the squalls of youthful zeal, and the idle gusts of curiosity. For, looking down from arcades in the reading room of the Paris National Library, the painted summer sky stretched over them its dreamy, lightless ceiling.

While matching Benjamin's lyricism would prove difficult, I can say that *The ABCs of Classic Hollywood* began in the hot July and August of 1993 when my older daughter, Margaret, played the role of Tootie in a local theater's production of *Meet Me in St. Louis*, the favorite movie of my younger daughter, Eleanor. Seeing the same show night after night over a six-week run, and comparing it repeatedly to the film, confirmed Roland Barthes's insistence on the rewards of rereading (see *S/Z*). Doing so also suggested how each of a movie's details might be made to open up into what Reuben Brower once called (citing Henry James) "the fields of light," that space where reading turns from interpretation into the kind of work that Benjamin also described: "Say something about the method of composition itself: how everything that comes to mind has at all costs to be incorporated into the work one is doing at the time."

In my own case, "everything that comes to mind" has had a lot to do with the teachers and colleagues who have continually provided me with models for my own work: Dudley Andrew, Noël Burch, Thomas Childers, Christian Keathley, James Naremore,

Gregory Ulmer, and Peter Wollen. My thanks go to them, and to Margaret and Eleanor Ray for their original inspiration.

I am grateful to Adam Nikolaidis, who produced the book's frame enlargements, and to Craig Cieslikowski, who did emergency work to help me correct the image-text inconsistencies detected by Oxford's exceptionally alert production editor, Stacey Hamilton. I also especially want to thank Oxford's Shannon McLachlan, who provided me with more useful editorial suggestions than any editor I have ever had.

Finally, in this case, moving from concept to execution involved the effort of all the students who took an *ABCs* class from me and contributed to what has become this book. As I say in the introduction, I could not have written it without them.

Contents

Introduction

1. The Hidden Things: An Image, a Story, and a Project

Speaking about the kind of filmmaking now known as classic Hollywood, the most popular and influential cinema ever invented, Vincente Minnelli once gave away its secret: "I feel that a picture that stays with you is made up of a hundred or more hidden things. They're things that the audience is not conscious of, but that accumulate."[1] How would we go about finding those things? What method would enable us to retrieve them and, by doing so, to understand better how Hollywood films got made? This book attempts to answer those questions by looking closely at four movies from classic Hollywood, the 1930–1945 period when the American studio system had reached the peak of its economic power and cultural influence. In an ideal world, I would provide two simultaneous introductions, one justifying the choice of subject matter (why *these* four films?), another explaining the method of study (why the discrete, alphabetized entries?). The spirit of what follows, however, suggests that even this introduction should issue from a specific cinematic detail.

Thus, I will say that this book began for me with a single image from *Grand Hotel*, that ghostly MGM antique, winner of the 1932 Academy Award for Best Picture. To the extent that it is remembered at all, *Grand Hotel* survives as the source of Greta Garbo's defining line, "I want to be alone," spoken with utter desolation and weariness by her character, the fading ballerina Grusinskaya, returning to her hotel room after yet another aborted performance. The next moments, however, interest me more. Having dismissed the hotel's housekeepers and her own attendant, Grusinskaya goes to the window, where a night breeze stirs the curtains. She closes the window and draws the heavy drapes, thinking she has achieved the privacy she needs to take her own life. In fact, she is not alone; an aristocratic jewel thief (John

Barrymore), surprised by her unexpected arrival, watches from a closet. As Grusinskaya sits on the floor to remove her costume, the movie provides us with this shot:

    In the midst of *Grand Hotel*'s creaky melodrama and steamy overacting, this image—mysterious, beautiful, unmoored from any character's perspective, narratively unnecessary—offers a challenge: what can we say that will do it justice? The movies, of course, are full of such moments, and the discipline of film studies arose, at least in part, to explain them. That task has proved more difficult than it once appeared: "[T]he movies are difficult to explain," Christian Metz once admitted in his famous epigram, "because they are easy to understand." For Metz, explanation would ultimately involve calling the cinema to an ideological accounting, but film's enormous appeal led him to an impasse expressed as a renunciation. "To be a theoretician of the cinema," Metz concluded, "one should ideally no longer love the cinema."[2]

    Despite its austerity, Metz's position has dominated film studies since the early 1970s. Each of a discipline's most significant movements thinks it has got things right. But since intellectual fashions can change justlikethat (as e. e. cummings put it), film scholars might do well to post above their desks this warning from Wallace Stevens: "Little of what we have believed has been true. Only the prophecies are true." Almost seventy years ago, Walter

Benjamin made one such prophecy, as he struggled to devise a means of writing that would work as powerfully as the movies:

> *Uprising of the anecdotes. . . . The constructions of history are comparable to instructions that commandeer the true life and confine it to barracks. On the other hand: the street insurgence of the anecdote. The anecdote brings things near to us spatially, lets them enter our life. It represents the strict antithesis to the sort of history . . . which makes everything abstract.*[3]

Here is what Benjamin might have called a "dialectical anecdote" about the cinema, one I happened upon while writing a book on the Andy Hardy series. One morning in 1933, MGM story editor Samuel Marx arrived at his office to find scriptwriter F. Hugh Herbert waiting for him. Herbert had worked in Hollywood since the silent days and loved MGM so much that he had been married in a church *set* on the studio's back lot; but with the coming of sound, his career had waned, and although still on salary, he was used less often. Marx tried to brush him off, but Herbert said that Irving Thalberg himself had told him to come for an assignment.

"When did Thalberg say that?" Marx asked skeptically.

"Last night. He dropped in to see me at my house."

Convinced Herbert was inventing an excuse, Marx persisted: "How was he dressed?"

"In a tuxedo."

"And does he usually dress like that when he drops in on you?"

Admitting that Thalberg had never paid him a visit before, Herbert nevertheless insisted that Irving had come calling around 10 o'clock the previous night and that, after drinking some brandy, had asked whether Herbert was working. Told that he wasn't, Thalberg suggested he go to Marx for an assignment. "When I woke up the next morning," Herbert confessed, "I thought I had dreamt it, so I went downstairs and there was the brandy bottle, with two glasses on the dining room table." Still incredulous, Marx saw Thalberg later that day and asked him about Herbert's story, which, surprisingly, Thalberg confirmed:

"I went to see someone who lives on the same street, but I rang the wrong doorbell. He asked me in, and I couldn't refuse."

"It seemed odd," Marx remembered, "he didn't explain what had happened and go on to his planned destination."

"Hughie's not a bad writer," Thalberg added. "See if you can find something for him." Marx bought a story from Herbert that became a B-movie, *Women in His Life*, the first picture at MGM for George B. Seitz, the director of the Andy Hardy series that made Mickey Rooney the leading box office attraction from 1939 through 1941.[4]

The anecdote's contradictory elements seem almost allegorical: an abandoned party, implied but not described; a Fitzgeraldian Hollywood night long ago; filmmaking's supreme rationalizer, lost on a suddenly strange street; a chance encounter, prolonged out of politeness; a coincidence leading to a new routine of perfectly planned serial production. When, inspired by the movies, Walter Benjamin proposed a historical method based on such images, Theodor Adorno could only reply: "Your study is located at the crossroads of magic and positivism. That spot is bewitched. Only theory could break the spell."[5]

Adorno meant to be dismissive. In fact, he had produced the perfect definition of the cinema ("the crossroads of magic and positivism") and of film studies' traditional project (to "break the spell"). In the 1920s, the surrealists and French impressionists focused almost exclusively on magic, offering the idea of *photogénie* as the essence of cinema. After May 1968, magic became the problem, the source of the movies' ideological menace. Thus, breaking the spell became film studies' object, a goal explicitly announced by Laura Mulvey in her brilliant "Visual Pleasure and the Narrative Cinema," the 1975 *Screen* essay that became the breviary for two decades of theory. "It is said that analyzing pleasure, or beauty, destroys it," Mulvey wrote. "That is the intention of this article."[6]

The anecdote about Thalberg, however, suggests that film studies errs whenever it forgets either of the cinema's two elements. If surrealism settled for mystification, *Screen* theory often ignored the reasons why people went to the movies in the first place. Where do we go from here? In his study of imperialist terror, *Shamanism, Colonialism, and the Wild Man*, Michael Taussig suggests that the task of understanding "calls neither for demystification nor remystification but for a quite different poetics of destruction and revelation":

> *Conrad's way of dealing with the terror of the rubber boom in the congo was* Heart of Darkness. *There were three realities there, comments Frederick Karl: King Leopold's, made out of intricate disguises and deceptions, Roger Casement's studied realism [in his official government-sponsored reports], and Conrad's, which, to quote Karl, "fell midway between the other two, as he attempted to penetrate the veil and yet was anxious to retain its hallucinatory quality." This formulation is sharp and important:* to penetrate the veil while retaining its hallucinatory quality.[7]

Here, then, is the proposition: the goal of this book is to penetrate the movies' veil while retaining their hallucinatory quality. The project is to invent a method that will achieve this balance.

2. A Method: How to Ignore Lady Brackenstall's Story

What method can accommodate *Grand Hotel*'s arresting image of Greta Garbo? How can we both "explain" this shot and convey its appeal? "If I am thinking about a topic just for myself," Wittgenstein once confessed, "I jump about all round it; that is

the only way of thinking that comes naturally to me."[8] As I began
to think about how I might apply Taussig's formulation to film
studies, I found myself unconsciously adopting Wittgenstein's
restlessness, with my only guides a few stray remarks, existing at
the margins of famous texts, implying without detailing a
different, emerging methodology:

> The eternal would be the ruffles on a dress rather than
> an idea. (Walter Benjamin)[9]

> It has long been an axiom of mine that the little things
> are infinitely the most important. (Sherlock Holmes)[10]

> To someone looking through piles of old letters, a
> stamp that has long been out of circulation on a torn
> envelope often says more than a reading of dozens of
> pages. (Benjamin)[11]

> The Lacanian subject (for instance) never makes him
> think of Tokyo; but Tokyo makes him think of the
> Lacanian subject. This procedure is a constant one: he
> rarely starts from the idea in order to invent an image
> for it subsequently; he starts from a sensuous object,
> and then hopes to meet in his work with the possibility
> of finding an *abstraction* for it, levied on the intellectual
> culture of the moment: philosophy then is no more
> than a reservoir of particular images, of ideal fictions
> (he borrows objects, not reasonings). (Roland Barthes)[12]

> The perspicuous presentation makes possible that
> understanding that consists just in the fact that we
> "see the connections." (Ludwig Wittgenstein)[13]

> When he comes up with a treatise "on" the Text (for
> an encyclopedia), without denying it (never deny
> anything: in the name of what present?), it is a labor
> of knowledge, not of writing. (Barthes)[14]

I approach deep problems like cold baths: quickly into them and quickly out again. (Friedrich Nietzsche)[15]

With intellectual things, we produce simultaneously theory, critical combat, and pleasure; we subject the objects of knowledge and discussion—as in any art— no longer to an instance of truth, but to a consideration of *effects*. (Barthes)[16]

The "reasoning" consists, in short, of a series of metaphors: he takes a phenomenon (connotation, the letter *Z*) and he submits it to an avalanche of points of view; what replaces argumentation is the unfolding of an image. . . . One might call "poetic" (without value judgment) any discourse in which the word leads the idea. (Barthes)[17]

I think I summed up my attitude toward philosophy when I said: philosophy ought really to be written as a *poetic composition*. (Wittgenstein)[18]

Let us not underrate the value of a fact; it will one day flower in a truth. (Henry David Thoreau)[19]

Even collectively, these epigrams do not articulate a method. And yet, in Wittgenstein's terms, they seem connected by a family resemblance. The faith in concrete details' capacity to animate theoretical speculation; a poetic approach to critical writing; the taste for fragments and speed; a mild suspicion of abstractions— these dispositions converge to imply a way of working different from that of traditional film studies.

Wittgenstein himself once proposed that "a man's philosophy is a matter of . . . a preference for certain similes."[20] As I began work on this book, one simile immediately occurred to me: every object in classic Hollywood cinema resembles a computer icon, storing menus of information that can be explicitly activated.

Touch *Casablanca*'s refugee trail map, for example, and you can retrieve, among other things, the story of Walter Benjamin, who took the same road to escape the Nazis but never reached Spain. While much contemporary film criticism proceeds allegorically, casting about for cinematic examples that will confirm (by giving flesh to) general propositions, I want to take up Eisenstein's admonition that "film is not to be simply seen and heard but *scrutinized* and closely listened to, *studied* by eye and ear alike." Citing that passage, Barthes suggested that such "interrogative readings" should begin with an image's details. Why?[21]

One answer to that question appears in historian Carlo Ginzburg's *Clues, Myths, and the Historical Method*, which argues for a "semiotic epistemology" practiced by Freud, Sherlock Holmes, and physicians. Starting from a case's smallest, apparently irrelevant details, this approach drew Ginzburg to history in the first place:

> I didn't even consider history because I found it so boring. What changed my mind was a seminar in which [I] was asked to spend an entire week analyzing only ten lines of a book written by a leading 19th-century historian.
>
> It was the slowness that fascinated me. Every phrase, every word had to be dissected for their possible implications. I came to understand that texts can have hidden, invisible meanings. It was not an easy lesson. In my speech, my writing, my judgments about people, I tend to be very quick. I learned the importance of reading and rereading one page, even a single passage, for days, weeks.[22]

I must admit that I also tend to be "very quick," and thus, this method, with its painstaking reliance on what Ginzburg calls *clues*, at first seemed forbidding. I pursued it, however, by teaching an entire 14-week course on just the four movies studied in this book. The result resembled what Ginzburg calls "squeezing the evidence," and as an approach, it proved exhilarating. Far from wearing out the films under investigation, the intense scrutiny enhanced both my own and my students' interest in them. In fact, as I wrote this book, I found myself reluctant to move on when I had finished each chapter; each movie I had been studying seemed, in its turn, the richest and most entertaining of the group. (Since I took them up in chronological order, *Meet Me in St. Louis* now seems to me the greatest movie of all time.)

Literary study, of course, offers ready examples of squeezing the evidence. In *S/Z*, a line-by-line analysis of Balzac's novella *Sarrasine*, Barthes began by dividing his object of study into brief passages, some no more than a few words. These *lexia*, as he termed them, enabled "a *slow motion* reading" that revealed associations made imperceptible by a narrative's headlong rush. Thus, from Balzac's simple statement *Midnight had just sounded from the clock of the Elysée-Bourbon*, Barthes could infer *wealth*, "since the Faubourg Saint-Honoré is a wealthy neighborhood." As Barthes saw, Balzac's detail implied further particulars, presumably activated by contemporary French readers: "This wealth is itself connoted: a neighborhood of *nouveaux riches*, the Faubourg Saint-Honoré refers by synecdoche to the Paris of the Bourbon restoration, a mythic place of sudden fortunes whose origins are suspect." Barthes insisted that such lexia, however arbitrary, would prove "the best possible space in which we can observe meanings."[23]

In *S/Z*, he used these entry points not only to unpack Balzac's details, but also to take up larger issues about storytelling. His simile "a *slow motion* reading" came, of course, from the cinema, and the connection is acute. Filmmaking proceeds by unruly, discontinuous fragments, disciplined into ex post facto sequences by parsing editors. This fact, which Hollywood cinema has always worked to conceal, suggests that to match its object of study, film analysis should itself *begin with the details*, the isolated objects and moments potentially obscured by a movie's inexorable momentum. This approach, like Barthes's in *S/Z*, would involve an initial resistance to narrative and a fetishistic reliance on details. However exotic that strategy may seem, it simply corresponds to the way most movies get made. Minnelli's "hidden things," after all, were the result of painstaking attention to *everything*, including what might appear as minutiae. "He took enormous—and to some fellow-participants, sometimes infuriating—trouble composing the frames," Gerald Kaufman wrote of Minnelli. "A former window-dresser, he regarded the apt placement of almost unobtrusive objects as essential. One daily report of the filming recorded, '3.20–3.26 Wait for perfume bottle (special container with satin lining asked for by director).'"[24]

In some ways, André Bazin offered a model for moving from detail to theory. The romantic force of his writing almost always began in reverent enthusiasm for particulars. Typically, his review of Jean Renoir's *Boudu Saved from Drowning* finds its emotional climax in the celebration of a scene:

> The last scenes from Boudu *could serve as the epigraph to all of Renoir's French work. Boudu, nearly wed, throws himself into the water. . . . When he comes up on the bank, an extraordinary slow 360-degree pan shows us the countryside. . . . At the end of the pan, the camera picks up a bit of grass where, in close-up, one can see distinctly the white dust that the heat and the wind have lifted from the path. One can almost feel it between one's fingers. Boudu is going to stir it up with his foot. If I were deprived of the pleasure of seeing* Boudu *again for the rest of my days, I would never forget that grass, that dust, and their relationship to the liberty of a tramp.*[25]

The surrealists and French impressionists would have stopped there; Truffaut and Godard would have used this scene for connoisseurship purposes, the attribution of its power to a director and the ranking of that director in a hierarchy of taste. Distrustful of *la politique des auteurs*, Bazin had other aims. *Boudu*'s grass and dust were, of course, the signs of Renoir, Bazin's favorite director, but "Renoir" was a name for what Bazin referred to as

the cinema's "ontology," its privileged relationship to a reality
trembling with potential revelation.

In one sense, therefore, Bazin demonstrated how to move
between cinematic details and grand theory. In his work, ideas
have what Barthes called "a *flush of pleasure*," as if the poetic and
conceptual registers had merged.[26] But Bazin's commitment to
one view of the cinema encouraged him to deploy even the scenes
that enchanted him as *evidence* of his one big idea. Certainly, that
idea had emerged from details like *Boudu*'s dust and grass, but
once he had formulated it, Bazin brought it with him to every
movie theater he entered. Inevitably, he became like Oscar Wilde's
image of Wordsworth, finding under rocks and stones the
sermons he had hidden there.

Here is a story about that problem. Summoned to Kent on a
wintry morning by a rural colleague's urgent message, Sherlock
Holmes and Dr. Watson arrive at the Abbey Grange, a sprawling
neoclassical country estate, whose owner, Sir Eustace Brackenstall,
has been murdered. Their correspondent, Inspector Stanley
Hopkins, greets them with an apology: "I should not have troubled
you, for since the lady has come to herself she has given so clear an
account of the affair that there is not much left for us to do. . . . I
think you had best see her and hear her account of the facts. Then
we will examine the dining-room together." Lady Brackenstall, the
beautiful young widow, recounts for Holmes the fatal events:
making a final round of the downstairs before retiring, she had felt
the wind on her face as she passed the curtained French door
leading to the lawn. Flinging the curtain aside to reach the window,
she had found herself face to face with an intruder. She had lifted
her candle slightly and seen two more men behind the first. The first
robber had struck her over the eye, briefly rendering her unconscious. When she came to, she had found herself gagged and
bound, with the room's bell rope, to a large oaken chair. From that
position, she had watched helplessly as her husband, awakened by
the noise, was beaten to death as he arrived to help her. To steady
their nerves, the three men had each drunk a glass of wine before

departing, taking with them a half dozen silver plates from the sideboard.

The dining room itself corroborates Lady Brackenstall's story: the French door, the oaken chair, the knotted bell rope, the three wine glasses, the body of Sir Eustace all confirm the prior account. Complaining that his "special knowledge and special powers" predispose him to a more "complex solution" than the simple one at hand, Holmes can only resign himself to accepting that this problem will yield to routine police work: find the robbers, solve the crime. He and Watson will have to go home.

And then the abrupt turn, so characteristic of the Holmes stories. Suddenly, as their return train is about to depart from a suburban station, Holmes pulls Watson out onto the platform:

> I am sorry to make you the victim of what may seem a mere whim, but on my life, Watson, I simply can't leave that case in this condition. Every instinct that I possess cries out against it. It's wrong—it's all wrong—I'll swear that it's wrong. And yet the lady's story was complete, the maid's corroboration was sufficient, the detail was fairly exact. What do I have to put up against that? Three wine glasses, that is all. But if I had not taken things for granted, if I had examined everything with the care which I would have shown had we approached the case de novo and had no cut-and-dried story to warp my mind, would I not then have found something more definite to go upon? Of course I should.[27]

Holmes's moral, so closely resembling Freud's recommendation to psychoanalysts ("not directing one's notice to anything in particular and . . . maintaining the same 'evenly-suspended attention'"), is, of course, a brief against deductive logic. It is also a lesson about how to read a scene. In effect, contemporary film studies has often approached movies with the equivalents of Lady Brackenstall's story, ready explanations that obscure the actual facts. But although subject to classification, films and crimes are specific, idiosyncratic, unpredictable. Like the Abbey Grange's French windows, their particulars offer too many escape routes. In Siegfried Kracauer's words, cinematic details reveal "the *provisional* status of all given configurations." To respond to them, we need a more unpredictable way of working.[28]

I found one method in the assignment I gave my students:

Working with one of the four course films, produce a text of 26 entries, one for each letter of the alphabet. Each entry must start with a detail from the movie you have chosen (e.g., U = umbrella, B = ballerina). The best entries will use details that you find especially intriguing or enigmatic to do the following:

- first, generate knowledge about the movie at hand;

- second, speculate about classic Hollywood film-making;

- third, reflect on the cinema in general.

Every entry does not have to contain all three levels, but you should worry if you never get beyond the first step, which will often simply amount to thematics.

Avoid initiating entries with ideas imposed on the film (e.g., "intolerance," "unhappiness," "the male gaze"). Regard such abstractions as "Lady Brackenstall's story"; they will inhibit your own discoveries.

For *The Avant-Garde Finds Andy Hardy*, I had written a chapter that roughly followed these directions, although I had not yet realized the advantage of avoiding such generalized starting points as "life imitates art," "*mise-en-abyme*," "opacity," and "thesis." When I began to teach this approach, I quickly discovered how insidiously tempting such terms can be. At this stage, almost every advanced undergraduate film student arrives with a rich vocabulary of fashionable (and often useful) critical terms. Although Walter Benjamin once insisted that an image's opaque silence would make captions "the most important part of the photograph," the dominant ideas "captioning" the cinema have begun, especially for sophisticated students, to replace the movies themselves. By disallowing the standard-issue captions, which often provide a priori conclusions about a detail's significance, the *ABC* method restores the images and sounds themselves for renewed inspection.[29]

This way of working can cause confusion. The discrete entries, the persistent attention to cinematic particulars, the avoidance of sweeping claims can leave a reader wondering; most books, after all, have something like a conventional thesis. Two of Wittgenstein's students once expressed their own discomfort with a similar method deployed for what became his *Philosophical Investigations*: "[I]t was hard to see where all this often repetitive concrete detailed talk was leading to—how the examples were interconnected and how all this bore on the problem which one was accustomed to put to oneself in abstract terms."[30] Of course, the problem lies precisely in our habit of starting with "abstract terms." To oppose this reflex, Wittgenstein himself advised, "Don't think, but look!" justifying his approach in a passage that complements Minnelli's insistence on how movies get made: "In order to see more clearly, here as in countless similar cases, we must focus on the details of what goes on; we must look at them *from close up*."[31]

The Wittgenstein of *Philosophical Investigations* was fighting against Western philosophy's abiding preference for abstract thinking. *The ABCs of Classic Hollywood* has a slightly different goal; it doesn't shun abstractions but suggests arriving at them by less conventional routes. This book works primarily as a *demonstration* of what happens when you ask film students to forgo (at least initially) conceptualization in favor of trusting the generative power of a particular operation—in this case, the *ABC* method. In effect, it translates Stéphane Mallarmé's advice to poets, "yield the initiative to words," into a directive for film students: *Yield the initiative to images and sounds.*[32] Barthes's remark quoted earlier ("One might call 'poetic' . . . any discourse in which the word leads the idea") suggests the proximity of this approach to what the academy distinguishes as "creative writing," a field whose teachers normally prompt student work by means of specific instructions (e.g., "write a poem of ten lines using the following words: *taxi, purple, medicine, preoccupied*"). Certainly, the entries' brevity encouraged both me and my students to apply some epigrammatic pressure to our prose, to work more "poetically." But it also encouraged us to think more freely about the movies we were studying. I designed the *ABC* method as a classroom device, one that "teaches" an approach to film study. If you write an *ABC* paper of your own, you can't avoid some intuitive sense of the larger issues involved. My bet is that, in fact, you will understand those issues better than someone who has simply heard them stated.

The results exceeded my expectations. Adhering to my instructions, students, primarily undergraduates, produced the most consistently interesting work I have seen in my 25 years of teaching. In the chapters that follow, almost every entry has involved a collaboration with one or more of them, whose work I have used, revised, extended, corrected, and occasionally argued with. I could not have produced this book without them.

I could also not have produced it without a few select books, articles, and even passages that have proved abidingly stimulating for me and my students. In some ways, *The ABCs of Classic Hollywood* amounts to a kind of lab report concerning what can still be done with four famous movies and a few basic critical texts. The results involve some repetition, but if, as Wittgenstein maintained, the "only way to do philosophy is to do everything twice," then perhaps film study also requires some retracing. "In teaching philosophy," Wittgenstein explained to his own students:

> *I'm like a guide showing you how to find your way round*
> *London. I have to take you through the city from north to*

south, from east to west, from Euston to the embankment and
from Piccadilly to the Marble Arch. After I have taken you
many journeys through the city, in all sorts of directions, we
shall have passed through any given street a number of
times—each time traversing the street as part of a different
journey. At the end of this you will know London; you will be
able to find your way about like a born Londoner.[33]

I hope that this book will enable its readers to know classic
Hollywood cinema, to be able to find their way about the movies
as readily as the people who once made them.

3. The Four Movies

Grand Hotel (1932), *The Philadelphia Story* (1940), *The Maltese Falcon*
(1941), and *Meet Me in St. Louis* (1944) are representative films from
the years 1930–1945, the period now known as classic Hollywood.
For those sixteen years, the movies averaged 80 million in weekly
attendance, a sum equaling more than half of the U.S. population
at the time. In other words, every week, week in and week out, one
out of every two Americans—man, woman, and child—went to the
cinema. Indeed, from 1930 to 1945, out of every U.S. dollar spent
on recreation (including sports and all rival entertainment), the
movies attracted 83 cents. Even these remarkable numbers fail to
convey the extent of Hollywood's influence. By also dominating the
international market, the American cinema ensured that for the vast
majority of the audience, both here and abroad, Hollywood's
classic period films would establish the definition of the medium
itself. Henceforth, different ways of making movies would appear as
aberrations from some intrinsic essence of cinema rather than
simply as alternatives to a particular form that had resulted from a
unique coincidence of historical accidents. We should realize,
therefore, that in examining the movies of classic Hollywood, we are

studying the single most important body of films in the history of the cinema, the one that set the terms by which all movies, made before or after, would be seen.

Why *these* four films? I recognize, of course, one obvious objection to my choices: three out of four come from a single studio, MGM. Would this book have been different had it concentrated instead on Paramount or RKO or Fox? Perhaps, but classic Hollywood's success resulted above all from what André Bazin famously called "the genius of the system," and no studio was more committed to systematic production than MGM.[34] Thus, I have chosen to sacrifice variety in favor of typicality: MGM was not only classic Hollywood's most commercially successful, most glamorous enterprise; it was also its most representative.

I have also chosen these four films simply because I like them: Since the *ABC* method demands a significant amount of reviewing, it works better when you enjoy what you're studying. Objective criteria, however, also determined my selections.

- All four of the movies are readily available on DVD, in libraries, and on television.

- Each represents one of classic Hollywood's principal genres: melodrama (*Grand Hotel*), screwball comedy (*The Philadelphia Story*), the detective story (*The Maltese Falcon*), and the musical (*Meet Me in St. Louis*).

- Collectively, they afford the chance to see many of classic Hollywood's most important stars: Greta Garbo, Joan Crawford, John Barrymore, Wallace Beery, Cary Grant, James Stewart, Katharine Hepburn, Humphrey Bogart, and Judy Garland.

- The stories these movies tell have proved abidingly appealing; each of them has been revived at least once.

▤ Beginning as a novel before being adapted for the theater, *Grand Hotel* was remade by MGM as *Week-end at the Waldorf* (1945) and, in 1989, turned into a Broadway musical.

▤ Originating as a Broadway play, *The Philadelphia Story* became a movie musical in 1955 (*High Society*) and a Broadway musical in 1998.

▤ John Huston's *The Maltese Falcon* was itself a third-time's-the-charm remake of two earlier Warner Brothers attempts to turn Dashiell Hammett's novel into a movie. It has been parodied (*The Black Bird*, 1975) and spoofed in countless comedies.

▤ Originating as a collection of *New Yorker* stories, *Meet Me in St. Louis* reappeared in 1989 as a Broadway musical.

• Each of these movies appears on the Library of Congress's National Film Registry, signifying their importance and ensuring their preservation. They have also been recognized in other ways.

▤ *Grand Hotel* won the 1932 Academy Award for Best Picture. Pauline Kael once observed of *Grand Hotel* that "if you want to see what screen glamour used to be, and what, originally, 'stars' were, this is perhaps the best example of all time."[35]

▤ James Stewart won his only Best Actor Oscar for *The Philadelphia Story*, which received nominations for Best Picture, Best Director (Cukor), Best Actress (Hepburn), and Best Supporting Actress (Ruth Hussey). Leonard Maltin's newest reference book, *Classic Movie Guide* ("more than 9,000 movies"), uses for its cover a publicity still from *The Philadelphia Story*.

▦ *The Maltese Falcon* received Academy Award nominations for Best Picture, Best Supporting Actor (Sydney Greenstreet), and Best Screenplay (Huston). It won nothing, but it did initiate the Bogart cult.

▦ *Meet Me in St. Louis*, while earning no Academy nominations, remains one of Judy Garland's four most important roles (the others: as Betsy Booth in the Andy Hardy series, as Dorothy in *The Wizard of Oz*, and as Esther Blodgett, Mrs. Norman Maine, in *A Star Is Born*).

I would not argue that these four movies suggest more than any others about classic Hollywood, or the cinema in general. The *ABC* method seems capable of turning almost any movie into an instruction manual for filmmaking. Squeezing the evidence, after all, means looking at something closely until it yields some precious information that has been hidden. What have Hollywood movies hidden from us? The work that went into them, the endless negotiation between commercial efficiency and seductive enchantment, the "hundred or more hidden things . . . that the audience is not conscious of, but that accumulate," as Minnelli put it. The movies are made bit by bit, in increments that pile up in developing rooms, and on the sound stages, and in the editing suites. The details in those fragments, in the shots and images and sounds, contain the record of the work and ideas that produced them. In our unconscious memories, we recognize something there, tantalizing and just out of reach. The goal of this book is to unlock those memories, to make them conscious and explicit, so that they will help us understand the most powerful and important storytelling system ever designed.

The ABCs of Classic Hollywood

Grand Hotel

A  rt Deco

An experiment: in a History of Film class, 40 undergraduate students, shown *Grand Hotel* six weeks earlier, are asked to name the three moments they most readily recall from that movie. Here are the four most often chosen:

These images suggest the importance of something that film theory has always struggled to define. Atmosphere? Mood? Mise-en-scène? Raymond Chandler once offered a practical sense of the matter:

> *A long time ago when I was writing for the pulps I put into a story a line like "He got out of the car and walked across the sun-drenched sidewalk until the shadow of the awning over the entrance fell across his face like the touch of cool water."*

*They took it out when they published the story. Their readers
didn't appreciate this sort of thing—just held up the action. I
set out to prove them wrong. My theory was that the readers
just thought they cared about nothing but the action; that
really, although they didn't know it, the thing they cared
about, and that I cared about, was the creation of emotion
through dialogue and description.*

With *Grand Hotel*, students who often struggled to remember the
plot (why did the Baron get killed?) could provide vivid descriptions of certain images, especially the ones above. Of these, only
the shot of Crawford and Barrymore has any real narrative
function, and its plot strand (Flaemmchen's flirtation with the
Baron) will lead to nothing. The other three exist at best *alongside*
the narrative, competing for the viewer's attention.

One way to think about classical Hollywood filmmaking is
to imagine a process occurring simultaneously on two axes. The x
axis involves a movie's forward momentum, its equivalent of
melody, or what Roland Barthes's *S/Z* called the "hermeneutic
and proairetic codes"—the enigmas and unfolding actions that
keep the viewer wanting to see what happens next. In the studio
system, producers, scriptwriters, directors, and editors had
responsibility for this domain, the film's story, often regarded as
its most decisive element. The y axis, on the other hand, resembles
a melody's particular harmony: every narrative moment must be
inflected by choices of set design, costumes, casting, camera
work, and music. In general, the Hollywood studios reserved their
highest rewards for the x axis: producers and directors, in other
words, made more money than cameramen and costumers. The
auteur critics would retroactively insist that directors had operated
precisely at the two axes' juncture; Hollywood's production
records, however, undermine that claim. With men like MGM's
W. S. "Woody" "One-Take" Van Dyke completing *two* features in
nine days, and Warners' Mervyn LeRoy, in Thomas Schatz's words,

"quite capable of cranking out six to eight pictures per year, on schedule and under budget," while "averaging 5'30" of finished film a day," directors often slighted the y axis in the pell-mell process of satisfying the studios' quota of 50 features a year. In a conversation about Van Dyke, MGM producer J. J. Cohn once bestowed the studio system's highest praise: "God, he was *fast*." Stars, of course, proved the exception to the x versus y rule. After producers, they commanded the highest salaries, perhaps because their work actually *did* involve both axes: Major stars became at once narrative axioms (Garbo-as-tragic-artist, Cagney-as-hoodlum) and a story line's mise-en-scène (compare *Grand Hotel* to its remake, *Week-end at the Waldorf*: Garbo is not Ginger Rogers, John Barrymore is not Walter Pidgeon). Replacing a star could simultaneously disable a plot (John Wayne cannot play screwball comedy) and transform a film's mood more decisively than any change in cinematographer, art director, or costumer.

Grand Hotel raises an unusual case: at MGM, the most producer-dominated of all the studios, art director Cedric Gibbons was, according to Elia Kazan, "the most influential person on the lot except for the owners." Gibbons was already working at Goldwyn when its 1924 merger with Metro and Mayer Pictures created MGM. Between 1930 and 1957, as Christina Wilson reports, he received 40 Academy Award nominations, winning 11. All the while, he "'reigned supreme' in all matters artistic at MGM," supervising a staff of as many as 80 technicians: architects, model builders, upholsterers, painters, etc. By contract, every MGM feature credited Gibbons as its art director, and he typically began work on a film long before its director, meeting with the producers to plan not only a movie's sets, but the camera angles from which they should be shot. Significantly, in a system where the small details of hierarchical status always mattered, subsequent preliminary meetings with the producer, director, and composer would take place in Gibbons's office.

Given Gibbons's power at MGM and the large budget assigned to *Grand Hotel*, we should not be surprised that the movie's sets achieve what Charles Affron and Mirella Jona Affron refer to as a high degree of "design intensity." The students' memories of *Grand Hotel* indicate, in fact, that the film moves beyond what the Affrons call *set as denotation*, where "decor carries a low level of narrative weight," remaining generically appropriate, but more or less invisible (e.g., *The Maltese Falcon*). *Grand Hotel* treats the set as *punctuation*: remarkable designs, "released from their status as background," "acquire the potential to punctuate the narrative and thus make claims on the attention of the viewer." Gibbons would have claimed more, and the Affrons' highest-intensity category, "set as narrative," seems to match his sense that "the Berlin hotel in which the entire drama was enacted became a personality rather than a mere background." "Here," Gibbons observed:

> the sets take the place of an actor. . . . The "Grand Hotel" is bigger than all the people who come and go within its walls. We therefore went about designing the sets with the view of bringing the background forward on the same plane as the players.

Grand Hotel's sets, of course, are art deco, a style that took its inspiration from both mass production techniques and high art, especially cubism, futurism, and Russian constructivism. Although it exerted its greatest influence on American design in the early 1930s, the movement acquired its name posthumously, when 1960s art historians replaced the earlier designation *moderne* with a term derived from the 1925 Paris Exposition Internationale des Arts Décoratifs Industriels et Modernes. While accounts often describe Gibbons as attending that fair, MGM's records indicate that work on *Ben Hur* and *The Big Parade* prevented his doing so. Gibbons, however, did design art deco's most well-known incarnation, the Oscar statuette.

Grand Hotel's sets exhibit all of the standard art deco iconography: repetition, symmetry, geometrical patterns, stylized bouquets, the reduction of color to a stark black and white. These attributes depended on machine-age production; deco's streamlined patterns and synthetic materials (plastic, aluminum, chrome) exceeded artisanal capabilities. And yet, deco also *felt* like art; indeed, in many ways, it amounted to a popularized version of cubism and Mondrian. It also provided one of the most prominent answers to a basic question: *what does it mean to be modern?*

Art deco's most important effect involved its commitment to *reductionism*, the circumscription of the visual field to simplified patterns. Long after deco had waned as a dominant style, it continued to exert its influence on classic Hollywood, whose greatest pictures appear, on examination, remarkably *abstract.* Comparing *Grand Hotel*'s introduction of Garbo to *Week-end at the Waldorf*'s less-effective first appearance of Ginger Rogers suggests that at their best, studio Hollywood movies resembled maps, whose value, as Nick Cullather observes, "derives from *the removal of information.*" *Week-end at the Waldorf*'s clutter competes with its star; *Grand Hotel*'s dramatic chiaroscuro leaves unshown almost everything but Garbo.

In *Raiding the Icebox*, Peter Wollen argued that modernism's official myth—the sleek urban skyscraper's celebration of engineering efficiency—was always shadowed by its opposite: an eroticized decorativeness descended from the Russian ballet. Function versus ornament, austerity versus extravagance—

modernism, Wollen proposed, always displayed both tendencies. And so did Hollywood cinema. In fact, F. Scott Fitzgerald's "whole equation of pictures" almost certainly involves the management of this opposition, which quickly translates into the inescapable tension between money and art. Almost no one in command at MGM ever lost sight of the studio's fundamental goal: financial profit. And yet, during *Grand Hotel*'s preproduction planning, Irving Thalberg often proved more willing to spend money than director Edmund Goulding. "It's just as important to see that it's spent," he insisted, "as to see that it isn't." *Grand Hotel* embodies both modernisms: lavish decoration designed to embellish a Pythagorean plot.

Grand Hotel also effects this merger at another level, by reconciling the functional and the decorative in the film's art deco set. The hotel's architecture is at once streamlined and sumptuous, with the overhead shots of the lobby lingering on a design whose straight lines are always sliding into curvature: the spiraling checkerboard floor, the circular front desk, the cylindrical interiors. These shots depict both a modernist geometry, uniform and industrial, and a polished extravagance, glamorous and ornamental. This mix also appears in the film's other sets, in the doors' angular inlays and in the furniture's lavishly clean lines. The set is at once pure decorative ornament and narratively efficient structure: its circular lobby and hallways funnel the movie's characters into meetings, as if they were balls thrown simultaneously into a spinning roulette wheel. In sum, the aesthetic reconciliation achieved by the art deco set mirrors both the plot, at once systematic and embellished, and the characters themselves, torn between economics and pleasure. The set makes this reconciliation visual and omnipresent; it works even when the story is idling.[1]

(*with Morgan Burroughs, Denise Cummings,*
Jennifer Simmons, Jennifer Wangerien)

B lue Danube

Film history offers *Grand Hotel* as one of the first Hollywood movies to layer scenes with nondiegetic music. Here, however, that process betrays its own immaturity by sending contradictory signals. Thus, beginning with the opening overhead lobby shot, Johann Strauss's *Blue Danube Waltz* plays continuously for several minutes on the soundtrack, presumably issuing from the ballroom's orchestra (boasting about his new residence, Kringelein claims, "[There's] music all the time"). No objection arises about hearing music disconnected from its source; as Stanley Cavell points out, "we are fully accustomed to hearing things that are invisible, not present to us."

The waltz first becomes audible in the lobby, where it accompanies the characters' gathering. When the Baron, Flaemmchen, Kringelein, and Pimenov take the elevator to the second floor, the music recedes, indicating that they (and we) have moved away from its diegetic source. The music stops completely when Flaemmchen, having entered Preysing's room, closes the door to the hall. Acting consistently, it resumes when she leaves, now accompanying the Baron's and Flaemmchen's conversation, stopping abruptly at the point when they arrange their rendezvous for the next day.

But something is askew. If we can hear an orchestra playing offscreen, why can't we hear the voices of the guests milling about the lobby? And why has Berlin's best hotel hired an orchestra that can apparently play only one song? A later scene confirms the confusion. As the Baron paces anxiously in Grusinskaya's room, trapped by Preysing's emergence onto an adjacent balcony, we hear no music. It reappears *exactly* when the maid opens the door, suggesting a diegetic source. But after the maid shuts the door behind her, the music continues, now apparently become non-diegetic. And yet, later, another about-face: packing for Vienna, but unaware of the Baron's death, Grusinskaya suddenly notices something: "The music has stopped," she remarks portentously, thereby reattributing the soundtrack's waltz to an offscreen diegetic source. A mature, confident Hollywood system will make jokes out of this kind of uncertainty. In *Bananas* (1971), Woody Allen lies on his hotel bed, daydreaming about dining with "President Vargas" as harp music emerges on the soundtrack. Suddenly noticing it, Allen opens the closet door to reveal a man playing the harp: "Oh, excuse me, señor," the musician apologizes, "I was trying to find someplace for practice."

This kind of sophistication lies ahead. In the meantime, *Grand Hotel* is working toward the kind of nondiegetic score perfected by *Casablanca* (*Grand Hotel* made topical), where the music, issuing from diegetically performed melodies ("As Time Goes By," "The Marseillaise"), hovers around the action like a word processor's boldface or italics, waiting for the right moment to put pressure on a gesture, a line of dialogue, a scene.

And why, to portray a Berlin hotel, use *Blue Danube*, an *Austrian* waltz? When MGM art director Cedric Gibbons objected to a scene showing Paris with a moonlit ocean in the background, Thalberg overruled him:

> *We can't cater to a handful of people who know Paris.*
> *Audiences only see about ten percent of what's on the screen,*
> *anyway, and if they're watching your background instead of*
> *my actors, the scene will be useless. Whatever you put there,*
> *they'll believe that's how it is.*

Hence, one possible lesson: since the audience, like Hitler, cannot distinguish between Austria and Germany, *Blue Danube*'s misplaced attribution doesn't matter. In fact, the tune serves to indicate less "Germany" than some vaguer notion of what Roland Barthes would have called *continentalicity*. The *Blue Danube* amounts to an instance of Hollywood's "camel principle": show the audience a camel, even in the margin of a frame, and it will think

"Egypt." Play the audience *Blue Danube*, and it will think "Old World Europe." Lesson two: The *Blue Danube* signifies one of studio Hollywood's three possible Germanies: first, the Bavarian beer hall (evoked by drinking songs); second, Weimar cosmopolitanism (*Blue Danube* as the Grand Hotel's ambient music); and third, Nazi tyranny (Wagner and "Deutschland über Alles"). This third possibility is the specter haunting *Grand Hotel*.[2] (See *The Maltese Falcon*: Golden Gate Bridge.)

(with Katherine Arpen and Ryan Johnson)

C offin

In a shot unlike any other in *Grand Hotel*, the Baron's coffin is loaded onto a Dickensian horse-drawn hearse and taken away. Outside the hotel's luxury, beyond the film's carefully planned sets and calculated lighting, something leaks through. Workers go

about their unnamed business, moving in and out of overexposed sunlight and underlit shadows, as if in a documentary, or a dream. Men load packages, laughing and shouting, as the Baron's body leaves the hotel. Any detailed description of this scene would necessarily include these elements:

the shot's unusual duration, 41 seconds, compared to 1928–1933 Hollywood's average of 11 seconds

the rough initial leftward pan, apparently resulting from a hand-held camera the off-center flood of light, falling on a man with a chef's hat and cigarette standing to the hearse's left

the large number of people (at least 22) milling in and out of the frame, apparently at random, none of them a recognizable actor

the odd counting, issuing from an unseen source and undefined by any readily identifiable activity: *44! 46! 38! 40! 42! 44! 44–no–46! 48!*

the inappropriate laughter, stifled as the coffin arrives, renewed when it leaves

the single trolley car in the background, splashed with light

the two men in suits and ties lounging by the trolley

the man unloading a crate from a wagon

the background sign, partially obscured and thus illegible: *L A R G — M*

This scene, resembling what appears through the windows of *Sunrise*'s trolley, requires an accounting, if for only this reason: nothing in *Grand Hotel* interests me more.

On the one hand, a simple thematics: the shot reinforces the movie's consistent association of what lies beyond the hotel with crisis. Thus, leaving its sanctuary will involve career setbacks (Grusinskaya), crime (the Baron), imprisonment (Preysing), or death (the Baron). This danger and the potential for outside contamination appear even in the way these excursions are filmed. The Baron's leap across the balconies exposes a shoddy rear projection atypical of Thalberg pictures, while his moments with the "chauffeur" seem borrowed from Warner Brothers. Although Thomas Schatz correctly insists that "grim realism and 'serious' drama had no place at MGM, where quality and style were a function of polish, poise, and glamour," the coffin sequence's grainy presentation of an unspecified alleyway, where meatpackers haul cattle carcasses and formally dressed men place the casket on a hearse, amounts to *Grand Hotel*'s abrupt shift into another register. The scene not only identifies death with the world outside the Grand Hotel; it represents death as *something beyond MGM's stylistic realm*. Instead of Douglas Shearer's normal, polished soundtrack, the coffin scene's decentered cacophony, uncushioned by music, makes it seem as if sound from another unrelated film-shoot were spilling into this one. Suddenly, the movie appears to have been relocated to a back lot of another studio that ignores MGM's rules of polish and glamour.

The scene's visual and aural polycentrism, the grainy overexposure, the location look, the unprivileged hand-held camera, the haphazard movement of the extras—all these elements evoke nonclassical Hollywood filmmaking. In fact, the coffin scene faces in two directions, backward to primitive cinema, forward to Italian neorealism. It represents, therefore, an image of the continuity system's *undoing*. Hollywood's commercial success had always depended on reducing the polysemousness of its images to make them effortlessly legible. What resulted, however, was a world like *Grand Hotel*'s—abstract, sealed off from the teeming world outside. Neorealism and the New Wave would attack this way of doing things, reopening the cinema like a rediscovered country. *Grand Hotel*'s coffin scene, which could readily appear in a film by Lumière, Rossellini, or Godard, shows what else the movies might have been.

Why is this moment moving? Stanley Cavell has said that *intuitions* about the movies require *a tuition*, a making intelligible to oneself and to each other. This entire book issues from an intuition about this scene, an intuition whose tuition I am struggling to articulate here. The intuition begins with Barthes's notion that the "third meaning compels an interrogative reading." That is, you should start with what piques or compels you. The coffin scene in *Grand Hotel* is such a moment for me. Here is my intuition.

As I was thinking about this shot, I was listening to a song from Moby's album *18*, "I Don't Worry at All." Moby works from samples, building up tracks from fragments, working them into a song, music's equivalent of a film's sequence. As I listen to this piece, however, I notice the fragments (I am intended to do so), and I have the sense of a ghostly transmission being sent, parts of which reach me, while others have been lost. Imagine a recording of signals from the *Titanic* radioing for help, intermittent, shadowy, desperate—a voice from far away.

To what extent have classic Hollywood movies now become such intermittent broadcasts—mysterious, incomplete, ghostly— that we only partially understand? The movies, of course, result from fragments, whose careful sequencing conceals that fact. Occasionally, however, static comes through in the signal (Griffith's wind in the trees, *On the Waterfront*'s dropped glove), and at that moment, we recognize not only the message, *but also the act of transmission itself*, which commercial cinema generally goes to such great lengths to hide. For a brief moment, we have made contact with a real, prior event, the effort involved in picturing anything on the screen. (Imagine the effect of two different *Titanic* recordings, one with static, one without: the latter, the equivalent of most Hollywood films, would have far less power to move us.)

The crucial lesson of cybernetics remains its refusal of the distinction between noise and information. For film studies, this idea suggests that the apparently marginal (Barthes's "the filmic," the *Cahiers*' mise-en-scène), the way the information is conveyed, becomes the information itself. Thus, in *Grand Hotel*'s coffin scene, the narrative events are inseparable from the struggles involved in representing them. Those struggles—the choices made, the ones abandoned—imply the cinema's history.[3]

(*with Patrick Brennan, Brian Doan, Heather Visser*)

D achshund

Grand Hotel's choice of pet confirms how even peripheral objects contribute to a movie's meaning. For Americans, the dachshund's exaggeratedly silly appearance and lapdog size *soften* the Baron's character, making even this jewel thief seem less threatening than  threatened. To measure this effect, one has simply to imagine replacing the dachshund with another appropriately German breed—Doberman pinscher, rottweiler, German shepherd—whose more menacing aspects and connotations would convert the Baron from dandy to predator.

 In 1912, Italian futurist painter Giacomo Balla's *Dynamism of a Dog on a Leash* had made the dachshund, its legs whirling like bicycle tires, an emblem of modernity. But in the United States, World War I provoked hostility toward all things German, including dachshunds, which occasionally became the victims of stoning. By 1932, even the Americans who had once labeled dachshund owners "traitors" probably no longer objected to the Baron's Adolphus, but the dog's name would certainly have reminded them of the man soon to become Germany's chancellor. Indeed, *Grand Hotel*'s Adolphus, a Berlin dachshund, predicts things to come. Jealously proud of their pure-bred shepherds, Dobermans, and Weimaraners, German dog lovers had long worried that the

dachshund would suffer from English and American mixed breeding. *Grand Hotel* uses the Baron to articulate this anxiety: "When you meet little lady dogs on the street that are not dachshunds," he admonishes Adolphus, "you must exercise some self-control." In retrospect, this concern seems an early warning of the German obsession with racial purity, whose vulgarized Social Darwinism would justify the Nazis' murderous racial policies. The dachshund, bred to hunt pests (especially rats and badgers), also evokes Nazi anti-Semitic propaganda films, which typically portrayed Jews as vermin.

(*with Ashley Bowen and Jennifer Wangerien*)

Daniels

Of Garbo's 24 American films, made with 14 different directors, all but 5 were shot by her preferred cameraman, William Daniels. Here is the list, with director named first:

1925	*The Torrent* (Monta Bell/Daniels)
1926	*The Temptress* (Fred Niblo/Tony Gaudio)
	Flesh and the Devil (Clarence Brown/Daniels)
1927	*Love* (Edmund Goulding/Daniels)
	The Divine Woman (Victor Seastrom/Oliver Marsh)
1928	*The Mysterious Lady* (Niblo/Daniels)
1929	*A Woman of Affairs* (Brown/Daniels)
	Wild Orchids (Sidney Franklin/Daniels)
	The Single Standard (John S. Robertson/Marsh)
	The Kiss (Jacques Feyder/Daniels)
1930	*Anna Christie* (Brown/Daniels)
	Romance (Brown/Daniels)

1931   *Inspiration* (Brown/Daniels)

       Susan Lenox: Her Fall and Rise (Robert Z.

       Leonard/Daniels)

       Mata Hari (George Fitzmaurice/Daniels)

1932   *Grand Hotel* (Goulding/Daniels)

       As You Desire Me (Fitzmaurice/Daniels)

1933   *Queen Christina* (Rouben Mamoulian/Daniels)

1934   *The Painted Veil* (Richard Boleslawski/Daniels)

1935   *Anna Karenina* (Brown/Daniels)

1937   *Camille* (George Cukor/Daniels)

       Conquest (Brown/Karl Freund)

1939   *Ninotchka* (Ernst Lubitsch/Daniels)

1941   *Two-Faced Woman* (Cukor/Joseph Ruttenberg)

Hollywood's other famous pairs (Billy Bitzer with D. W. Griffith, Joseph Walker with Frank Capra) confirm the *auteurist* insistence on direction as filmmaking's privileged site. Garbo-Daniels, however, suggests a revision: the star-photographer team as *auteur*, dominating the production process.

    Auteurism always rested on a paradox. While the term evoked the favored analogy, the cinema as a kind of writing, the *auteurists* themselves were the intellectual children of André Bazin, whose famous essays had championed the camera's wondrous *automatism*: For the first time in human history, an exact representation of the world could be made *by accident*. This miraculous revelatory power, Bazin argued, made the Soviet or expressionistic imposition of subjective meanings (by editing or distorted compositions) seem a kind of misguided vanity. Bazin's position amounted to a revival of the French impressionist filmmakers' *photogénie* and the surrealists' beloved automatism, related (but not identical) concepts: the movies' ineffable moments (an actor's walk across a room, the light from a candle) seem to result from the camera's innate ability to record them. For the impressionists, however, *photogénie* was untranslatable but intentional. For the surrealists, it was accidental and omnipresent.

Bazin, however, preferred to associate his cinematic ideal not with accidents, but with a particular set of strategies deliberately employed by a select group of filmmakers. Renoir, De Sica, Murnau, Flaherty, Wyler, and Welles were great because in relying on long takes and deep focus, they had modestly permitted reality to speak for itself. With this argument, Bazin was retreating from his thought's most radical implication, his sense of the fundamental difference between previous representational technologies like writing and the new "random generators" like the camera. In the hands of his followers, the *Cahiers* critics, this attitude toward intentionality became even more ambivalent. *La politique des auteurs* seemed to renounce altogether the surrealist faith in chance, celebrating even Bazin's beloved "reality" less than the filmmaking geniuses who could consciously summon its charms.

Here was the problem: *auteurism* required *authors*, and authorship assumed intentionality. How could Bazin's protégés simultaneously celebrate the effects of automatism and praise the choices of directors? Would only Jean Renoir embody the paradoxical ideal of the *automatic auteur*? The problem deepens when we consider the proposition that the cinema's dramatic capacity depends on editing, which Bazin had disparaged: "The camera shows, and the editing tells." The *auteurist* insistence on the analogy of writing threatened this division of labor's equilibrium. Writing seems more obviously connected to telling than to showing, the realm of automatism and mere recording.

The *Cahiers* solution was the term "mise-en-scène." As those writers used it, mise-en-scène quickly left behind its conventional meaning ("setting") to become a sacred word, shared by friends who could invoke it knowing the others would understand. At first, it appeared to be simply another version of *photogénie*, a way of talking about the untranslatable "essence of the cinema." Hence, Jacques Rivette on Otto Preminger's *Angel Face*:

> *What tempts Preminger if not the rendering audible of*
> *particular chords unheard and rare, in which the inexplicable*
> *beauty of the modulation suddenly justifies the ensemble of*
> *the phrase? This is probably the definition of something*
> *precious, its enigma—the door to something beyond intellect,*
> *opening out onto the unknown.*
>   *Such are the contingencies of* mise-en-scène.

Auteurism's basic problem, however, involved just this kind of attribution. More than even most theoretical groups, the *Cahiers* critics had a sense of themselves as a visionary, well-educated, sensitive elect. As long as they were associating the delights of mise-en-scène with filmmakers like Jean Renoir, they could continue to insist on the conscious aspect of a director's decisions. Renoir, after all, was aesthetically well-bred, politically liberal, and personally sympathetic. But the *auteurist* position increasingly prompted them to celebrate directors who had often made bad films and who sometimes seemed neither particularly smart nor especially nice. Directors, for example, like Otto Preminger. Faced with this situation, the *Cahiers* writers revised their praise, directing it less at individual filmmakers than at the medium itself. Thus, the *Cahiers*' American operative Andrew Sarris could explicitly modulate *la politique des auteurs* into a revival of surrealism's praise for automatism:

> *For me,* mise-en-scène *is not merely the gap between what*
> *we see and feel on the screen and what we can express in*
> *words, but it is also the gap between the intention of the*
> *director and his effect upon the spectator. . . . To read all*
> *sorts of poignant profundities in Preminger's inscrutable*

urbanity would seem to be the last word in idiocy, and yet there are moments in his films when the evidence on the screen is inconsistent with one's deepest instincts about the director as a man. It is during those moments that one feels the magical powers of mise-en-scène *to get more out of a picture than is put in by a director.*

The Garbo-Daniels team raises a basic question about *auteurism*: to what extent can that policy modify the analogy to writing by also giving credit to film as *recording*? In one of the most profound remarks ever made about the cinema, David Thomson once observed, "[I]t is often preferable to have a movie actor who moves well than one who 'understands' the part. A director ought to be able to explain a part, but very few men or women can move well in front of a camera." Garbo could, and the camera that recorded those movements was most often operated by William Daniels.[4] (See *The Maltese Falcon*: Bogart.)

D**oors**

The art deco, cubist-inspired door to Kringelein's room is an emblem of the Grand Hotel's sleekly engineered modernity. But with its zigzag decoration, the door also resembles a series of sliding panels, intersecting with each other to create odd patterns. This design alludes

to, by rejecting, the boredom of doors leading to predictable places—i.e., almost all real doors. Sliding panels, trap doors, secret locks—these are the accoutrements of the adventure stories of H. G. Wells ("The Door in the Wall"), Louis Feuillade ("The Underground Passages of the Chateau-Rouge"), and the Hardy Boys (*The Secret Panel, The Disappearing Floor, The Secret of the Lost Tunnel*), whose

haunted wonderlands remain wonderfully unpredictable. Transformed from their existence as hinges-between-machine-tooled
parts, *Grand Hotel*'s doors offer an escape from the routines of
Taylorism and Fordism. They become entries into modernity's secret
sharer, what Peter Wollen calls the "phantasmagoric East." Thus,
Grand Hotel's doors allude to the magic promised by Hollywood
itself, where at any moment, in F. Scott Fitzgerald's description of
MGM's back lot, "On top of a huge head of the god Siva, two
women [might float] down the current of an impromptu river."[5]

(*with Alan Clinton*)

Drunken Man

Over a half-century after *Grand Hotel*, film historian Kristin Thompson would suggest that *The Bicycle Thief*'s "realism" depends partially
on a loose narrative, willing to tolerate "interpolated events incidental to the action." If classical Hollywood had insisted that "all
moments must contain significant action," Vittorio De Sica's movie
"seems to recreate the rhythm of real events, with trivial and

important happenings alternating." As an example of this
open-ended structure, Thompson points to the scene of Ricci's
supervisor teaching him how to
put up movie posters. When a
prosperous-looking man passes
by, the camera temporarily
abandons Ricci to follow two
pursuing beggar boys, who will
not figure in the film's plot.

Long before *The Bicycle Thief*, *Grand Hotel* seems similarly
casual about maintaining the optimum narrative vantage point. As
the movie rushes toward its climax, Grusinskaya frantically
searches the fifth floor for the Baron, who, although she does not
yet know, is already dead. Pimenov and Suzette shepherd her into

the waiting elevator, from which emerges a drunken man, still dressed in evening clothes from the night before.

As the door closes on Grusinskaya, the camera remains with its new discovery, who bows solemnly to the departed elevator before collapsing in a comic heap, to be rescued by a hotel attendant. Only then does the movie resume its attention to Grusinskaya, now entering the lobby below. This brief, narratively insignificant moment, suggests something unstable about *Grand Hotel*'s plot, its *seriality*. At any moment, we can be disconnected from one story line and rerouted to another, old or new. As Grusinskaya leaves the hotel, a honeymooning couple is checking in. The metaphor is obvious: the hotel-as-movie-studio, its rooms (like MGM's sets) infinitely available, its guests (like the cinema's performers) briskly superseded.[6]

 rrors

Hollywood cinema's continuity system developed as a means of managing the hundreds of choices involved in every stage of the filmmaking process. That system addressed itself primarily to two crucial sites: the contents of individual shots and the articulation between them. For individual shot decisions (known as mise-en-scène), mainstream commercial cinema settled on *centering*, using various devices to keep narratively important elements prominent in the frame. Typically, this process involves framing and character positioning: in *Grand Hotel*, for example, Garbo's scenes keep her spatially centered, rarely allowing her to dissolve into the mise-en-scène's background. Designed to overcome early movies' illegibility, centering could also work more subtly, especially with sound: by merely speaking, for example, even a marginalized character would at least temporarily command the viewer's attention.

Regulating sequences, however, proved more difficult. With every shot change creating the potential for spatial and temporal discontinuity (see Buster Keaton's *Sherlock, Jr.*), early movies often left their audiences confused. Continuity's solution was *matching*, a set of protocols designed to achieve a transparent linearity that would shift attention from the filmmakers' effort to the movie's story. Matching involves some obvious rules: if a bearded man's glance at a house prompts a cut to its entrance, he can't be clean-shaven in the reverse-shot. (Godard would play with this rule in *La Chinoise*, changing the color of his actress's dress from shot to shot.) More elaborately, continuity devised the 180-degree system, a procedure of filming all takes in an establishing-shot/breakdown-shot sequence from the same side of an imaginary 180-degree axis. The 180-degree system not only allowed filmmakers to maintain consistent screen direction (particularly important with horizontal movement in the frame); it also enabled them to break down the overall space of a scene into smaller units without confusing the audience about their spatial relationship.

Film historian Noël Burch has argued that, after emerging during the movies' second decade, the continuity system had achieved legitimacy by the early 1920s. Throughout the 1920s, continuity manuals, detailing the system's protocols, circulated within Hollywood's studios. And yet, for all of Thalberg's inexhaustible attentiveness and MGM's commitment to perfection, *Grand Hotel* seems remarkably indifferent to continuity errors. Take these examples:

1. In their first meeting on the balcony overlooking the lobby, the Baron and Flaemmchen flirt, mostly in

two-shot. In Shot 1, having arranged a rendezvous for the next afternoon, Flaemmchen stands by the Baron's right shoulder, looking up at him to her left, the two caught in a medium close-up. In the same shot, she crosses in front of him to his left, then turns back to him, now on her right. Cut to Shot 2, a medium full-shot that *repeats this exact change of places*.

Shot 1:

Shot 2:

Although Shot 2 does not literally duplicate the contents of Shot 1 (it is the Baron who moves in Shot 2, not Flaemmchen), the editing, despite the continuous dialogue, violates Hollywood's principle of strict linearity. By providing another version of a just-shown action, Shot 2 introduces the kind of overlapping cut deployed by avant-gardists like Sergei Eisenstein (see, for example, *Potemkin*'s famous scene of an angry sailor smashing a plate). By Hollywood's own standards, however, the cut simply amounts to a continuity error.

2. The Baron hides in Grusinskaya's closet, waiting for the housekeepers to leave her alone. A series of shots of the room and the characters' movements establish a 180-degree axis that places Grusinskaya to the Baron's right. Yet as he watches from his hiding place, the close-up shows him looking left.

He starts his exit from the closet moving right to left, but the cut completing that action has him moving left to right, a 180-degree violation.

Here, the sequence suggests MGM's deference to its stars: Barrymore's preferred left profile trumps continuity's rules.

3. When Grusinskaya telephones the Baron just after he has left her room the next morning, shot 1 shows her on her knees as she picks up the receiver.

The second shot, another temporal reversal confounded by continuous dialogue, shows her standing with the telephone. She then gradually sinks to her knees.

At some point, especially after May 1968, film theory began to celebrate such continuity breaks in terms of what David Rodowick has called "the discourse of political modernism." If the continuity system intended to hide filmmaking's processes, anything that revealed them became the equivalent of Bertolt Brecht's alienation devices—a progressive means to consciousness-raising. In fact, as Noël Burch warned, mistakes don't necessarily make good politics; Ed Wood, after all, was not Godard. Burch's own study of Japanese cinema, however, attempted to recruit conservative artists like Ozu for leftist politics. From the 1930s on, Burch argued, Ozu had regularly violated the 180-degree system, thereby undermining the eyeline match, "the cornerstone" of the Hollywood system's "illusionist rapture," the source of its regressive effect.

But as Burch admitted, when Ozu screened two versions of the same conversation, one obeying the 180-degree system, the other not, the director's only comment was, "There is no difference." Certainly, *Grand Hotel*'s continuity errors never break the movie's spell. Merely noticing them requires extraordinary scrutiny. Why, then, note them at all? Perhaps because *discontinuity implies events without causes*—gaps, lapses, secrets, the undisclosed. *Grand Hotel*, we begin to see, is remarkably casual about causation. Why, for example, has Grusinskaya's career declined? As played by Garbo, she is far too young to be suffering Pavlova's fate, the inevitable loss of physical abilities. Why does Preysing's business require a merger with the Saxonia Company? Why does the Baron owe 5,000 marks? Why can't Flaemmchen make an honest living? What is Kringelein's fatal illness? *Grand Hotel* will not answer these questions, but it rushes headlong from one story to the next, using its stars to cover up every mistake in the filmmaking, every defect in the plot. These errors amount to *punctures*; they leave behind peepholes through which, leaning close, straining our eyes, we catch a glimpse behind the scenes.[7]

(*with Seth Keller, Samantha Murrell, Maitreya Sims*)

F laemmchen

Flaemmchen (or *Flämmchen*, as Baum writes the name), is the diminutive of *Flamme*, "little flame." While her name suggests the character's sexual appeal and casual virtue, it also evokes the German expression *auf kleiner Flammen kochen*, literally "to cook over little flames" or "to make do with very little," a connotation suiting Flaemmchen, who, as she admits to the Baron, gets by on "one meal a day." The translation into English, however, sheds these connotations, and by doing so shifts *Grand Hotel*'s register from allegory to novel. In a famous objection to what he referred to as Anthony Trollope's "fantastic names," Henry James proposed:

> *It is impossible to imagine what a novelist takes himself to be unless he regard himself as an historian and his narrative as a history. It is only as an historian that he has the smallest* locus standi. *As a narrator of fictitious events he is nowhere. . . . he must relate events that are assumed to be real.*

Thus, James went on, by naming a poor clergyman with a dozen children "Mr. Quiverful," Trollope had injected a "primitive" element that disrupted his story. "It would be better," James insisted, "to go back to Bunyan at once." For "we can believe in the name and we can believe in the children, but we cannot manage the combination." Noël Burch has suggested that, as the cinema evolved from its own primitive mode, it attracted middle-class patrons by adopting their preferred forms, the nineteenth-century realistic novel and play. Allegorical names cannot survive this move, for they recall the earlier, abandoned forms of presentational melodrama. To confirm this speculation, to sense the proximity of an earlier *suppressed* cinema, one need only imagine *Grand Hotel* with Crawford as "Little Flame."[8]

(with Charles Meyer)

 Garbo

1

Although to a modern audience, the Greta Garbo of *Grand Hotel* appears at least in her mid-30s, she was only 26 during the movie's filming and thus 6 years younger than Julia Roberts in *Notting Hill*, 10 years younger than Sandra Bullock in *Miss Congeniality*, and 11 years younger than Meg Ryan in *You've Got Mail*, all of whom seem, to contemporary eyes, far younger. Why? We know, of course, that standards of beauty evolve and that Garbo's statuesque perfection (celebrated by Roland Barthes) has given way to a more idiosyncratic "cuteness." When did this transformation begin? A quick answer: at some point between 1932, with *Grand Hotel*, and 1945, when the remake, *Week-end at the Waldorf*, replaced Garbo with the cute-not-beautiful Ginger Rogers, 34 at the time, but still capable of doing (as Garbo never was) what David Thomson calls "her child impersonations" (see *The Major and the Minor*, where the

31-year-old Rogers played a teenager). Almost certainly, World War II encouraged this shift, making Garbo's kind of continental beauty seem threateningly "European." It may also have seemed increasingly *abstract*. If Christian Keathley is right to locate the cinephiliac moment in a mise-en-scène's idiosyncrasies (the wind in the trees, the dust on Boudu's road), then Garbo's model beauty may have eventually proved less appealing to a modern audience eager for the eccentric detail: Julia Roberts's mouth, Meg Ryan's hair.[9]

(with Ashley Bowen)

2

MGM treated Garbo like a valuable jewel, avoiding liberal display for elaborate vaults, opened every now and then to allow a viewing. From 1931 until her retirement in 1941, Garbo made only 12 films; in that same period, Warner Brothers put its biggest female star, Bette Davis, in 49. Most of Garbo's movies delay her entrance. In *Grand Hotel*, for example, she does not appear onscreen for the movie's first 20 minutes, although by then, her character's name has been spoken 13 times. In the 110-minute film, her time onscreen amounts to barely 26 minutes, and at one point, as the plot conducts Preysing and the Baron to their fatal collision, Garbo disappears from *Grand Hotel* for over 19 minutes. And yet, despite the movie's collection of stars, she dominates the film. It is the first movie to bill her simply as *Garbo*, which in Swedish means "wood nymph," but in Italian suggests "politeness," "elegance," "good manners."

3

In *Grand Hotel*, Garbo's histrionic acting finds its rationale in what Barthes called the "reference code of the artist": ballerinas are temperamental. More immediately, this style, which can now appear dated and campy, descends from François Delsarte (1811–

1871), who, as James Naremore summarizes, "made one of the earliest attempts to codify expressive gestures for actors and public speakers." The "Delsartean system" linked specific facial expressions and body movements to particular emotions like fear, anger, grief, boredom. In fact, Delsarte's formulaic approach anticipated Frederick Taylor's industrial management, with both convinced that every task had its "one best way" of execution. Laying down rules ("any interrogation made with crossed arms must partake of a threat"), Delsarte developed a dictionary of gestures that actors could simply memorize and use, the way a Taylor worker could mindlessly deploy procedures presented by management. Delsartean acting's great antithesis is what Naremore calls the "psychological school," identified with Stanislavski and his progeny: Lee Strasberg's Group Theater, the Actor's Studio, and "the Method." While Method acting would emphasize "private moments" and "motivation," the style of *Grand Hotel*'s performers is exteriorized, a set of gestures dictated by an imaginary codebook.

Here are two stories:

In 1911, Frederick Taylor's famous *The Principles of Scientific Management* prescribed the four rules for achieving a fully rationalized workplace:

1. "the development of a true science": studying the task at hand to derive the "one best way" of executing it

2. "the scientific selection of the workman": choosing the workers whose physical attributes best suit them to a particular job

3. "his scientific education and development": teaching the worker the "one best way"

4. "intimate friendly cooperation between the management and the men": Taylor meant that

supervisors would give orders to workers who would unquestioningly obey

Hired in 1899 by Bethlehem Steel to devise a system for loading pig iron, made suddenly valuable by the Spanish-American War, Taylor followed his own rules. He quickly assessed the task, producing a recipe for its ideal execution. Selecting the workers took more time. "In almost all of the mechanic arts," Taylor wrote,

> the science which underlies each workman's act is so great and amounts to so much that the workman who is best suited actually to do the work is incapable (either through lack of education or through insufficient mental capacity) of understanding this science.

Taylor put the matter even more bluntly: "the man suited to handling pig iron is too stupid properly to train himself." In fact,

> one of the very first requirements for a man who is fit to handle pig iron as a regular occupation is that he shall be so stupid and so phlegmatic that he more nearly resembles in his mental make-up the ox than any other type. The man who is mentally alert and intelligent is for this very reason entirely unsuited to what would, for him, be the grinding monotony of work of this character.

Taylor "scientifically selected" one laborer in particular, a Pennsylvania Dutchman whom he called "Schmidt." Getting down to work, Taylor convinced Schmidt that by doing exactly what his supervisors told him to do, he could load 47 tons of pig iron a day and make more money. Schmidt, "a man of the mentally sluggish type," agreed. He would work at Taylor's prescribed pace, resting at "scientifically" scheduled intervals. With Schmidt as the model for other workers, Taylor claimed to have solved Bethlehem's problem.

By breaking jobs down to their most elementary components, Taylor was *deskilling* tasks, making them less dependent on
experienced workers who were not easily replaceable. Taylor's
ideal was "the ready-made man," a phrase recalling his near-
contemporary Marcel Duchamp, who just six years after *The
Principles of Scientific Management* would produce *Fountain*, his first
"ready-made" art object. Even more significantly, Taylor's system,
especially as it developed under Henry Ford, provided the Hollywood studios with an organizational blueprint. Hollywood
translated Taylor's rules into its own protocols:

1. Taylor's "development of a true science," his one
best way, became the Hollywood movie, a big-
budget, feature-length fiction, whose director and
stars would operate within a strict grammar known
as continuity.

2. Taylor's "scientific selection of the workman" led
to screen tests and typecasting, with physiology
determining an actor's possible roles.

3. The studios took Taylor's "scientific education and
development" to encourage training that brought
actors and technicians up through the ranks, from
shorts to B-pictures to supporting roles to principal
parts in a lot's most prestigious films.

4. In Hollywood, Taylor's utopian "intimate friendly
cooperation" between management and labor meant
one thing: producers would control the filmmaking
process. An independent maverick like von Stroheim,
used to having his own way, would soon fall victim to
Taylor's most fundamental edict: "All of those who,
after proper teaching, either will not or cannot work in
accordance with the new methods and at the higher
speed must be discharged by the *management*."

And the second story: Preparing to shoot *Queen Christina*'s famous final scene, which required her to gaze into the distance from the prow of a rapidly moving ship, Garbo asked director Rouben Mamoulian for instructions.

"What do I express in this last shot?" she inquired. "Nothing," Mamoulian replied, "absolutely nothing. You must make your mind and heart a complete blank."

Hence a potential exam question:

Imagine a polemical essay that begins with the following sentence: "In Grand Hotel, *Greta Garbo has become Frederick Taylor's Schmidt, another unskilled laborer practicing a routinized task." Write the outline of this essay and then a reply that refutes its arguments.*

A response to this question could begin with these points:

1. Like Schmidt, Garbo was chosen for her physical attributes, not her "skill." Her beauty is the equivalent of Schmidt's brawn.

2. Walter Benjamin's famous essay "The Work of Art in the Age of Mechanical Reproduction" describes film acting as a deskilled activity, the composite of small takes stitched together in the editing room. The camera operator, director, and editor create the performance more than the actor does.

3. By devaluing acting skill and replacing it with "presence" and *photogénie*, the star system further Taylorized film performance. Mamoulian can tell

Garbo to "think of nothing," relying on mere physiology to "do the job." In 1949, Garbo thought about returning to the cinema for a Walter Wanger–produced version of Balzac's *La Duchesse de Langeais*. She agreed to a screen test. Cameraman James Wong Howe recalled that she arrived alone, looking utterly ordinary, without retinue, make-up, or elaborate clothes. When the camera started to turn, Howe remembered, "her face changed, her expression, her whole emotional mood came to life and transformed her completely. It was incredible, wonderful." Then the test was over, as Howe put it, "and she was nothing again." Does this effect have anything to do with *skill*?

4. Both stardom and typecasting encouraged standardization, routinization, deskilling, all in the name of control and predictability. Furthermore, Garbo's Delsartean acting style relies on a repository of coded gestures that make performance somewhat automatic.

And yet (the rebuttal):

1. Garbo-as-craftsman had some control over the filmmaking process: she had her choice of cameraman (William Daniels), directors (often Clarence Brown), and co-stars (she chose her erstwhile lover, the fading John Gilbert, for *Queen Christina*).

2. Garbo's persona is not the same thing as the real Garbo. Garbo has a skill: to project "Garbo," an image that results not only from her looks, but also from her previous roles, MGM's publicity, and her own self-created aura. After all, Archibald Leach created "Cary Grant," and only he could play that part.

3. Taylorism rests on the premise that deskilled labor is both replicable and replaceable. *But Garbo cannot be replaced by anyone in the world.* MGM could not develop "a true science" capable of teaching someone (else) to become "Garbo." Hence, stardom is the kink in the machine, the chief impediment to the Taylorism of Hollywood production.

4. In telling Garbo to make her face a blank, Mamoulian was intuitively relying on an insight about movie stardom made explicit by Ralph Richardson, who said of John Wayne that "his face projected the mystery required of a great actor."[10]

(See *Grand Hotel*: Manchester.)

4

Most descriptions of Garbo characterize her as "broad-shoul-dered," "lanky," "big-boned," "mannish"—too large to play a ballerina. Charles Affron puts the case against casting her as Grusinskaya: "She cannot impersonate away her physical bigness that verges on gawkiness. . . . Garbo as a dancer is something of a joke. . . . a role so suited to her temperament is completely alien to her physique." Alexander Walker, one of her best chroniclers, emphasized her androgynous athleticism: "She cannot take six steps without making it look like the start of a hike." In fact, Garbo was only 5'7" and 126 pounds, hardly a giant. This discrepancy suggests the *relativity* of all screen dimensions. How big are *Grand Hotel*'s rooms? How tall is John Barrymore? Lewis Stone? Joan Crawford? How far *exactly* is the lobby from Preysing's room? As Grusinskaya, Garbo registers as "big" precisely because the actors who surround her—John Barrymore (the Baron), Rafaella Ottiano (Suzette), and Ferdinand Gottschalk (Pimenov)—are unusually small. Like all cinematic universes, *Grand Hotel*'s world is self-contained; its space and time refer only to themselves. Thus, the question of Garbo's size can be solved only in terms of Galileo's principle of relativity, the key to Einstein's own: all cinematic dimensions are "relative and cannot be detected without reference to an outside point." They are an effect of light, as artificial as Einstein's mental experiments, moving as rapidly as the railroad car he used to illustrate the theory of relativity. The film is moving, and its viewers are also moving, and the distance between *Grand Hotel* and us is unstable. Hence, by changing the word *time* to *size* in this formulation of Einstein's question, we see the problem of Garbo's dimensions:

> *How then could* [size] *be measured? Most importantly, how could* [size] *be measured in two different reference systems when the distance between them was constantly changing? Was it possible, in other words, to tell* [the size of] *vehicles moving at near light speeds by an exchange of light signals?*

"You see," *Grand Hotel*'s cameraman, William Daniels, once explained, "*we try to tell the story with light as the director tries to tell it with his action.*"[11]

(with Samantha Murrell)

5

"Garbo," David Thomson writes, "is the extreme definition of stardom in the cinema." At first, this pronouncement seems to suggest her absolute *noncommutativity*. Semioticians have suggested that an actor's most significant features become identifiable when we mentally imagine another playing the same role. A "commutation test," for example, replacing Garbo with Marlene Dietrich would pinpoint which distinguishing star features "read" for an audience: accent, hair color, size, movement, etc. To a certain extent, Garbo's exaggerated stardom resists such attempts at comparison. But, of course, MGM did perform its own applied commutation test, replacing, at its loss, Garbo with Ginger Rogers in the remake, *Week-end at the Waldorf*.

Garbo's stardom, however, does seem vaguely threatening. While the attraction of MGM's other major actors depended on their ability to embody and *bestow* glamour, Garbo's appeal seems predicated on *withholding* it. She inevitably withdraws from those around her ("I want to be alone"). In *Grand Hotel*, she appears onscreen with none of the other stars except John Barrymore, who functions solely to direct attention back to her. Garbo's stardom, in other words, rests on a paradox: radiation without fallout. Thus, while MGM regularly joined established stars with newcomers, in the hopes that something would rub off, the studio rarely juxtaposed Garbo with would-be equals. When it did, as in *Camille* (with Robert Taylor) and *Queen Christina* (with John Gilbert), the effect proved negligible: Gilbert's career did not revive, and Taylor never grew into a major figure. Garbo's stardom explodes on the screen, but it always gravitates back to her, rarely settling on her accompanists. She is a supernova always on the verge of becoming a black hole.[12]

(with Patrick Brennan)

History

31 March–29 June 1929: Vicki Baum publishes *Menschen im Hotel* (rendered in English as *Grand Hotel*) as a serialized novel in the *Berliner Illustrite Zeitung*. The novel will appear later that year in book form, this time under the title *Menschen im Hotel: Ein Kolportageroman mit Hintergründen* (*Hotel People: A Pulp Novel with Undercurrents*).

January 1930: *Menschen im Hotel* opens as a play in Berlin, directed by Gustaf Gründgens, who will soon play underworld boss Schränker in Fritz Lang's *M*. Gründgens will became famous as a director and actor, particularly for his stagings of *Faust*; he will compromise himself by remaining in Germany and regularly cooperating with the Nazis.

1930: *Grand Hotel* translated into English. MGM buys the rights to it and backs November 1930 Broadway opening of the play, a commercial success.

September 1930: Nazi party wins 18.3% of the vote in a German national election.

October 1931: MGM begins work on turning *Grand Hotel* into a movie, assigning Edmund Goulding to direct. Thalberg supervises casting and holds script conferences with Goulding.

January–February 1932: *Grand Hotel* filmed at MGM. Shooting actually begins on Christmas Eve 1931 and is completed by 19 February 1932. The Thalberg-ordered retakes are done by 29 March.

12 April 1932: *Grand Hotel* has its Hollywood premiere.

31 July 1932: Nazis win 37.3% of the vote in national elections, becoming the largest political party in Germany.

6 November 1932: *Grand Hotel* wins the Academy Award for Best Picture.

24 December 1932: Irving Thalberg has a second heart attack. He takes an extended leave from MGM.

30 January 1933: Hitler becomes German chancellor.

4 February 1933: Hitler issues "Emergency Decree" banning public meetings and freedom of the press, and private assembly.

6 February 1933: All power in Prussia (roughly three-fifths of Germany) transferred to Goering, who bans

campaigning by leftist parties, outlaws Communist and Social Democratic newspapers, gives the police free rein to conduct searches and seizures of offices and homes, and encourages the SA (1 million strong, compared to the army's 100,000) to conduct terrorism against the Left.

14 February 1933: L. B. Mayer hires David O. Selznick, who is seen as a partial replacement for Thalberg.

28 February 1933: Reichstag Fire Decree ends *all* civil rights, including freedom of speech and privacy of mails and telephone. Nazis, in effect, install martial law.

3 March 1933: Goering arrests 10,000 political prisoners in Prussia alone. As jails begin to fill, concentration camps are started to hold the overflow of political prisoners.

5 March 1933: In a nonfree election, Nazis still do not get a majority of the vote (only 44%), doing very poorly in what Hitler calls "Red Berlin."

21 March 1933: Hitler sworn in as chancellor at Potsdam, near the palace of Frederick the Great. Hitler asks for "Enabling Law" which would give him unlimited emergency decree powers without having to consult the Reichstag. The law will require a two-thirds majority vote in the Reichstag.

23 March 1933: Reichstag votes on the Enabling Law. Communists are not allowed to vote, but if both the Catholic Center party and Social Democrats vote against the law, it will fail. SD leader Otto Wels makes a courageous speech: "If we allow this law to pass, we are saying farewell to everything we know as civilization and decency in Germany." The Catholic party

votes for the law; Wels and other SD leaders are arrested on the steps of the Reichstag.

28 March 1933: Thalberg leaves Los Angeles to see heart specialist Dr. Franz Groedel in Bad Nauheim (a spa near Frankfurt). He travels by boat, going through the Panama Canal; in Panama City, he learns that local brothels advertise prostitutes by giving them the names of famous movie stars. Thalberg sees one brothel with his wife's (Norma Shearer) name in lights. He is angry, but Shearer seems pleased by the tribute.

1 April 1933: Nazi government calls for a boycott of all Jewish businesses. In Thalberg's absence, MGM releases *Gabriel over the White House*, a movie shot in two weeks that glamorizes dictatorial solutions to America's problems.

7 April 1933: Nazis remove all Jews from courts, universities, media, professions, and civil service.

1 May 1933: Nazi government declares National Day of German Labor and that evening arrests labor leaders, sending them to concentration camps.

10 May 1933: German universities, led by the German Student Union, burn books by "un-German" authors (especially Jews). Among the condemned writers is Vicki Baum.

May–June 1933: Thalberg in Germany to see Dr. Groedel, who removes his tonsils. While in Germany, Thalberg and Shearer see just outside their hotel room storm troopers beating up a couple in the street below. Police do not respond to Thalberg's call. Nevertheless, Thalberg seems unfazed. Back in New York in July, Thalberg declares that although "a lot of

Jews will lose their lives, Hitler and Hitlerism will pass; the Jews will still be there." (He sees Communism as the greater threat.) Dr. Groedel, himself Jewish, will soon leave Germany for a New York practice. In 1936, he will attend Thalberg on his deathbed.[13]

Want to Be Alone

This famous line, forever associated with Garbo, occurs for the first time in *Grand Hotel*, where its effect demonstrates star-acting's dependence on the viewer's extratextual knowledge. By 1932, Garbo's aloofness—in part her natural disposition, but also a persona carefully nurtured by MGM—had become central to her performances.

Merely by playing them, Garbo could now endow her characters with a world-weary remoteness requiring little narrative motivation. Garbo, in other words, like almost all great movie stars, had become a *shorthand*, an extraordinarily efficient way of rendering a person, a situation, an atmosphere. (To realize this phenomenon's immediate effect, one need only imagine a scene into which walks John Wayne or Cary Grant or Woody Allen—each producing an entirely different set of audience expectations.)

Nevertheless, although Grusinskaya's famous line is consistent with Garbo's offscreen image, by now it almost certainly invokes the actress more than the character. The case of Judy

Garland as Betsy Booth (in the Andy Hardy series) suggests that extratextual knowledge directly *contradicting* narrative tone can prove fatal to a movie's diegetic effect, its power to absorb the viewer in a fictional world. Indeed, such knowledge is the beginning of camp. *Grand Hotel* offers a more subtle problem: what happens when a star's persona *overwhelms* the character? When that persona itself dates more rapidly than the roles she has played, the movie's ability to convince begins to wane: interest in the story gives way to a fascination with the performance. *Grand Hotel* provides an important demonstration of this result. Thus, Pauline Kael's brief summary completely dismisses plot as the movie's source of interest:

> *There is every reason to reject* Grand Hotel *as an elaborate chunk of artifice; there are no redeeming qualities in Vicki Baum's excruciating concepts of character and fate, and anyone who goes to see the movie expecting an intelligent script, or even "good acting," should have his head examined. Most of the players give impossibly bad performances—they chew up the camera. But if you want to see what screen glamour used to be, and what, originally, "stars" were, this is perhaps the best example of all time.*

The Garbo image gave rise to rumors about prima donna behavior during *Grand Hotel*'s filming, supposedly requiring Goulding to film her scenes separately, using cross-cutting to achieve the illusion of conversation with another actor. In fact, however, while tempers flared between the enormously ambitious Joan Crawford and the scene-stealing Wallace Beery, Garbo expressed ready admiration for John Barrymore. "You have no idea," she told him, "what it means to me to play opposite so perfect an artist." Goulding had no need to isolate Garbo; *Grand Hotel*'s plot had already done that job. As this chart shows, of the five leading characters, only Grusinskaya is limited to one other contact; the other four all interact with each other.

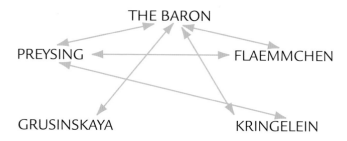

THE BARON

PREYSING   FLAEMMCHEN

GRUSINSKAYA   KRINGELEIN

This arrangement enables the movie's plot, which, as Barthes observed in *S/Z*, depends on "a rule of communication [that] keeps the networks of destination separate, so that each one can continue to operate even if its neighbor is already 'burned out.'" This metaphor, literalized by *Grand Hotel*'s recurring shots of the hotel's telephone switchboard, suggests the rapid branching of plot lines: when one story temporarily runs dry, we are connected to another circuit, just as the operators shuffle phone lines. When one channel wears out (e.g., when the Baron is killed), a new inquiry begins (what will Flaemmchen do now?).

Garbo's early retirement at 36 and her "bachelor" life retroactively enhanced the resonance of "I want to be alone." Her retreat, by preventing her audience from seeing her age, kept her young. By then, Walter Benjamin had already suggested that mechanical reproduction threatens the distinction between the original and its reproduction. In 1941, Garbo erased the distinction by eliminating the original, retiring into seclusion.[14]

(*with Katherine Arpen, Ryan Johnson, Samantha Murrell*)

 J **azz**

Disgusted by Grusinskaya's premature departure from the theater, her manager (Meierheim) pronounces the death-knell of the ancien régime. "After this," he tells Pimenov, "it's no more ballet for me. Jazz, just jazz." Arno J. Mayer's famous book long ago detailed "the persistence of the old regime," the aristocratic tastes and values that survived all of Europe's bourgeois revolutions, enduring until World War I. With its ballerina heroine and *Blue Danube* soundtrack, *Grand Hotel* represents that "persistence." "I am only old fashioned," Grusinskaya admits to the Baron in Baum's novel. "I am from another world, another century." The name for the *new* century, on the other hand, will be the Jazz Age, and this shift from high to vernacular culture represents many of the other postwar transformations: the relocation of power to America, the search for non-European musical influences, the aristocracy's final collapse.

Just three years after *Grand Hotel*'s premiere, Walter Benjamin's famous essay "The Work of Art in the Age of Mechanical Reproduction" would offer the cinema as the model of post-ancien régime culture and politics. The movies' radical potential, Benjamin argued, lay precisely in their status as *recordings*. What is an event, Benjamin would ask, that has no independent status, that exists only for the sake of being reproduced? The answer was—a film. "Technical reproduction," Benjamin observed, "can put the copy of the original into situations that would be out of reach for the original itself. Above all, it enables the original to meet the beholder halfway." In this reproducibility lay the cinema's progressive effects:

> One might generalize by saying: the technique of reproduction
> detaches the reproduced object from the domain of tradition.
> By making many reproductions it substitutes a plurality of
> copies for a unique existence. And in permitting the reproduc-
> tion to meet the beholder or the listener in his own particular
> situation, it reactivates the object reproduced. These two
> processes lead to a tremendous shattering of tradition.

What distinguished rock and roll from the music that preceded it—especially classical—was its elevation of the *record* to primary status. While classical recordings for the most part had aimed only at approximating live performances, regarded as the significant event, many of rock's most important musicians, beginning with Elvis, made records before ever appearing in public. In doing so, they imitated the many movie stars who had never acted in a theater. In semiotic terms, therefore, a record, like a film, became a sign without a referent: behind *Grand Hotel* or "Fight the Power" lies no single, "real" event that has been transcribed and reproduced. Instead, there are only fragments of behavior, snatches of sound: a turn of the head filmed one Monday for a sequence completed a month later, a drumbeat sampled for mixing with a radio announcement.

In its relationship to recording, jazz stood halfway between classical music and rock. While jazz has always privileged live performance, its advent and diffusion depended enormously on recordings. As Evan Eisenberg's *The Recording Angel* puts the matter, "records and radio were the proximate cause of the Jazz Age. . . . Records not only disseminated jazz, but inseminated it. . . . they created what we now call jazz." Eisenberg traces how the act of recording (with its producers' concomitant eagerness to avoid paying royalties for existing songs) prompted Louis Armstrong's early Hot Five compositions, and the records themselves carried his solos into every corner of the country, where they could be studied, memorized, and duplicated by the new music's emerging players.

But Hollywood cinema's relationship to jazz involved a paradox. Although the movies and jazz shared both a basis in mechanical reproduction and a status as "modern," *Grand Hotel*'s baron and ballerina, waltzes and horse-drawn hearse testify to the old regime's persistence. In fact, for much of the sound era's first 20 years, Hollywood would often use jazz as a signifier for moral decay—listen, for example, to the soundtrack of *It's a Wonderful Life*'s Pottersville sequence, where jazz instantly represents the slide into the landscape of urban noir. In its early days, as Eisenberg admits, jazz was usually heard "while under the influence of alcohol, lust, or gaming table greed"—all prominent in *Grand Hotel*. The Nazis had the same idea about jazz, promulgating their own notorious 1938 "official position" about the music they quickly banned:

> *Prohibition: It is forbidden to play in public music that possesses*
> *to a marked degree characteristic features of the method of*
> *improvisation, execution, composition and arrangement adopted*
> *by Negroes and colored people. It is forbidden in publications,*
> *reports, programs, printed or verbal announcements, etc.:*
>
> (a) to describe music played or to be played with the
> words "jazz" or "jazz music."

Ballet, on the other hand, did not suffer under Nazi cultural policy. Despite the ordered closing of modern dance studios and performances, even party officials did not refrain from attending ballets. On a 1939 trip to the Soviet Union, Foreign Minister Joachim von Ribbentrop needed to pass some time while waiting for a meeting with Stalin. He watched the first act of *Swan Lake*, the ballet Grusinskaya performs in Berlin.[15]

(with Katherine Arpen and Ryan Johnson)

K ringelein's Disease

Kringelein is dying, but the movie cannot name his disease, whose narrative function resembles that of Rick's mysterious crime in *Casablanca*. Rick "cannot return to his country," as Major Strasser summarizes. "The reason is a little vague." Like Gatsby's past, Rick's offense must remain unspecified, for while anything less than murder (e.g., theft, forgery) would make Rick simply a common criminal, any capital crime would disqualify him as Ilsa's suitor. Similarly, *Grand Hotel*'s narrative evades particulars. Naming Kringelein's disease (e.g., cancer, ALS) would evoke both existing symptoms and inevitable outcome, thereby disabling the movie's fragile happy ending, Kringelein's flight to Paris with Flaemmchen. Since in her memoirs, Vicki Baum was less discreet (Kringelein, she revealed, has stomach cancer), we suspect that *Grand Hotel*'s silence results from an attempt to avoid what Susan Sontag identified as cancer's connotations: scandal, contamination, the violation of a taboo. Thus, *Grand Hotel*'s spectator becomes like a cancer patient, "lied to, not just because the disease is (or is thought to be) a death sentence, but because it is felt to be obscene." Sontag's *Illness as Metaphor* contrasts cancer with tuberculosis, romantically associated with heightened artistic sensibilities (the myth of Keats, *The Magic Mountain*). Just four years before Baum's *Grand Hotel*, another novel appeared, also in German, written by a clerk, dying like Kringelein: *The Trial*. Kafka, whose shabby hero, Joseph K., anticipates Baum's own, died of tuberculosis, the disease Baum originally intended for Kringelein.[16]

L earning to Dance

To Flaemmchen in the Yellow Room, Kringelein confesses that he has never before danced in public. He stumbles, concentrates on his feet, and moves hesitantly. Why doesn't Kringelein know how to dance? *Grand Hotel*'s "realistic" answer is Kringelein's status as a poor factory bookkeeper ("Room 23, Building C, third floor") who doesn't get out much. The real answer is because he doesn't go to the movies. During the studio era, for a provincial audience unaccustomed to travel or sophistication, the cinema served as an ongoing instruction manual, teaching its viewers how to do unfamiliar things: check into a luxury hotel, walk a dog through a lobby, order a cocktail, get in and out of a limousine, tip a bellboy, flirt with a pretty young stranger, dress for dinner, dance.

(with Eleanor Helm)

Likes and Dislikes (after Roland Barthes)

I like: the scene with the Baron's coffin, the overhead shot of Garbo undressing on the floor, the switchboard operators, the hotel's circular lobby and landings, Grusinskaya's "I was *frantic*," Flaemmchen and the Baron flirting by the fifth-floor railing, the mirrors that appear in so many scenes, Pimenov, the chiaroscuro of Garbo's first appearance, the Baron on the ledge, Preysing's exercises, "I want to be alone," the mise-en-scène's abstraction.

I dislike: Lionel Barrymore as Kringelein (except when he returns drunk to his room), the Baron speaking baby-talk to his dachshund, the Yellow Room scenes, the Senf plot, the Saxonia negotiations, Preysing's "arrangement" with Flaemmchen, Wallace Beery's "German" accent, the Baron's "chauffeur," the arrogant reservation clerk, the refusal to acknowledge the film's dateline: "Berlin, 1932."

Louisiana Flip

Responding to the bartender's suggestion, Kringelein orders a Louisiana Flip, already rejected by both Flaemmchen and the Baron. The scene will reiterate the drink's name six times, enforcing its emerging connotations: femininity, naïveté, silliness. If no one who drinks a Louisiana Flip can be taken seriously, the man who orders champagne (Dr. Otternschlag) is cultured, while the woman with absinthe (Flaemmchen) is doomed. Nevertheless, the drink's obscurity (unlisted in indexes containing 10,000 recipes) makes the viewer feel the Grand Hotel's power to intimidate. What is a Louisiana Flip? A mixture of rum, triple sec, grenadine, orange juice, ice, and one egg yolk. Like *Grand Hotel*, it is, as the bartender advertises, both "sweet and *cold*."

(*with Morgan Burroughs, Elliot Gale, Charles Meyer, Ryan Johnson*)

Lucille LeSueur

Born as Lucille LeSueur, raised as Billie Cassin (for her mother's live-in, criminal boyfriend), Joan Crawford required a name that did not sound like "sewer." After her discovery by MGM, she proved relentlessly ambitious, especially about her appearance. In 1930, Crawford decided to remake her body, carving her face through extensive dental work and make-up into a new fashion.

> *After altering the shape of her face by having her back teeth removed to give her cheekbones, she had her teeth, which were spaced and filled with dental cement during the early days of filming, filed down to allow temporary caps to fit over them. The painful procedure, however, infected her gums, which stretched her mouth. When the swelling subsided, it left her with a large upper lip.*

By *Grand Hotel*, Crawford's face had become a structured, highly recognizable creation, ripe for parody and impersonation. As she flirts with John Barrymore as the Baron, she sucks in her cheeks to show off their new planes.

In the meantime, Crawford was being dressed by Adrian, MGM's chief costumer and the man charged with creating her distinctive look. From 1929 to 1943, Adrian designed everything Crawford wore onscreen and most of what she wore off. Increasingly padded shoulders accentuated her own angular shape, and Crawford became a generic deco work, with figurines of her selling widely.

Grand Hotel, as Thomas Schatz has said, represents "the triumph of style." Flaemmchen, the "little stenographess" who would "love to be in the movies," eagerly explains to Preysing that she has "a rather nice figure" and poses for "art studies," presumably nudes. Here, actress and character merge (Crawford had worked at similar modeling jobs) in their obsession with surfaces. Balzac's Sarrasine, as Barthes saw, "tries to undress appearances, tries always to get *beyond, behind*, according to the idealistic principle that identifies secrecy with truth: one must go *into* the model, *beneath* the statue, *behind* the canvas." Crawford, on the other hand, sculpted herself, thereby demonstrating that Hollywood's star system had made operable Nietzsche's metaphoric description of the Greeks:

> [O]ne will hardly ever find us again on the paths of those
> Egyptian youths who endanger temples by night, embrace
> statues, and want by all means to unveil, uncover, and put
> into a bright light whatever is kept concealed for good reasons.
> No, this bad taste, this will to truth . . . have lost their charm
> for us: for that we are too experienced, too serious, too merry,
> too burned, too profound. We no longer believe that truth
> remains truth when the veils are withdrawn. . . .
>   Oh, those Greeks! They knew how to live. What is
> required for that is to stop courageously at the surface, the
> fold, the skin, to adore appearance, to believe in forms, tones,
> words, in the whole Olympus of appearance. Those Greeks
> were superficial—out of profundity.

Research assignment: Use Nietzsche's remarks as a means of understanding Garbo.[17]

(*with Kate Casey-Sawicki, Denise Cummings, Samantha Murrell*)

 **anchester**

Everything depends upon news from Manchester.

Waiting, waiting . . . I've been waiting for news from Manchester.

The Saxonia Company will never sign unless your firm is definitely tied up with the Manchester people.

"Deal with Manchester definitely off." Is that something bad?

A man in the textile industry must know Manchester.

Have you any connections with Manchester?

Manchester—that's what we want to know.

Well, gentlemen, the situation seems to be perfectly clear. How clear is Manchester?

But don't you think for one moment that I am such a fool as not to have something to say about Manchester.

In *Grand Hotel*, the word "Manchester" recurs like a fatal curse, dooming Preysing when his deal with that city's firm falls through. The formulations, insistent, rhythmical, edge toward modernist haiku:

> *everything depends*
> *upon*
>
>
> *news from Man-*
> *chester*

and a tele-
graphed message

about the group
merger

But why "Manchester"? Preysing, after all, is German, and the movie's story takes place in Berlin. "Manchester," of course, is the name for a catastrophe, one based on speed and one relevant to studio-era filmmaking. As the industrial revolution developed in England, Manchester became its center, mush-rooming between 1800 and 1851 from a town of 90,000 people to an appalling city of over 450,000, where the smoke-filled air caused the sun to disappear, and a person's life expectancy was half that of someone living barely 20 miles away. The name Manchester symbolized an entire culture's commitment to Britain's utilitarian version of the Enlightenment, a redefinition of rationality as the means-to-profit. As power shifted from its previous centers ("What Manchester thinks today, London will tomorrow" went the proverb), the "Manchester men" became famous for their "progressive" business sense, their wealth, and their ruthlessness. Eight-year-old children were roused from their beds after five hours' sleep and forced to walk miles to a 15-hour shift in blanket factories, where sleepiness was punished by savage beatings. In Manchester, where he worked in his father's mill, Friedrich Engels invented Communism, publishing in 1845 *The Condition of the Working Class in England* as a response to what he had seen around him.

But the Manchester system made fortunes: as visiting Frenchman Alexis de Tocqueville said of Manchester in 1835, "From this filthy sewer pure gold flows." Manchester's industrial discipline, to which its men, women, and children had to conform, was perfected by Frederick Taylor and Henry Ford, whose management systems Hollywood eagerly adopted. Mass production, standardized designs, concentration of the whole production cycle in a single place, even the after-hours surveillance of employees—all of these Fordist practices became Hollywood's own. Thus, at the peak of its early 1930s power, the time of *Grand Hotel*, MGM could produce one feature film per week, a quota enabled by its standardized genres, enormous physical plant, and a star system whose performers often remained as alienated from their tasks as any factory worker. *Grand Hotel*, in other words, issued from the system known throughout the nineteenth century as "Manchester," and the industrialist Preysing's resort to murder seems as inevitable as the effects of Hollywood's own child labor practices on Judy Garland.

Engels had detected the terrible paradox, describing a day spent in Manchester with a middle-class gentleman:

> *I spoke to him about the disgraceful, unhealthy slums and drew his attention to the disgusting condition of that part of the town in which the factory workers lived. I declared that I had never seen so badly built a town in my life. He listened patiently and at the corner of the street at which we parted company, he remarked, "And yet there is a great deal of money made here. Good morning, Sir."*[18]

(See *Grand Hotel*: Garbo, section 3.)

(with Ryan Johnson, Jason von Lembke, Maitreya Sims)

umbers

Like *Pride and Prejudice*, *Grand Hotel* assigns precise value to every detail. Thus, we know:

Kringelein's monthly salary is 320 marks.

Every minute on the lobby telephones costs 2 marks 90.

Flaemmchen was to earn 1,000 marks, plus clothing expenses, for becoming Preysing's temporary mistress.

The Baron owes the burglary ring 5,000 marks.

Kringelein has 13,600 marks in his pocketbook: 3,400 from his savings and 10,200 from his gambling winnings.

Kringelein gives Flaemmchen 3,200 marks to go with him and promises her the rest of his money after he dies.

With Jane Austen, the origins of such specificity seem obvious: a class system whose marital arrangements, brokered like securities, turned on minutely scrutinized incomes. In *Grand Hotel*, however, the motivation involves deadlines, the preoccupation of the Hollywood studios, obsessed with "working" their fixed costs: actors, technicians, writers, equipment, land. Thus, the movie encourages us to calculate its characters' desperation. Given the exact amount of Kringelein's fortune, *we know that it can run out*. Similarly, the number assigned to Kringelein's life savings (3,400 marks) makes the Baron's 5,000-mark debt seem to require *un coup de théâtre* for its solution ("I have no time," he tells Kringelein). In fact, except for Grusinskaya, all of *Grand Hotel*'s main characters have money problems, as did all of the Hollywood studios in 1932. And yet the film suppresses the value of its most important object, Grusinskaya's pearls, set at 500,000 marks by Baum's novel. Silencing this disproportionate number makes the Baron's choice of love over money more credible, albeit less noble.

(with Samantha Murrell)

verhead Shots

Grand Hotel opens with one of
its most memorable images,
an overhead shot of the hotel
switchboard, the depersonal-
ized operators (the film never
shows their faces) busily
routing incoming and outgo-
ing calls. This overhead angle,
unsponsored by any diegetic

motivation (it issues from no character's point of view), will
recur intermittently throughout the movie. The shots of the
circular staircase and lobby, the image of Garbo removing her

ballet costume, the view of
Kringelein's drunken return to
his room—taken together,
these moments indicate
Goulding's taste for, and
Thalberg's tolerance of, design
over plot.

In each case, the over-
head angle deemphasizes the
human element, transforming
character into geometry, actor
into pattern. Although classical
Hollywood remained preoccupied with narrative momentum,
it occasionally seemed willing
to acknowledge the fourth of
Thalberg's "Ten Command-
ments for Studio Readers":

Remember you are dealing with a pictorial medium. Thus, if a film's story line resembles a river, rushing headlong to its destination, *Grand Hotel*'s overhead shots amount to pauses, places where the movie is *eddying* (by chance, a close homonym of Goulding's first

name). Thalberg's approval of these shots—narratively inefficient, often expensive—depended on his recognizing that even commercial filmmaking could not be reduced to plot. F. Scott Fitzgerald's "whole equation of pictures" required an algorithm, a method for continuously reconciling the competing demands of narrative and mise-en-scène.

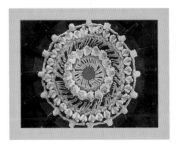

Within months, *Grand Hotel*'s occasional demonstrations of the pattern latent in every event would erupt into *42nd Street*'s extravagant sequences, in which Busby Berkeley's overheads would realize Kracauer's "mass ornament."

This beauty's provenance, however, lay in industrial management's inflexible demands. Like Berkeley's kaleidoscopic dancers, *Grand Hotel*'s switchboard operators evoke Frederick Taylor's system, with its implacable logic of routinized tasks performed by deskilled labor. Taylor's *The Principles of Scientific Management* presents the apposite case. Summoned in 1896 by the Simonds Rolling Machine Company, Taylor designed a method for young women to hand-sort ball bearings, a task at once so exacting and tedious that "after about an hour and one-half of consecutive work they began to get nervous." Taylor's solution was to prohibit all socializing, separating the inspectors to prohibit talking, while scheduling regular, precisely measured work breaks. In effect, he had turned the women into machines. Kracauer had discovered "the mass ornament" in the Tiller Girls, a European dance troop he mistook for American. This new, "modern" glamour, Kracauer intuited, was always produced by its exact opposite, the repetition of tiny, monotonous actions. Every image of flight, each spinning wheel, requires a Taylor Girl, "engaged in picking out all [the] defective balls." In public, the Taylor Girls dressed up as Tiller Girls, becoming dancers who "formed an undulating snake, [and] radiantly illustrated the virtues of the conveyor belt." But *Grand Hotel*'s telephone operators, even reduced to a visual pattern, suggest that the Tiller Girls were never as "de-eroticized" as Kracauer had claimed. Hollywood would prove that eroticism is not incompatible with mass production.

In *Grand Hotel*, the unmotivated overhead shots contribute to a visual strategy that also seems bent on avoiding shot/reverse-shot, regarded as the key to classical Hollywood's diegetic effect. Reverse-angle editing attributed images to a character's point of view, "suturing" a sequence into a self-contained world: If shot 1's man looked offscreen, shot 2's ocean appeared to be the result of the character's gaze, not the director's choice. By thus providing shots with sources within the story, Hollywood cinema encouraged identification with characters, while forestalling the viewers' sense that someone had constructed what he was seeing. "It was this procedure," as Noël Burch observed, that "made it possible to implicate the spectator in the eye contact of the actors . . . to *include* him or her in the mental and 'physical' space of the diegesis." The film's events acquired an apparently independent status, which the camera merely seemed to record. As the studios perfected the invisible style, this technique assumed increasing importance. By 1942's *Casablanca*, in many ways the ultimate studio era movie, reverse-angles would account for 50% of all shot changes.

Grand Hotel, however, prefers the two-shot, used by Goulding especially for the Baron's sustained conversations with both Flaemmchen and Grusinskaya. This approach has an obvious advantage: it keeps *two* of MGM's expensive stars simultaneously in view. But it also keeps the movie's characters at a distance; we rarely occupy their space, see what they see. When coupled with the recurring unmotivated overheads, the paucity of reverse-angles endows *Grand Hotel* with an atmosphere different from that of the usual Hollywood film: cool, abstract, untethered. One name for this mode is "Brechtian." Only a few months before *Grand Hotel*, Fritz Lang, admittedly influenced by Brecht, had made *M*, a movie starring Brecht's discovery Peter Lorre. Like *Grand Hotel*, *M* avoided reverse-angles, while repeatedly returning to unmotivated overhead shots in which the film's events were subsumed by a suddenly apparent, inescapable geometry.

Noël Burch detected a similar set of strategies in the films of Yasujiro Ozu. The Japanese director regularly confounded reverse-angle cutting with 180-degree violations while also employing what Burch called "pillow shots," transitional images of objects or landscapes with at most an imprecise relationship to the movie's fictional world: the side of a house, a railroad station, clothes on a wash line. These curious shots—lengthy, still, unpopulated—"*suspend the diegetic flow*," marking, in Burch's words, "the gradual abandonment of that narrative density of the West, that relentless chain of diegetic events." Ozu's pillow shots, Burch implicitly argued, had a Brechtian effect, undermining Hollywood cinema's insistence on invisibly produced, insistently enthralling stories.

Do *Grand Hotel*'s overheads produce the same alienation effect? Unlike Ozu's pillow shots, *Grand Hotel*'s images of the switchboard operators, circular staircase, Grusinskaya's disrobing, and Kringelein's confusion all contain *diegetic* information. They do not leave the story's world or its characters. And yet, these shots seem part of a different system, one more concerned with sheer pictorialism, less committed to plot. In places, the strain of calibrating the two registers becomes visible. Flaemmchen's

approach to the railing makes the overhead of stairwell and lobby seem a reverse-angle from her perspective, the object of her gaze.

In fact, however, *she appears in this shot*, and the movie offers no prior justification for it. The subsequent cut back to the landing, revealing the Baron at Flaemmchen's side, amounts to a continuity error since he cannot be found in the overhead.

Here is a way of thinking about *Grand Hotel*'s overhead shots. Gilberto Perez has suggested that the movies are "both a dramatic and a narrative medium." Perez follows Brecht in using "dramatic" to mean something like classical Hollywood cinema, a filmmaking process that conceals its own workings. "Narrative" moments, on the other hand, like Brecht's Epic Theater, emphasize a story's telling. The distinction appears, as Perez shows, in Brecht's *Caucasian Chalk Circle*, where a woman, initially reluctant to help an abandoned baby, eventually, after approaching it, picks it up.

> Brecht has this played in pantomime, with a singer alongside telling about it in the words of a song, which refer to [the woman] in the third person and to what is happening in the past tense. "As if it was stolen goods she picked it up. / As if she was a thief she crept away."

Here, the song's words convert the events from drama into narrative, thereby raising "the possibility of other ways in which the action could have been played." If, as Perez maintains, "the point-of-view shot is a dramatic rather than a narrative technique," and if that technique depends precisely on the motivation denied by *Grand Hotel*'s overheads, then *Grand Hotel*'s subtle strangeness seems explainable. The movie is a drama *punctuated by narrative*. It is Brechtian *avant la nouvelle vague*.[19]

(with Alan Clinton)

Pavlova

Baum modeled the fading ballerina Grusinskaya on the Russian Ballet's Anna Pavlova (1882–1931), who lived most of her life in hotels and trains. As her career wound down, she cut difficult sections and performed only less-demanding pieces. Her world-weary epigrams—"Life would be so wonderful if we only knew what to do with it," "Happiness is like a butterfly that appears and delights us for one brief moment, but soon flits away"—seem to modern ears even more outlandish than Grusinskaya's complaint about an evening without applause: "I was *frantic!*"

Baum had presumably seen Pavlova in 1925, when the Russian had performed *The Dying Swan* in Berlin to a half-empty house. Pavlova was 43 then, 17 years older than Garbo during *Grand Hotel*'s filming. Indeed, Garbo was born in the same year as

Pavlova's official appointment to the rank of prima ballerina. Photographs of Pavlova as the swan clearly inspired *Grand Hotel*'s overhead shot of Grusinskaya removing her ballet shoes. This replication of bodies, however, seems unusual for classic Hollywood, a period when the studios confidently advertised their stars' individuality: Garbo, MGM insisted, could not be duplicated.

In fact, Hollywood's moguls had intuited the difference between stage and screen acting. Stanley Cavell sums it up: "[I]n a play the character is present, whereas in a film the actor is. . . . a role in a play is like a position in a game, say, third base: various people can play it." But the great movie stars subsume all roles into themselves. Cavell quotes Panofsky on this point: "The character in a film . . . lives and dies with the actor. It is not the entity 'Othello' interpreted by Robeson or the entity 'Nora' interpreted by Duse, it is the entity 'Greta Garbo' incarnate in a figure called Anna Christie." Garbo, in other words, is not playing "Pavlova" or "the dying swan." She can only play "Garbo."[20]

(with Charles Meyer and Drew Shackelford)

Q uestions

In *The Avant-Garde Finds Andy Hardy*, I suggested that the surrealist game of "irrational enlargement" might offer a tool for thinking about classic Hollywood. The game asks questions of the sort expressly forbidden by New Criticism, whose paradigmatic example of an improper question was, "What did Hamlet study in Wittenberg before the play begins?"—i.e., a question unaddressed by the play. Hollywood films, however, never provide answers for all of the questions they imply. Their realism, for one thing, is elliptical, metonymic (one minaret + one parrot = "Casablanca"); its stories unroll with a speed that forestalls objections. (See *Grand Hotel*: *Blue Danube*; *The Maltese Falcon*:

Golden Gate Bridge.) Irrational enlargement questions point to the places in a movie where realism struggles, where the viewer, however unconsciously, wants to know more. Often, the irrational enlargement game asks questions that occur to us during a movie, but which we suppress because the narrative proves them irrelevant. The questions' appeal, therefore, represents a moment of delayed recognition: we hear spoken, made explicit, something we wondered about without realizing it, which we censored as inconsequential to the story. The speed of Hollywood's sense-making renders it invisible; the irrational enlargement game alerts us to its having occurred. Here, then, are some questions about *Grand Hotel*:

> Who gets the cramped room (with the water pipes that "go *bing, bong* all day") originally assigned to Kringelein?

> Was the Baron at Verdun?

> How near is the Grand Hotel to Wansee?

> When Kringelein complains to the front desk about his room, he displaces a young woman in a fur coat who is trying to make a reservation for nine people: herself, "my mother, two sisters, and a secretary." Who are the other four?

> Did Hitler leave early from one of Grusinskaya's performances?

> Where are Suzette's and Pimenov's rooms?

> As Grusinskaya leaves to catch the Vienna train, the hotel clock reads 6:30 a.m. Why have Grusinskaya's handlers scheduled such an early-morning departure after an evening performance?

> What disease is killing Kringelein?

What is in the message the front desk gives to Flaemmchen as she leaves for Paris with Kringelein?

What becomes of Senf's son?

Where did Grusinskaya appear immediately *before* Berlin?

What are the other ends of the opening telephone conversations?

When does the hotel restaurant close?

What is "Dr." Zinnowitz a doctor of?

What do Preysing's wife and daughters look like?

What do the Baron and Grusinskaya eat the morning after?

At the movie's end, young honeymooners, apparently Americans, arrive in a two-door convertible. Why is the steering wheel on the *right* side?

In the scene with the Baron's coffin, what are the men counting?

If the characters' *fifth*-floor hotel rooms have numbers in the 100s, what numbers do the *first*-floor rooms have?

Does Flaemmchen use a German typewriter?

How did Grusinskaya discover Tremezzo, where she has a villa?

R oom Assignments

Somewhere en route from novel to film, *Grand Hotel*'s characters have changed rooms.

Room Assignments in the Novel

68	69	70	71	72
Grusinskaya	Baron	Kringelein	Preysing	Flaemmchen

Room Assignments in the Film

176	174	172	170	168	166
Kringelein	?	?	Grusinskaya	Pimenov	Preysing

164	162	160
Flaemmchen	Conference Room	Baron

The new arrangement's ability to imply a realistic space depends on its being asserted only *in passing*. In classic Hollywood filmmaking, a descendant of the nineteenth-century novel, overt schema appear as what Barthes called "prattle," a vestige of earlier narrative forms' insecurity about communication. The modern viewer will experience any obvious communiqués as "corny" and heavy-handed. Thus, although the film either shows or tells us exactly where most of the main characters are staying (Dr. Otternschlag is the exception), this information almost never calls attention to itself. It remains available for retrieval, but only by the kind of fetishistic re-viewing discouraged by the studios, always eager to sell their next product. Room numbers, therefore, simply appear on doors, usually in the background, unannounced. When someone actually mentions a number, the film works to divert our attention, like a magician using sleight of hand. Ballet master Pimenov's request for his room key, "Number 168," for example, occurs so quickly and inconsequentially (we never see him enter or leave his room) that noticing the number requires actively looking for it—as opposed to following the story.

The revised room assignments represent the kind of decision that seems unimportant until we remember that *someone had to make it*. (The principle: the controlled world of studio filmmaking will leave nothing to chance.) Why relocate the main characters? Some possibilities:

1. Separating the Baron from his prey, Grusinskaya, makes his cat burglary more visually arresting: as he clings to the hotel's exterior walls and balcony railings, *he has farther to go*. (But the separation also calls into question the Baron's plan: can he really expect to pass undetected by *three* occupied rooms? By abridging his trip—we only see him outside Preysing's room—the movie forestalls this objection.)

2. Increasing the sequence of rooms from five to nine stretches the hallway, providing the illusion of a hotel with, in Dr. Otternschlag's words, "a hundred doors to one hall."

3. Rooms 172 and 174, whose occupancy status the movie withholds, indicate that *Grand Hotel*'s story does not exhaust its diegetic space—something is left over, a world indifferent to these characters, these events. In that territory, the film implies, unknown people engage in unknown activities. The empty rooms, in other words, heighten *Grand Hotel*'s realistic effect. Imagine the contrary as an experimental exercise, a movie hotel whose every occupant must take part in a plot, a fairy tale whose exacting rigor seems worthy of Georges Perec or Jacques Rivette.[21]

(with Charles Meyer)

S eduction

In *S/Z*, Barthes demonstrated how an apparently innocent description of Sarrasine's visits to La Zambinella's performances might be replaced by a structurally identical erotic anecdote. "This operation," Barthes suggested, "is based not on a lexicon of symbols but on systematic cohesion, a congruence of relationships" that appear in rereadings. Similarly, *Grand Hotel*'s dictation scene between Flaemmchen and Preysing provides an analogue of the sexual-act-interrupted-by-impotence.

> *Seduction*: Preysing's repetition of the phrase "mutual advantages."
>
> *Foreplay*: Flaemmchen accepts and teases him with her magazine picture.
>
> *Impotence*: Receiving the news that his Manchester deal has failed, Preysing loses power.
>
> *Denial*: Preysing claims that he has no problem ("It doesn't mean that at all. . . . that's a mistake").
>
> *Withdrawal*: Flaemmchen asks, "Do you want to go on?" Preysing tells her to come back the next morning.

This scene's casual acceptance of lust, a pre-Code symptom, differs from the Baron's first meetings with Flaemmchen and Grusinskaya, which taken together suggest the simplest rule of film courtship: when presented with two seductions, the one that mentions dieting will date less than the one that involves intervention in a suicide attempt. And prove more realistic, too. Although her character seems shocked by the Baron's question, Crawford was, in fact, "reducing" her appearance (see *Grand Hotel*: Lucille LeSueur), and Garbo's late-20s world-weary apathy had probably resulted from an MGM-enforced diet. As L. B. Mayer told her interpreter, "Tell her she has to take off weight. We don't like fat girls in my country." Garbo's reply: "If that is so important, you'll see, I will be so thin like a reed when I come to America."[22]

(*with Katherine Arpen and Ryan Johnson*)

Surfaces

When compared to *Week-end at the Waldorf*, whose even, high-key lighting anticipates television, *Grand Hotel*'s rooms and sets can seem extraordinarily empty. The heavy chiaroscuro favored by Goulding and Daniels contributes to this effect, restricting attention to small illuminated areas, while reducing the rest to black. This strategy appears most decisively in Garbo's first scene, where a single bedside lamp forms a narrow triangle of light falling only on her.

Closer inspection, however, reveals that art director Cedric Gibbons varied the decor in *Grand Hotel*'s rooms, even among

the same class of suites. Thus, the rooms of Preysing, the Baron, Kringelein, and Grusinskaya visually differ, while sharing the same floor plan and recurring graphic motifs. The inlaid designs on the doors and furniture, for example, appear in all of these suites, with two conjoined triangles meeting at their apexes, as if the corset, banished from fashions three decades earlier, had returned as architectural design. The rooms' distinguishing features, however, match the personality types that inhabit them. Hence, the Baron's room: smooth, sparse, angular, with an abstract painting on
the wall. By contrast,
Grusinskaya's room, similarly
laid out, appears much more
ornate, swathed in drapes
simultaneously heavy and
flamboyant. Above the bed,
the framed print of an unfinished line drawing resembles
an outline of Garbo herself.

This accomplishment—making modular units immediately distinguishable—mirrors MGM's own production methods, developed to satisfy the feature-film-a-week quota. Formulaic plots, conventional genres, typecast stars—these modular elements could be mixed in a variety of different combinations, like hotel rooms subject to continual redecoration. In effect,

both the Grand Hotel and MGM were imitating General Motors'
Alfred P. Sloan, Jr., who maintained his cars' essential structure
(engines, transmission, brakes), while modifying their surfaces to
make them "new."

(with Aron Pease and Patrick Brennan)

 elephone

In their celebrations of *photogénie*, proposed as "the purest
expression of cinema," the French impressionist filmmakers
often treated narrative as an obstacle to be overcome. "The
telephone rings," Jean Epstein complained, pointing to the event
that so often initiates a plot. "All is lost." Instead of stories, the
French championed the movies' intermittent intensities (a face,

a landscape, an actor's movement, the fall of light across a room) that break free from the sometimes indifferent movies containing them. As a production strategy, however, *photogénie* was complicated. The impressionists' own films proved static and dull: intensities, it turned out, work best when they emerge from a narrative background and seem to arrest the story that generated them. (*Sunrise*'s trolley sequence, a respite from the movie's conventional melodrama, provides this effect's ideal example.)

Nevertheless, if the impressionists were right to equate *photogénie* with the cinema itself, the Hollywood studios could not ignore the concept. Hence another "equation of pictures": how to balance the demands of narrative with the attractions of *photogénie*? *Grand Hotel* offers one solution. Even if we ignore the switchboard scenes, the movie contains 21 calls, many of them important to a plot that symbolically turns on Preysing's murder of the Baron, when the telephone becomes an instrument of violence. And yet, by consistently using an overhead angle to remake the switchboard into a visual design, *Grand Hotel* creates *photogenic* "intensity" out of what would otherwise function as simply a narrative building block. In those shots, the telephones are ringing, but nothing is lost.[23]

Types

Grand Hotel's main characters form a gallery of stock types: the sexual *grisete* (Flaemmchen), the hypocritical capitalist (Preysing), the shabby clerk (Kringelein), the scarred soldier (Dr. Otternschlag), the dandyish gambler (the Baron), the fading prima donna (Grusinskaya). These figures' explicit codification originates with the *physiologies*, which achieved enormous success in Paris between 1840 and 1842 by offering guides to the urban scene. The first mass-market, paperback, pocket-size books, the *physiologies* proved enormously appealing to readers wanting an immediately legible account, however misleadingly simplified, of the cosmopolitan crowd. Roughly 120 different *physiologies* appeared during those years, each offering what historian Richard Sieburth has called "pseudo-scientific portraits of social types": "the Englishman in Paris," "the drinker," "the creditor and the retailer," "the salesgirl," "the deputy," "the stevedore," and so on.

Whatever usefulness the *physiologies* purported to have rested on a single, profound faith in the reliability of appearances. As Walter Benjamin observed of these books, "They assured people that everyone was, unencumbered by any factual knowledge, able to make out the profession, the character, the background, and the life-style of passers-by." This assumption proved crucial to the detective story, whose first great example, Poe's "The Murders in the Rue Morgue," appeared in 1841 at the height of the *physiologies* craze. In fact, the detective story represents a transposition of the *physiologies*, an extrapolation from that earlier mode's purely descriptive purposes to narrative. Like the *physiologies*, the detective story offered to make the world, and particularly city life, more legible. To do so, it relied incessantly on the very reference codes the *physiologies* had propagated. Thus, for Sherlock Holmes, physical evidence is always unproblematically indexical: "the writer" will inevitably display a shiny cuff and worn elbow patch, the "laborer" a muscular hand, "the visitor to China" a particular Oriental tattoo. The *physiologies*' rule applies in all cases, including *Grand Hotel*: character, career, biography are clearly externalized.

Both the detective story and the *physiologies* offered strategies of *reading* based on a simplified hermeneutics. As in paleontology, a science emerging at the same time, the method enabled species to be construed from the smallest details. What can we tell about someone from the objects in his hotel room? *Grand Hotel*'s publicity repeated Vicki Baum's claim that her "research" had included several weeks as a hotel chambermaid. In 1981, conceptual artist Sophie Calle repeated this experiment, working for three weeks in a Venetian hotel, where she photographed and detailed the personal belongings of the guests in 12 fourth-floor rooms.

But from its invention, photography had undercut the *physiologies*. As part of the late eighteenth and early nineteenth centuries' rage for classification and surveillance, the *physiologies* had subsumed all idiosyncrasies under the rule of the controlling term: "the banker," "the Spaniard." Photographs, on the other hand, swarming with accidental details unnoticed at the time of shooting, evoked precisely what eluded classification—the distinguishing feature, the contingent detail. By showing that, contrary to *Sarrasine*, every Spaniard was not dark, every banker not dull, photographs effectively criticized all classification systems and ensured that any such system attempted in photography (for example, August Sander's) would inevitably appear not as science but as art.

Popular narrative cinema, which converted the *physiologies'* hermeneutic into a production strategy, always faced the paradox involved in photographing stock types. *Grand Hotel* illustrates the results: the standardized parts dissolve into the stars' idiosyncrasies—Crawford's mouth and eyes, Garbo's brow and lashes, Beery's stubble, Barrymore's nose.[24]

 **U**nderwear

At least three of *Grand Hotel*'s actors—Beery and, more provocatively, Crawford and Garbo—appear at certain points in their underwear. This casual eroticism suggests the movie's precise date, during the brief four-year period (from 1930 to 1934) when the industry's self-censoring Production Code had not yet acquired its enforcing agency. As film historian Thomas Doherty puts it, this was the pre-Code era, "when censorship was lax and Hollywood made the most of it." *Grand Hotel* implies a chic, modern attitude about sexuality while also managing a certain discretion about it: we only see Grusinskaya and the Baron on the morning after. For the most part, however, the film seems cavalier about morality. The Baron is a thief we are never encouraged to condemn, and Flaemmchen's willingness to prostitute herself appears as merely a kind of world-weary fatalism and the character an extension of Crawford's previous flappers, with their modern world views. In fact, all of the sex in *Grand Hotel* is needy and desperate, especially that between Grusinskaya and the Baron.

In his first job as head of production at Universal, Irving Thalberg famously clashed with Erich von Stroheim, whose *Foolish Wives* (1921) had spiraled beyond normal feature length. At stake was an issue crucial to the future of commercial filmmaking: where is the ideal site of control? Having emerged from the director-dominated pre-studio world of cottage-industry cinema, von Stroheim had no patience for any law but his own. But with Hollywood pursuing the analogy of Fordist mass production, the producer's ascent seemed inevitable. When von Stroheim refused to cut his three-and-a-half-hour version of *Foolish Wives*, Thalberg locked him out of the studio's editing rooms and supervised the job himself. Von Stroheim thus became Hollywood's first great example (Orson Welles would be the next) of the prodigal genius, suitable for reverence from a distance, but not for employment. By 1922, Thalberg would remove von Stroheim at an even earlier stage of production, replacing him during *Merry-Go-Round*'s filming. The newspapers reported Thalberg's reason: Von Stroheim's extrava-gance had now extended to clothing his aristocratic characters in specially produced, monogrammed underwear that would never appear onscreen.

In both style and theme, *Grand Hotel* fits comfortably with the Viennese tradition of filmmaking, most often associated with von Stroheim, Josef von Sternberg, and Max Ophuls. (Vicki Baum, *Grand Hotel*'s author, was born in Vienna.) In these directors' movies, time often seems to have come to a stop, and the future no longer exists—exactly the attitude evoked by *Grand Hotel*. Thalberg usually gets cast as the villain in his battles with von Stroheim, but *Grand*

Hotel suggests how much Thalberg admired some aspects of von Stroheim's work and sought to reproduce it in more fiscally responsible and more marketable conditions. Thus, *Grand Hotel* amounts to an early example of commercial entertainment's fantastic powers of recuperation, which reach one peak with the late 1960s ads "The Revolution is on Columbia Records!" Thalberg, himself, appeared unapologetic about what he had taken from von Stroheim. MGM story editor Samuel Marx reports that "when he [Thalberg] wanted to know a character better he would ask, 'What kind of underwear does he have on?'"[25]

(with Paul Johnson and Jennifer Wangerien)

 Values

For American audiences in 1932, *Grand Hotel* may have seemed "grown-up" and "European" simply because its characters were so casually "corrupt," especially about sex and property:

> Flaemmchen is a prostitute, who admits to living off men. She agrees to Preysing's offer of "an arrangement."
>
> Preysing lies to the Saxonia Company about his deal with Manchester.
>
> Preysing means to have Flaemmchen as his mistress.
>
> The Baron steals both Grusinskaya's pearls and Kringelein's wallet.
>
> To get her to the theater, Grusinskaya's manager lies to her about how many tickets have been sold for the evening's ballet.

Showing no concern for her colleagues, Grusinskaya walks out of her Berlin performance.

Grusinskaya sleeps with the Baron without knowing his name.

The "chauffeur" threatens to kill the Baron.

Preysing kills the Baron and tries to convince Kringelein to help him cover up the crime.

Grusinskaya's handlers lie again to her by insisting that the Baron "will be on the train."

Victor

Summoned by Preysing with a rude finger-snap and a peremptory "Stenographer!" Flaemmchen wearily comments to the Baron and Kringelein, "Her master's voice." RCA Victor's slogan, with its famous image of company dog Nipper listening to a phonograph, was still new in 1932, RCA having acquired the Victor Talking Machine Company only three years earlier. In 1928, RCA had also created RKO, the only major studio established after the coming of sound. Thus, by alluding to RCA's trademark, *Grand Hotel* is inadvertently promoting a rival filmmaking enterprise, which in 1932 alone would sign George Cukor, Katharine Hepburn, Fred Astaire, and Merian C. Cooper, and the next year would make *King Kong*. *Grand Hotel*, in other words, offers evidence of a "tie-up" system not yet perfected. As the emphasis on production had generated a preoccupation with management (see *Grand Hotel*: Garbo, section 3, and Manchester on Frederick Taylor and Henry Ford), the resulting overproduction crisis shifted late-1920s industry attention to consumption and the means of stimulating it: advertising and publicity. Here, the movies would become an ideal tool for promoting products (Warner Brothers characters drove Buicks, MGM's drank Cokes) while getting paid to do so

(MGM received $500,000 from Coca-Cola in 1933). These mutual arrangements developed rapidly. By 1934, when *Grand Hotel*'s sequel, *Dinner at Eight*, appeared, its pressbook would trumpet the new regime: "The merchandising value of Jean Harlow's name was never better demonstrated than by the dozens of *Dinner at Eight* fashion and shoe windows. . . . Tie Ups a Million Dollars Worth of Promotion. . . . 250,000 Coca-Cola dealers will exploit *Dinner at Eight*." That movie's producer would be David O. Selznick, who in 1932 was at RKO.

While the RCA Victor slogan refers to the master-servant relationship between man and dog, *Grand Hotel*'s allusion evokes the unequal relationship between men and women. Almost 75% of RCA Victor's factory workers were women, preferred by the company for being cheap, submissive, and nonunionized. Like so many Hollywood movies, however, *Grand Hotel* displaces Flaemmchen's political grievances into Manichaean melodrama and a Cinderella ending that anticipates *Pretty Woman*. When the movie again alludes to RCA's slogan, if only implicitly, it fulfills Marx's dictum that tragedy repeats itself as farce: with the Baron already dead, his dog, Adolphus, cocks his head to listen to the

ringing telephone, while on the other end, Grusinskaya whispers, "Come and fetch me, *cheri*."[26]

(*with Ryan Johnson and Charles Meyer*)

W ar Souvenirs

When "the chauffeur" inter-
rupts the Baron instructing
Adolphus on the rules of
courtship, the camera focuses
on the desk and its significant
objects: a kaiser helmet (used
by German troops in World
War I), a model airplane, and a
miniature artillery cannon.

These souvenirs, along with the Baron's wristwatch (which the war
had popularized), are what Barthes called *semes*, "flickers of
meaning" that "appear to float freely, to form a galaxy of trifling
data." As *S/Z* demonstrated, they work collectively to create a
character, whose proper name will act "as a magnet field for the
semes" traversing it. *Casablanca*'s introduction of Rick Blaine
(Humphrey Bogart) offers another ideal example. While temporarily withholding Rick's face, the shot defines him through
objects whose meaning repeated use has made clear: The champagne glass and cigarette suggest both sophistication and
jadedness, the solo chess game (an intellectual's solitaire)
cleverness and a solitude simultaneously proud and melancholy.

The trick, Barthes noted, is to achieve the effect of character
without the audience's noticing the machinery. Thus, "connotation
is concealed beneath the regular sound of the 'sentences'" (or a
movie's shots) in an impressionism that hides meaning's production. Overtly *naming* the Baron's character (aristocrat-morally-
wounded-by-war) would violate realism's code: "meaning," as
Barthes saw, "is antipathetic to nature." Instead, "the Baron"
emerges from a process that presents relevant details, in Albert J.
Guerard's words, "as a sensitive witness would receive [them]—

casually, digressively, without logical order." Taking up Joseph Conrad's dictum—"Life does not narrate; it makes impressions on our brains"—classical Hollywood would present information *in passing*. Thus, the Baron mentions his war experience only three times: to Dr. Otternschlag, where his offhand "I was in the war" gets buried in the front-desk hubbub; to his "chauffeur" ("I know all about chloroform; I had it in the War"), when his present need for money seems more urgent; and to Grusinskaya, in an ironic autobiographical aside that "the War" had taught him only "to kill and hide." Suzette's description, "he walks like a soldier," is the movie's only other reference to the Baron's military past. (See *The Maltese Falcon*: Curtains.)

If characterization in realistic fiction and cinema results from this indirection, these "flickers of meaning" (Barthes: "the person is no more than a collection of semes"), what provides the illusion of *individuality*? *S/Z* suggests an answer: the proper name, which "enables the person to exist outside the semes, whose sum nonetheless constitutes it entirely." Significantly, *Grand Hotel* gives the Baron more proper names than any other character; he is, introducing himself to Grusinskaya, "Felix Amadei Benvenuto Freiherr von Gaigern," nicknamed "Flix." (In fact, in *Grand Hotel*, only the Baron and Otto Kringelein have more than one name.) But this *German* Baron's individuality seems also assured by the set of golf clubs sitting by the door, which might also result from Hollywood's portrayal of all aristocrats as vaguely *British*.[27]

(*with Drew Shackelford*)

This figure, joining two (unfinished) triangles at a nexus, represents one image of *Grand Hotel*'s structure: Flaemmchen connects the two triangles of Grusinskaya-Baron-Flaemmchen and Preysing-Kringelein-Flaemmchen. By revealing her character as the movie's center, the fulfills Crawford's ambition to make the *soubrette* part more important than the grande dame's, an achievement not accomplished by the Broadway musical until *South Pacific*, which would banish the grande dame role into Bloody Mary's parody. In fact, at the time of *Grand Hotel*, Crawford and Garbo were the same age (26). And despite the X (which, as a butterfly, insinuates itself into her ballet costume), Garbo dominates the movie.

(with Brandon Duany)

X anthochroid

A person with pale hair and skin. Clarence Brown, one of Garbo's favorite directors, once said that she "had something behind the eyes that you couldn't see until you photographed it in close-up. You could see thought." Or imagine it, since Garbo biographies reveal very little thought going on. Nevertheless, this effect seems dependent on her fairness, at once opaque and transparent, which may in turn have encouraged her directors' preference for close-ups. Like Falconetti (Dreyer's *The Passion of Joan of Arc*), Garbo is represented in film history by her face alone. These still images now signify classic Hollywood and outmoded glamour, but the specific meanings of "Garbo" no longer exist. Most film students today know Garbo is a star only because they have read that she was one. As a result, her performances often leave them unmoved. Garbo offers perhaps the first great example (Elvis will provide another) of a celebrity whose fame, even at its peak, is inseparable from camp.[28]

(with Eleanor Helm and Ryan Johnson)

 **Y** **ellow Room**

Grand Hotel often mentions what Flaemmchen calls "the funny yellow room where they dance." There, strange events take place: the drinking of absinthe and Louisiana Flips, an affirmation of love's existence, dance lessons, attempts at murder, solicitation of a prostitute (even this partial summary will suggest the movie's proximity to the world of directors like Pabst). The Yellow Room's name also invokes an issue central to film history. In one of his most famous essays, André Bazin argued that the critics who regretted the coming of sound had failed to understand "the myth of total cinema," whose ideal had always been an asymptotic advance toward reality's perfect reproduction. If the movies' ontology involved, as Bazin thought, "an integral realism, a recreation of the world in its own image," then the advent of technological developments like sound and color warranted celebration. Hollywood, however, conflated "realism" with an "invisible style" that hid not only the process of filmmaking, but also the gap between the screen and the world. But the Yellow Room's name confounds the goals of both realism and stylistic self-effacement: in a black-and-white movie, the room's "yellowness" *calls attention* to the cinema's technological immaturity, its inability to render completely its own chosen subjects. Given the name, a viewer cannot help inferring that an actual Yellow Room exists somewhere, *and this is not it.*[29]

(with Ryan Johnson)

Z igaretten

This word, appearing as a
stenciled sign on a lobby
window, reminds us of *Grand
Hotel*'s setting. In fact, such
cues appear infrequently in the
movie. Of the main characters,
only Preysing has a German
accent, a result less of some
conscientious verisimilitude

than of Beery's demands for a showier part. Historical events,
unfolding contemporaneously with the movie's making, shifted
the connotations of its crucial signifiers, *Berlin* and *Germanicity*,
terms which now required repression or displacement into the
vaguer, safer notions of "the continental." Thus, if the film can
only rarely pronounce the word *Berlin*, it must deploy an occasional sign to replace it. The movie's realism, as a result, is
intermittent, like a radio signal broadcasting a familiar tune, whose
melody is inferable from a few notes. Here, the note is partially
jammed, first appearing backward (NETTERAGIZ), thereby further
disguising its newly pejorative associations.

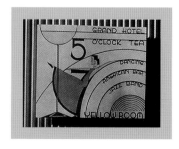

This fitful realism is itself
regulated by narrative demands. Although the set design
must incorporate *some* German
words as periodic reminders of
the movie's putative location,
when a sign relays story
information, its message will
suddenly appear, entirely
unrealistically, in English. In

Grand Hotel, English writing inevitably signals the reemergence of some temporarily abandoned plot line. Hence the sign outside the hotel bar, advertising dancing, drinks, and tea at 5 o'clock—important, since the Baron has arranged a rendezvous with Flaemmchen for this time and place—can only be in English.

(*with Katherine Arpen and Eleanor Helm*)

The Philadelphia Story

in Katharine Hepburn (after Roland Barthes's *S/Z*)

Katharine Hepburn's individuality appears not only in her screen persona, but also in the spelling of her name. The opening *K* defies countless Catherines, including several English and French queens and two Russian empresses. Nevertheless, the *K* better represents Hepburn's characteristic angularity than would the curvy C. More interesting is the uncommon vowel choice for Katharine's second syllable, where the usual *e* gets replaced by the eccentric *a*, inherited from her mother, a women's rights and birth-control activist. Since this syllable is silent, its purpose remains symbolic and aesthetic, offering the suggestion of several connotations: *a*ndrogyny, *a*chievement, *A*cademy *A*wards (12 nominations, 6 wins), *A* for the highest grade.

The *a* has led to a thousand misspellings, including one by *Philadelphia Story* author Philip Barry, who once got the name wrong in his credits. That mistake compromises Hepburn's identity, preserved onstage by her presence, onscreen by her reproduced image. But on paper, "Katharine Hepburn" depends on her name, which must include that second *a*.

(with Jason Mendro)

Alcohol

By identifying Tracy's wedding Saturday as "the longest day of the year," Philip Barry's play marks the previous evening, when most of the action occurs, as midsummer night. Like Titania in *A Midsummer Night's Dream*, Tracy Lord will roam a pastoral world, falling in love with whatever male her eyes awaken to. Stanley Cavell, who has detailed the similarities between Shakespeare's play and *The Philadelphia Story*, compares Puck's magic potion to Tracy's champagne or Dexter's "stinger," made "with the juice of a few flowers." Alcohol, in other words, enables the movie's resolution (Tracy's remarriage to Dexter) after having caused its initial crisis (their divorce due to Dexter's alcoholism). The film's staging, of course, implies his cure: while all of the main characters are portrayed drinking or getting drunk, only Dexter never appears drinking alcohol.

One of the first proponents of alcoholism as a disease was Dr. Benjamin Rush, a physician living and working at the turn of the nineteenth century in, of all places, Philadelphia. Rush's efforts prompted the eventual emergence of late nineteenth-century temperance movements, which in turn led to the Prohibition Act, whose 1933 repeal seemed to trigger Hollywood's blissful representations of happy drunkards (see, for example, 1934's *The Thin Man*). Despite Rush and his successors, however, alcoholism has never entirely shed its representation as moral weakness, a view consistently espoused by Tracy Lord. Dexter's drinking, she reproaches him, was "disgusting," making him "weak and unattractive," an uncompromising judgment tailor-made to fit Katharine Hepburn's starchy persona. In real life, just two years after *The Philadelphia Story*, Hepburn would enter into a long-running affair with another Tracy (Spencer), an alcoholic far more desperate and abusive than Dexter.[1]

(with Rochelle Mabry)

Argus C-3 Rangefinder

Liz's camera, apparently abandoned after Tracy deliberately causes its spill from a drink cart, is an Argus C-3 Rangefinder, one of the world's most popular cameras until its 1958 discontinuation. The Argus was the first affordable 35mm camera, and by mandat-

ing the switch from 120-roll film, it made candid photography a less costly hobby. For the movie, the Argus performs an aesthetic function: with its large black box, chrome knobs, and protruding lens, it *looks like* a camera. (Liz had carried a Contax in the play.)

The Argus also raises other issues important to *The Philadelphia Story*. As Mike explains to Tracy, Liz is not a photographer by choice; "[s]he's a born painter, and might be a very important one. But Miss Imbrie must eat. And she also prefers a roof over her head to being constantly out in the rain and snow." This casual remark reflects yet another class marker, the persistent aesthetic hierarchy that prefers painting to photography. The Lord mansion, stocked with portraits and landscapes, reflects the popular idea of patrician taste. And while Dexter and Tracy both break cameras (Dexter on their first honeymoon), nouveau riche George will welcome them, hoping for *Spy*'s appearance at his wedding.

Only four years before, in his famous essay "The Work of Art in the Age of Mechanical Reproduction," Walter Benjamin had addressed this prejudice favoring painting, dependent, he argued, on "a number of outmoded concepts, such as creativity and genius, eternal value and mystery." His brief for photography, however, had turned on politics: In the age of the Nuremberg rallies, photography's

> technique of reproduction detaches the reproduced object
> from the domain of tradition. By making many reproductions
> it substitutes a plurality of copies for a unique existence. And
> in permitting the reproduction to meet the beholder or
> listener in his own particular situation, it reactivates the
> object reproduced. These two processes lead to a tremendous
> shattering of tradition.

Benjamin's target had been the Hitler cult, whose ritual power depended on the Führer's carefully maintained inaccessibility. Photographic reproduction, on the other hand, undermined "aura" and "authenticity," concepts dependent upon unique originals. Reproductions of Hitler could appear in unguarded contexts, where they might be manipulated for progressive purposes—the working method of the famous anti-Nazi artist John Hartfield. The essence of the photograph, in other words, lay in what Jacques Derrida would later call its inherent "corruptibility." Photography speeded up "the possibility of disengagement and citational graft which belongs to the structure of every mark." "Every sign, linguistic or non-linguistic, spoken or written," Derrida would write, "can be *cited*, put between quotation marks; in so doing it can break with every given context, engendering an infinity of new contexts in a manner which is absolutely illimitable."

The Philadelphia Story associates Tracy Lord's hostility to photography with her frigid virtue. "Of all the filthy ideas," she snaps after seeing a *Spy* article on a couple, "coming into a private home with a camera." The movie's outcome, however, depends precisely on Tracy's corruptibility (champagne-induced), a *felix culpa* whose triumphant outcome, her remarriage to Dexter, will appear, fittingly, in Sidney Kidd's photographs.[2]

(with Chris Soldt)

 **B** **uenos Aires**

In its transposition from play to movie, *The Philadelphia Story* relocates missing brother Junius's embassy from London to Buenos Aires, while also assigning to Dexter the *Spy* job held in the play by another brother, Sandy Lord, eliminated entirely from the film. Dexter, too, has been working in South America since his divorce. In 1940, "Buenos Aires" represents both a capitulation to world events and a gesture toward verisimilitude. With England at war since 1939, London has become too important to house a dilettante journalist like Dexter and, in a comedy, too dangerous for even an offscreen Junius. Like almost all screwball comedies (*To Be or Not to Be* is the exception), *The Philadelphia Story* depends on a strict isolationism. Thus, the movie cannot acknowledge the European war, even implicitly. "Buenos Aires" represents a kind of euphemism—an actual place, too remote to evoke any immediate connotations that might interfere with the narrative's machinery. (See *The Maltese Falcon*: Honolulu.)

 **C** ontracts

Roland Barthes used *S/Z* to argue that, in a market society, which converts even art into "merchandise," popular fiction depends on an implicit contract obligating its authors to resolve every enigma and to honor conventional wisdom. Thus, Balzac will eventually have to reveal the source of the Lanty fortune and La Zambinella's real identity. Similarly, his "reference codes" ("dark as a Spaniard, dull as a banker") will adhere to the "already-written." As heir to the nineteenth-century novel, classical Hollywood will maintain this regimen, showing no tolerance for open-ended plots (à la Antonioni's *L'Avventura*) or surprising characterizations. And yet, as Barthes demonstrated, popular stories often produce contradictory *mise-en-abymes* in which characters openly repudiate contracts to which they had previously agreed. In *Sarrasine*, Barthes's case study, the contracts between La Zambinella and Sarrasine and between the narrator and his lover both get broken. And by spending a year repeatedly rereading the story, Barthes himself was refusing Balzac's proposition to move on to another book.

The presence of broken contracts in *The Philadelphia Story* confirms Barthes's point about their importance to this form of storytelling. Every woman in the movie is either divorced (Tracy, Liz) or about to be (Mrs. Lord). By refusing to turn in a story, Mike will break his deal with Kidd, who in turn will violate his agreement with Dexter by publishing photographs of the wedding. Tracy will refuse to honor her engagement to George, while Connor wanders from his implicit one with Liz. Thus by stopping here to read and reread *The Philadelphia Story*, we short-circuit the studio system, ignoring other contemporary MGM products (*Susan and God, Come Live with Me*) to concentrate on this one.[3]

(*with Stephanie Dykes and Richard Keenan*)

Cukor

In the 1960s, Andrew Sarris consigned George Cukor to his second tier of American directors, "The Far Side of Paradise." It was hardly a bad group, since it included Borzage, Capra, De Mille, Fuller, La Cava, Mann, McCarey, Minnelli, Preminger, Ray, Sirk, von Stroheim, Sturges, Vidor, and Walsh—*auteurs* all. And yet, despite additional championing by the *Cahiers* writers, including François Truffaut, Cukor remains one of *la politique des auteurs'* hardest cases. When the *Cahiers*-inspired *Cinema One* series devoted a book to Cukor, its author seemed stumped by *The Philadelphia Story*:

> *Cukor gambles everything on the players, the* mise-en-scène *being almost invisible in its discretion, a matter of glossy overlit sets and stagy groupings of three or four performers within the frame, all of which would pall were the performances not so mutually enriching.*

Or take these remarks, which betray the struggle to formulate specific praise for a plain, narratively efficient style:

> *The essential. The truth of the dialogue, the truth of the situations, the truth of the subjects, of the milieux, the characters: a dramaturgy derived from an agglomeration of facts, words, noises, movements, situations, as a motor is assembled. There is nothing superfluous: no stopping, no meandering, no fleshing out.*

> *Such art demands a basic honesty . . . no flashback, no
> ellipsis; the rule is continuity. No character disappears without
> us following him, and nothing surprises the hero which doesn't
> surprise us at the same time. . . . each shot has a functional
> beauty.*

In fact, these last two passages come from essays about one
of Sarris's "Pantheon" directors: Howard Hawks. Although the
case for Hawks-as-*auteur* is now probably settled, its initial
assertion once seemed scandalous, another neosurrealist provoca-
tion. Hawks, after all, had worked in every Hollywood genre,
making movies that both he and his audience regarded as simple
entertainments. Worse, his films, unlike Hitchcock's (the other
great *Cahiers* cause), offered no stylistic signature. Their form was
pure classic Hollywood—invisible, matter-of-fact, narratively
deferential.

As deployed by the *Cahiers* critics, *la politique des auteurs*
amounted to an argument about filmmaking's ideal site of
control. Truffaut rejected the scriptwriter-dominated productions
of the postwar French cinema, proposing that control be relocated to the decisive moment of shooting, the director's realm.
Hawks, however, who typically served as his own producer,
evidently attributed more importance to the preceding stages:

> *Hell, the first thing you've got to do if you're going to make a
> picture is to get a story. The next thing is to get a good script,
> the next thing is to figure out who the hell is going to play in
> it, your characters, and then after that to make it.*

Confronted by Hawks's own downplaying of style, his
advocates had to look elsewhere, shifting their attention to plots
and motifs. Gerald Mast summarizes the findings:

> Auteur *discussions of Hawks, insistent on demonstrating that
> there* is *a Howard Hawks beneath the genre conventions of*

his films, seize on the bits of themes and business that link the
films: the exchange of cigarettes, the professionalism of his
characters, the sexual role reversals and the use of animals in
his comedies, male friendship and the rites of passage that
allow a female entrance to the male group in the adventure
films, and so forth.

But this British *"auteur* structuralism" rested from the start on a
paradox: by reverting to thematic analysis, Hawks's supporters
found themselves annulling *auteurism*'s premise, the *Cahiers*
insistence on mise-en-scène. The French critics were fond of
quoting Sartre's pronouncement that "[o]ne isn't a writer for
having chosen to say certain things, but for having chosen to say
them in a certain way," and Fereydoun Hoveyda's reformulation
assumed canonical force: "[T]he originality of the *auteur* lies not in
the subject matter he chooses, but in the technique he employs. . .
. the thought of a *cinéaste* appears through his *mise-en-scène.*"

Jacques Rivette rendered that dictum even more specifically:

And when I talk about ideas, I really mean ideas of mise-en-
scène or—if I were to be shocking about it—of framing, or
the way shots are put together, which these days are the only
ideas whose profundity I wish to recognize.

Confronted by *auteurism*'s insistence on a formal accounting,
Hawks's supporters invented a new idea: Hawks's filmmaking
wasn't nondescript; it was *classical.* Analyzing a scene from *The*
Thing (?!), Robin Wood would make the case: "The sequence can
be taken as the epitome of . . . the classicism of Hollywood
(invisible technique, symmetry, orderly and logical narrative,
economy of means)." In other words, "Hawks" now stood for
almost all of the things that the New Wave filmmakers would
themselves repudiate.

The brief for Cukor-as-*auteur* follows the same trajectory.
Like Hawks, he visited almost every genre, even the western (*Heller*

in Pink Tights). His reputation for relying on, and improving, actors matched that of Hawks. And taken as a whole, his work offered recurring themes: role playing, life as theater, the delicate fragility of illusions. As a filmmaker, Cukor seemed marked by his origins in the theater. He often worked with adapted plays, and his approach to scenes relied more on blocking than editing. Thus, *The Philadelphia Story*, especially in its most typical moments, offers a series of long takes that allow the movie's stars to feel their way into scenes. George's arrival at the stables; Mike and Liz waiting to meet the family; Dexter's lie to Mrs. Lord, Tracy, and Dinah about bringing "friends of Junius"; and his revelation to Tracy of Kidd's blackmail—all these events transpire in shots lasting roughly a minute or more. In between, Cukor uses the standard devices of classical Hollywood: motivated camera movements and the out-in-out of establishing shot/breakdown reverse-angle/reestablishing shot that the British call "the concertina."

As it reaches a climax, the "friends of Junius" scene demon-strates this approach. Shot 1 begins on Tracy alone, but pans with her as she rejoins the group. As Tracy grows both more suspicious and more hostile, shot 2 isolates her with Dexter. The reestablish-ing shot 3 allows Mrs. Lord to be seen asking her question before shot 4's medium close-up of Dexter's confession. Shot 5, a reverse-angle medium close-up of Tracy's scornful look, is followed by another reverse-angle (shot 6), a repeat of shot 4's set-up. On the words "of the goddess," shot 7 repeats 5's medium close-up of Tracy, before the reestablishing shot 8, which by following Tracy and Dexter to the screen-right door, precisely reverses shot 1's opening pan.

Shot 1

Tracy: *I think it's queerer than that, I think it's paranoiac.*

Dexter: *Well, dear, you see it was Junius's idea. They've been very kind to him, and as they're in Philadelphia . . .*

Tracy: *You're lying, Dexter. I can always tell.*

Dexter: *Can you, Red?*

Mrs. Lord: *But, dear, if they're Junius's friends.*

Shot 2

Tracy: *You had to work after the divorce didn't you?*

Dexter: *Ah, yes, except for a brief interlude in a couple of alcoholic sanatoriums.*

Tracy: *But you took a job in South America. Who for?*

Dexter: *A magazine.*

Tracy: *And it wasn't by any chance* Spy *magazine?*

Dexter: *You are a* mass *of intuition.*

Tracy: *And I don't suppose that Junius's friends are photographers by any chance? I thought . . .*

Shot 3

Tracy: *you were low, but I never thought you'd sink to . . .*

Mrs. Lord: *What are you going to do?*

Tracy: *After I've telephoned Junius, I'm going to do plenty.*

Shot 4

Dexter: *Wait, Red, wait. You don't have to telephone Junius. I'll confess.*

Shot 5

[Tracy's scornful look]

Shot 6

Dexter: *No, you're slipping, Red. I used to be afraid of that look. The withering glance . . .*

Shot 7

Dexter: *of the goddess.*

Tracy: *I didn't think that alcohol . . . Oh, shut up.*

Shot 8

[reestablishing shot]

At points, *The Philadelphia Story* strings together long takes, with cuts occurring only when the narrative takes a decisive turn. Thus, a nearly minute-long shot of Tracy and Mike on the terrace

gives way to an even longer 1 minute, 45 seconds, one, the transition to the medium close-up falling on Connor's line, "you can't marry that guy"— precisely where the plot's momentum makes it most invisible.

The Philadelphia Story, in other words, is a movie that *covers its traces*. In fact, it looks in many ways like a big-budget version of the Andy Hardy series, in production on MGM's lot at the same time. The sets are more detailed, the lighting more careful (especially on Hepburn in her love scene with Stewart), the framing more graceful, the actors more prominent, but the filmmaking hand is equally discreet. Not surprisingly, Cukor once rejected the suggestion that he had been influenced by *Citizen Kane*, dismissing Welles's film as "rather too much UFA." The remark is telling: The studio era directors with reputations as "stylists" (e.g., Ford, Lang, Murnau, von Sternberg, Welles) were often those most marked by the German expressionism of the 1920s. That tradition, with its emphatic work on the image and its striking stills, called attention to the filmmaking process, which could no longer appear as mere recording. Cukor would occasionally borrow that style (see *Gaslight*), but he would never make it his own.

While Cukor's reliance on long takes certainly reflects his theatrical apprenticeship, it also required confident actors.

Hepburn, of course, knew her part inside out; she had played Tracy Lord almost 700 times on the stage (415 Broadway performances, 254 on the road). Cukor simply had to retain her spontaneity. Grant and Stewart, while not yet at their peaks, were already skilled professionals who could be trusted with extended shots. Given less-reliable performers, Cukor would work quite differently. Marilyn Monroe, he told Gavin Lambert, "couldn't sustain scenes. She'd do three lines and then forget the rest, she'd do another line and then forget everything again. You had to shoot it piecemeal. But curiously enough, when you strung everything together, it was complete."

That result should not have surprised him. Walter Benjamin's 1936 essay "The Work of Art in the Age of Mechanical Reproduction" had already described the process as essential to the cinema:

> The artistic performance of a stage actor is definitely presented to the public by the actor in person; that of the screen actor, however, is presented by a camera. . . . The camera that presents the performance of the film actor need not respect the performance as an integral whole. Guided by the cameraman, the camera continually changes its position with respect to the performance. The sequence of positional views which the editor composes from the material supplied him constitutes the completed film. . . .
>
> [The film actor's] creation is by no means all of a piece; it is composed of many separate performances.

When compared to theatrical acting, the cinema's way of constructing a performance had two immediate consequences. First, it shifted control from actor to director, but by discounting sustained technical skill, it also redefined movie stardom as less about expertise than something mysterious like *photogénie*. The theater, after all, had managed for centuries without what we would call "the director," a role apparently invented by W. S. Gilbert while staging the Savoy operas in the nineteenth century's last two decades. And many of classic Hollywood's greatest stars would have been lost on the stage.

Cukor understood both effects. "She never could do the same thing twice," he noted of Marilyn Monroe, "but, as with all the true movie queens, there was an excitement about her." Was Katharine Hepburn a "good actress"? Only six years before *The Philadelphia Story*, her performance on Broadway in *The Lake* had prompted Dorothy Parker's famous slam, "she ran the gamut of emotions from A to B." And yet, David O. Selznick had detected in her first film, 1932's *A Bill of Divorcement*, the signs of imminent stardom. "[V]ery early in the picture," he wrote, "there was a scene in which Hepburn just walked across the room, stretched her arms, and then lay out on the floor before the fireplace. It sounds very simple, but you could almost feel, and you could definitely hear, the excitement in the audience."

Cukor had directed that scene, of course, and he would go on to work with Hepburn eight more times. But even before that film, he had already sensed the difference between the theater, where he and Hepburn had trained, and the movies, which turned on other things. In 1932, Hepburn had done a screen test for RKO, choosing a moment from Philip Barry's *Holiday*, which she had understudied on Broadway. As Anne Edwards describes, Hepburn

> *perversely kept her back to the camera during most of the test. The scene was one where the very rich maverick Linda Seton, slightly inebriated from champagne, tells her sister's fiancé to run off before the wedding. Kate put the champagne glass on the floor beside her and had to swoop down to retrieve it for a drink to emphasize her statement.*

Watching this test, Cukor had been stunned:

> *She was quite unlike anybody I'd ever seen. . . . I thought, I suppose right away, "She's too odd. It won't work." But at*

one moment in a very emotional scene, she picked up a glass.
The camera focused on her back. There was an enormous
feeling, a weight about the manner in which she picked up
the glass.

Cukor was describing what the French impressionist filmmakers had called *photogénie*, which eluded precise definition while remaining the cinema's holy grail. In 1921, Jean Epstein had even described something remarkably similar: "Hayakawa crosses a room quite naturally, his torso held at a slight angle. He hands his gloves to a servant. Opens a door. Then, having gone out, closes it. *Photogénie*, pure *photogénie*, cadenced movement." To what extent do such moments depend upon direction? To what extent do they depend upon the cinema's automatism, the camera's magical capacity to endow even the most ordinary objects with the spell of what the surrealists called "the marvelous"? Was Cukor an *auteur*? Gavin Lambert told Cukor that even Hepburn "used to wish you'd put more of a stamp, your own stamp, on things." The best proof of Cukor's skill, however, is *The Philadelphia Story*'s remake, *High Society*, in which so little of the original's charm survives.[4]

 ive

With classic Hollywood movies, even the smallest details open into complexities. After quarreling with Dexter, who has called her (among other things) a "virgin goddess," Tracy sheds her bath-

robe and then, dressed only in a pale-striped white bathing suit, walks determinedly to the diving board. Having climbed up, she pauses, glances offscreen left (in the direction of the now-departed Dexter), squares her shoulders, and dives into the pool. The shot lasts under 15 seconds, unaccompanied by any dialogue or music. It seems longer. Tracy's dive is one of *The Philadelphia Story*'s most memorable images.

But why is it here? One possibility, of course, is thematic. Noël Burch once described studio era filmmaking as radically efficient: "[I]t was essential that there be no superfluous, 'gratuitous' marks which would call into question the economy of the system: the bourgeois codes are *thrifty*." This method of cinema, in other words, subordinates every detail to a steadily developing narrative, whose progress results from keeping every scene, every shot, every detail on the same teleological track. In Burch's terms:

> [*Hollywood filmmaking*] *is organized to facilitate the development of a diegesis whose economy consists in loading the slightest detail with signification, of flattening every signifier under the tyrannical weight of the signified. This economy of expressiveness, in which everything is determined by a single-purpose articulation, clearly defines one of the basic ingredients of linearity, the mechanical relationship of cause and effect.*

In a long interview with Peter Bogdanovich, Cukor was eager to describe himself as a good citizen of this regime:

> [Y]ou should remain unostentatious; because, if you do a lot
> of fancy footwork, maybe they notice you as a director, but I
> think it hurts the story. . . . No, I think one should not be
> aware of technique of any kind.

Given this view of filmmaking, we might assume that the image of
Tracy's dive, far from gratuitously displaying Cukor's pictorial
sense, must further *The Philadelphia Story*'s plot. How?

Placement seems important. The shot occurs between two
important conversations, Dexter's brutal diagnosis of Tracy as a
"virgin goddess" and "married maiden," and Kittredge's overly
deferential hymns to a "distant queen" and "beautiful statue." By
showing us Hepburn in a bathing suit, which reveals more of her
body than appears in any other scene, by indicating both the
actress's and the character's athleticism, the shot could be said to
offer an image of sensual physicality that contradicts the men's
epithets, while foreshadowing the conclusion's emerging "new
Tracy." In fact, however, that tidy reading, like any other description of this shot, depends almost entirely on one thing: the
audience's response to Katharine Hepburn. While "Tracy Lord
dives into the pool" is unnecessary to *The Philadelphia Story*'s
narrative (the play had managed without it), "Katharine Hepburn
dives into the pool" is something else again. For Tracy's dive to
soften her image, the audience needs to regard Hepburn as sexy.

In 1940, it apparently didn't. Even after being labeled as
"box-office poison" in 1938 by exhibitors, Hepburn had avidly
sought the role of Scarlett O'Hara in *Gone with the Wind*. David O.
Selznick, that film's producer, had discovered Hepburn, and he
remained an astute judge of a performer's rapport with viewers.
Late in 1938, with casting still under way, he wrote an emblematic
memo, indicating his reservations:

> Hepburn should be sent for immediately and her test should
> be carefully selected to include the scenes that require the
> most sex, because I think Hepburn has two strikes against

her—first, the unquestionable and very widespread public
dislike of her at the moment, and second, the fact that she is
yet to demonstrate that she possesses the sex qualities which
are probably the most important of all the many requisites of
Scarlett.

With her angular, small-breasted body and harshly metallic
voice, Hepburn has never conformed to the standard for movie
stardom. A favorable response to her depends on admiration of
her obvious intelligence, independence, and resourcefulness. In
fact, her case demonstrates how radically the status of an image
can change. If Selznick and the 1938 exhibitors were right, a 1940
audience would probably not have found Hepburn "sexy." In the
wake of feminism's gains, however, a twenty-first-century audience
might, especially since with her dive, she quickly puts Dexter's
remark behind her with a brisk athletic activity that reasserts her
autonomy while pleasing herself.

But the question refuses to be resolved so easily. Did 1940
women viewers find Hepburn more sexy than did men? What about
women who shared what Andrew Sarris called Hepburn's "premature feminism"? These questions approach film studies' terra
incognita, the actual responses of real audience members. And the
issue deepens. Like other filmmakers, Cukor maintained that the
director's job is to anticipate a future audience's response to
everything put onscreen. But Cukor was gay, and if contemporary
queer theory is right to reject broad-brush notions of "the viewer,"
he may not have seen things in quite the same way as most
filmgoers.

Let's try another tack. Filmmaking involves a series of
problems, and Tracy's dive amounts to a solution to one of them:
how to effect the transition from Dexter to George. Onstage, the
shift had been abruptly handled, with Kittredge simply picking up
the conversation abandoned by Haven. Cukor's device proves
more elegant, like a rest that subtly colors the music occurring

before and after. The scene benefits from a pause of a few beats; Cukor's skill lay in filling that pause with a striking image. Again, Thalberg's advice proves decisive: "Remember you are dealing with a pictorial medium."[5]

(with Jason Mendro and Heather Visser)

 lizabeth Imbrie

Playing the Eve Arden role, a wisecracking working woman, Ruth Hussey was nominated for the Academy Award for Best Supporting Actress. She didn't win, and although only 25 at the time of *The Philadelphia Story*, she would never get close to stardom again. A Brown philosophy major, she seems to have simply grown impatient with Hollywood. She shifted to Broadway, where she had her greatest success in 1945's *State of the Union*, in a role given to Katharine Hepburn for the movie version. Hussey provides yet another link to *The Great Gatsby*, a book that everywhere shadows *The Philadelphia Story*: In the 1949 film version, she would play Jordan Baker, Nick Carraway's friend who has cheated at golf.

Hussey may have been wrong to take the Elizabeth Imbrie part. Even at the peak of screwball comedy, Hollywood proved largely incapable of creating leading roles for verbally witty women. Carole Lombard (*My Man Godfrey*), Claudette Colbert (*It Happened One Night*), Jean Harlow (*Libeled Lady*), Irene Dunne (*The Awful Truth*), and even Katharine Hepburn (*Bringing Up Baby*) got laughs by being ditsy or causing pratfalls, but the more obviously clever Rosalind Russell (*His Girl Friday*) never quite became a star.

Only Myrna Loy (especially in *The Thin Man* series) could hold her own in rapid banter, and her movies almost always made her appear older than the typical leading lady. *The Lady Eve* went a step further, attributing Barbara Stanwyck's ready wit to her trade as a con woman. In *The Philadelphia Story*, Liz's wisecracks often work to bring Mike back to earth, but under 1940s prevailing gender codes, they also desex her (a process furthered by her unusually short hair). On Broadway, Elizabeth Imbrie had been played by an actress as unlike Ruth Hussey as one could imagine: Shirley Booth, a 41-year-old New Yorker with a freakish Betty Boop voice and a big, slatternly body. (Imagine Judy Holliday with every characteristic exaggerated.) The part seems incapable of accommodating both actresses, but Hussey's youth and beauty obviously made the role, barely mentioned by the play's reviewers, more visible.[6]

 **raming**

Cukor told Peter Bogdanovich that although he didn't believe in "meticulous," line-by-line rehearsing, he often asked his actors to practice "the *movement*" of a scene: "They walk through it and they indicate it; they try it themselves. And I'm looking for camera angles; it just helps *me*, really." Cukor, of course, was talking about framing, an aspect of filmmaking neglected by most critics. Eisenstein's abiding prestige has always made editing seem the cinema's most important tool, and unless a movie's framing deploys the obvious devices inherited from German expressionism (grotesque tilts, extreme low or high angles), it usually gets ignored. Cukor's choices, however—subtle, almost perfectly transparent—contribute enormously to *The Philadelphia Story*'s effect. They amount to the movie's *invisible writing*, which can be made to appear only through comparisons to other, less-successful films. Juxtaposing identical scenes in *The Philadelphia Story* and *High Society*, the musical remake, confirms that the aptness of Cukor's framing is primarily a function of his camera's distance from the events being recorded.

    High Society consistently resorts to long shots of its characters, who, as a result, appear isolated from each other and dwarfed by cavernous, high-ceilinged rooms. In *The Philadelphia Story*, on the other hand, the tighter blocking and closer framing make the Lords' rooms seem warmer and the people more important. Cukor's intimate framing encourages investment in the movie's characters, whom *High Society* transforms into objects of study, kept at a distance.[7]

 G rant

Cary Grant, according to David Thomson, "was the best and most important actor in the history of the cinema." Inevitably, the Academy ignored him. Of *The Philadelphia Story*'s four principals, only Grant failed to receive even an Academy Award nomination. (James Stewart and screenwriter Donald Ogden Stewart won; Hepburn, Cukor, and the picture itself were nominated.) Recognizing this slight, the film's producer, Joseph L. Mankiewicz, wrote to Grant:

> *Whatever success the picture is having . . . is due, in my*
> *opinion, to you in far greater proportions than anyone has*
> *seen fit to shout about. . . . your presence as Dexter, and*
> *particularly your sensitive and brilliant playing of the role,*
> *contribute what I consider the backbone and basis of*
> *practically every emotional value in the piece. I can think of no*
> *one who could have done as well or given as much.*

Grant thanked Mankiewicz and donated his $125,000 fee to British War Relief.

Thomson attributes Grant's effectiveness to the ambivalence he conveys:

> [*H*]*e can be attractive and unattractive simultaneously; there*
> *is a light and dark side to him but, whichever is dominant, the*
> *other creeps into view. . . . the effect he achieves is one of art;*
> *it shows malice, misogyny, selfishness, and solitariness*
> *beneath good manners and gaiety; and it reveals a sense of*
> *grace-in-humor buoying up a near sadistic playing upon lesser*
> *people's nerves and good nature.*

The Philadelphia Story's "emotional value," Mankiewicz's telling phrase, depends on these mixed signals. As Dexter, Grant often proves physically aggressive, starting with the prologue's brutal shove of Hepburn, a gesture turning James Cagney's infamous grapefruit-in-the-face to Mae Clarke (*Public Enemy*) into slapstick humor.

Arriving in the family sitting room for the first time, Dexter insistently advances on Tracy, bullying her into retreat.

Even his smallest gestures indicate his contempt: as he prepares to leave the pool house, he hands his empty glass to Kittredge as if George were a servant.

Dexter's wit, directed at Connor, Kittredge, and Tracy, frequently becomes malevolent, and as the movie rushes toward its concluding marriage, we infer that this couple may not live happily ever after.

Cary Grant's career, of course, turned on a famous paradox: the ultimate symbol of upper-class elegance came from the British working class. As biographer Graham McCann points out, he "sprang from his Platonic conception of himself" like Fitzgerald's Jay Gatsby, born James Gatz of West Egg, Long Island. As Archie Leach turned himself into "Cary Grant," he repudiated once and for all the premise of the nineteenth-century *physiologies* (see *Grand Hotel*: Types), which had assured their readers of the direct connection between physical appearance and class, profession, and ethnicity.

The *physiologies* project was challenged by the advent of photography, which continually displayed precisely what eluded classification—the idiosyncratic feature. All "country priests" (or "lovers," "lawyers," "bachelors"), it turned out, did not look alike. (See *The Philadelphia Story*: Yacht.) "Cary Grant" confirms this effect. By becoming the movies' most famous emblem of upper-class sophistication, Grant repeatedly demonstrated a simple fact: *appearances are unreliable*. As a theme, this proposition became the basis of the detective story, whose murderers are never quite what they first seem. But it had already sustained Shakespeare's comedies and Jane Austen's novels, two of screwball's principal sources. Disconnecting character from appearance cut both ways: the gruff, rude Mr. Darcy could be revealed as ultimately kind and generous, but Mr. Wickham's far greater charm merely concealed his villainy.

When this uncertainty becomes *comic*, it perfectly suits Cary Grant, the leading male screwball actor. But it also appealed to Alfred Hitchcock, who would use it most effectively in *Suspicion* (1941) and *Notorious* (1946). *The Philadelphia Story* always intends Dexter as a sympathetic character. But Grant himself taught us to distrust appearances as a dependable guide to character. Thus, at the heart of *The Philadelphia Story* lies a Hitchcockian ambiguity that makes it more than a simple parable of class consolidation. After all, if a working-class boy could become "Cary Grant," then C. K. Dexter Haven could turn out to be a skunk.[8]

 **H**epburn

By now, the story is well known: reeling from being denounced as "box-office poison" by Harry Brandt, president of the Independent Theater Owners of America, Hepburn retreated to her parents' house in Connecticut, where, nearing 30, she feared her movie career was over. She continued to seek the part of Scarlett O'Hara, but would get nowhere on that front. Suddenly, playwright Philip Barry, whose earlier Broadway hits (1923's *You and I* and 1928's *Holiday*) had only led to a string of failures, appeared with the rough idea for two different plays. The first, about a suicidal diplomat, Hepburn quickly rejected, but the second was a marital comedy whose heroine Barry had based both on his Philadelphia socialite friend Hope Montgomery Scott and on Hepburn herself. Hepburn retired with Barry to his Maine summer house, where they worked on the play together. As Sheridan Morley observes, "Few actresses in the entire world history of theater can ever have had such close attention from a playwright." George Jean Nathan detailed Barry's method:

> [H]e spent two long months observing at close quarters, recording carefully every attractive gesture she made, every awkwardly graceful movement of her body, every odd little quirk of her head and every effective dart of her eye, then to incorporate them all into the play he was writing for her. A line was interpolated to allow her to swing her lithe figure across the stage; another was so contrived that a toss of her lovely brown hair would pictorially embellish it; still another was so framed that it would permit her, while seated, relevantly to cross her knees and display her pretty legs to the critical professors out front. If her voice was found unable to cope properly with a line, it was altered until she could handle it nicely.

The result, of course, was *The Philadelphia Story*, the play that resurrected Hepburn's Broadway stardom and ultimately her film career. "The play," Carlos Clarens declares, "is beyond revival," and even the movie has its detractors. "I have never liked the movie version of *The Philadelphia Story*," Andrew Sarris announced, and explained why in what has become the most damaging critique ever written about it:

> It was not until I actually saw Blythe Danner, almost invariably a luminous stage performer, groping desperately with the part of Tracy Lord that I perceived for the first time the real subject of The Philadelphia Story. *The play was not about a spoiled socialite* like *Katharine Hepburn. The*

play was about Katharine Hepburn herself, and what the American people thought about Katharine Hepburn in 1939, and what Katharine Hepburn realized she had to do to keep her career going. The Philadelphia Story *is quite simply the breaking, reining, and saddling of an unruly thoroughbred for the big races to come on Broadway and in Hollywood. It is Katharine Hepburn getting her comeuppance at long last, and accepting it like the good sport she was.*

Sarris is right, of course, but *all* star vehicles are about their leading performers and what the audience thinks of them. *The Philadelphia Story* confronts us with a slightly different question: Why do some actors *overflow* a movie's diegesis more than others? Why is the viewer so aware of Hepburn-the-person?

Every movie star is simultaneously (1) a real person, (2) a persona, and (3) the aftereffect of a series of roles. Hollywood's publicity and typecasting worked to conflate these three things, despite their almost inevitable differences. Most commonly, the real person differed from the persona (as with James Cagney and Edward G. Robinson), but inconsistent casting could also erode the relationship between persona and role (see Cary Grant in *The Howards of Virginia*). The myth persisted that, as Cukor himself put it, "You can't be phony in a picture because the camera's right up close to you—and looks right through you." But as Jon Lovitz's *Saturday Night Live* skits insisted, acting almost always involves "lying" or "being phony." The more a star's acting involves theatrical impersonation, the more her self will disappear into the part.

Hepburn represents the extreme case of an accord among real self, persona, and roles. For a start, she never played anything but starring parts, most selected to accommodate an unusually distinct temperament, marked by particular enthusiasms, prejudices, and limitations. This consistent casting reinforced a persona that Hepburn's own exceptional distaste for studio publicity prevented from straying very far from her actual self. The result is a star who always seems larger than any role she plays. *The Philadelphia Story* takes advantage of that fact, and with Hepburn's complicity, worked to transform the persona that threatened her career.[9]

(with Kate Casey-Sawicki)

 ntoxication

Sometimes what has become objectionable behavior can date a film as much as its characters' clothes. Dexter pushes Tracy to the ground, and a modern audience thinks "domestic abuse." As he waits to meet the Lords, Connor lights one cigarette after another, and we think "lung cancer." So drunk she can barely keep her eyes open, Tracy drives Mike home from Dexter's house. Indeed, all the movie's visible signs of intoxication, and the resulting hangovers, are played for laughs, with censure reserved for Dexter's prior, and hence conveniently offscreen, alcoholism. "I'd sell my grandmother for a drink," Mike proclaims at noon on wedding day, blithely adopting the prevailing mores. Eventually, someone will be watching us. "In the future," Irving Thalberg once predicted, "the movies will be the best record of how we once lived."

(with Brian McCullough and Heather Visser)

 oe Smith

Somewhere back among what Fitzgerald called "the lost Swede towns" of the upper Midwest, always Hollywood shorthand for

the "real America," Macaulay Connor has grown up in South
Bend, Indiana (Tracy: "South Bend! It sounds like dancing"), and
Liz Imbrie of Duluth ("it's west of here, isn't it?") has been
married to "Joe Smith, hardware." Like Tracy's missing brother,
Junius, Joe Smith will remain offscreen, fostering some anxiety in
the viewer accustomed to having all characters present and
accounted for. (The obvious analogy: sounds issuing from
unidentified offscreen sources, a recurring feature of horror films.)
Nevertheless, "Joe Smith, hardware" offers the pleasures of the
uncanny. Jimmy Stewart, whose Best Actor Academy Award for
The Philadelphia Story seemed a payback for the more deserving, but
nonwinning, performance in *Mr. Smith Goes to Washington*, kept the
Oscar statuette proudly displayed in his father's hardware store on
Philadelphia Street in his oxymoronically named hometown,
Indiana, Pennsylvania.

(with Stephanie Dykes and Rochelle Mabry)

John Howard

Although *The Philadelphia Story*
provides Tracy with three
possible husbands—Kittredge,
Connor, and Haven—only the
latter two seem at all dramatically possible. The movie, of
course, teaches us to perceive
George's inappropriateness
long before Tracy does: he is eager for *Spy*'s publicity, afraid to
dirty his riding clothes, uncomfortable on horseback, unrespon-
sive to jokes, overly deferential to Tracy, and eager to leave Uncle
Willie's party. Only when he suspects the worst of her dalliance
with Mike does Tracy recognize what we have known all along.
And yet, none of this behavior seems decisively condemning:
Fitzgerald, after all, could make a similar outsider, Jay Gatsby,

into a sympathetic figure. If we imagine *The Philadelphia Story* with only one major change, John Howard and Cary Grant swapping roles, we begin to see how our sense of "Kittredge" depends less on his "flaws" than on casting. In the cinema, physiognomy is destiny: John Howard, a Phi Beta Kappa war hero, cannot compete with Cary Grant and Jimmy Stewart. He is shorter than both, and though the youngest of the three, much the oldest looking. With his neat mustache and more-formal suits, he seems a figure left over from the 1930s, like a poor man's John Barrymore or William Powell, precisely a type being abandoned by 1940.

Barry King has suggested that the cinema largely replaces theatrical acting's goal of "impersonation" (the actor loses himself in the part) with "personification" (the actor takes only those parts consonant with his looks and persona). Even actors committed to impersonation, however, are limited by their looks. As King points out, "Ernest Borgnine can be made into a better looking Ernest Borgnine, not another Robert Redford." Hence, the obvious strategy:

> The predominant tendency is for the norm of impersonation
> to be abandoned at the level of casting in favour of a strategy
> of selection based on personification—let the actor be
> selected by physical type anyway and let these physical
> attributes mean in and of themselves.

"Remember," Irving Thalberg wrote in his "Ten Commandments for Studio Readers," "you are dealing with a pictorial medium." The logic is inexorable: Describing an unfortunate female character in a British horror film, Truffaut would pitilessly remark, "[W]e don't feel sorry for her since she isn't pretty." In effect, we don't feel sorry for Kittredge because he doesn't look like Cary Grant.[10]

(*with Jason Mendro*)

K ittredge

Brendan Gill once identified Philip Barry with a group of Irish-American writers, including Eugene O'Neill, John O'Hara, and F. Scott Fitzgerald, "drawn to the rich and well-born." Each of the four had Ivy League connections: O'Neill and Fitzgerald attended Princeton, where O'Hara ended up living; Barry graduated from Yale, for which O'Hara had so longed that he kept scrapbooks detailing the exploits of his imaginary class. Barry even named Kittredge for a Harvard English professor, famous at the time.

As Gill points out, all four of these writers—Irish Catholic and of modest means—regarded the world of privilege from an outsider's vantage point. "That was always my experience," Fitzgerald wrote, in words that also apply to Barry. "A poor boy in a rich town; a poor boy in a rich boy's school; a poor boy in a rich man's club at Princeton. . . . I have never been able to forgive the rich for being rich, and it has colored my entire life and works." *The Great Gatsby* was Fitzgerald's revenge. "They were careless people, Tom and Daisy," Nick Carraway summed up, in a judgment that Kittredge might have made about Tracy Lord and C. K. Dexter Haven. "[T]hey smashed up things and creatures and then retreated back into their money or their vast carelessness or whatever it was that kept them together, and let other people clean up the mess they had made." Kittredge's angry epithet, "You and your whole rotten class," delivered to Dexter after Tracy has broken off the engagement, would not be out of place in Fitzgerald's novel.

In fact, *The Philadelphia Story* is *The Great Gatsby*, written from Tom and Daisy's point of view, and showing no mercy for its own *arriviste* Gatsby figure, George Kittredge, whom the movie humiliates at every turn. Like Tom and Daisy, Dexter and Tracy are privileged, reckless, and ultimately cruel. Like Gatsby, Kittredge is humorless, a fatal flaw in a screwball comedy, and his money, coming from coal, is "dirty." "When I was a coal miner," he says, objecting to Tracy's attempts to rumple his nouveau riding outfit, "the idea was to get enough money to buy clean clothes." Cukor had a feel for this story: his first major success as a director had come in 1926 with a Broadway version of Fitzgerald's novel. Production stills from both the 1926 and the 1949 Hollywood films of *Gatsby* appear like missing scenes from *The Philadelphia Story*: the elegant sets, the formal ball, the chandeliers, the omnipresent cocktail glasses.

The Philadelphia Story's reverence for the upper classes derives, of course, from Barry's play. Because Hollywood's own aristocracy of moguls, producers, directors, and stars came almost entirely from humble origins, the movies typically made fun of the rich; see, for example, *It Happened One Night, My Man*

Godfrey, and *The Palm Beach Story*. When things turned serious, as in *Meet John Doe*, *Citizen Kane*, or *It's a Wonderful Life*, the rich became villainous. *The Philadelphia Story*'s decided preference for the upper class is an exception to Hollywood's general rule.[11]

Light

The greatest classic Hollywood films seem endlessly mysterious, evocative, surprising. Despite the increasingly sophisticated analytical tools developed by film studies, the effect of these movies, so often dependent on formulaic plots and stock characters, continues to elude complete explanation. In the 1920s, the French impressionist filmmakers struggled to make explicit the intuition they called *photogénie*, "the purest expression of cinema." Jean Epstein's approach suggests a discourse seeking to account for the cinema's magic while approximating its spell:

> *The cinema is essentially supernatural. Every thing is transformed. . . . All volumes are displaced and reach flashpoint. Life recruits atoms, molecular movement is as sensual as the hips of a woman or young man. The hills harden like muscles. The universe is on edge. The philosopher's light. The atmosphere is heavy with love.*
>   *I am looking.*

This kind of writing resembles, as Walter Benjamin said of Kafka, "the *rumor* of true things (a sort of theological whispered intelligence dealing with matters discredited and obsolete)." With the cinema, Epstein seems to say, "only the most indistinct sounds reach the listener."

Do the best movies rely the most on something indistinct, just beyond words? Why does *The Philadelphia Story*, and not other movies, reward repeated viewings? What about it do we remember? To what extent do the elements that we *cannot* remember contribute to the film's success? Where does it surprise us every time? These questions, so resistant to explicit answers, may prove the key to Hollywood's approach to cinema. A musical analogy can help us think about them.

Classical Hollywood's apparent simplicity finds its analogue in rock and roll, which as Theodore Gracyk argues, "shuns compositional complexity, either horizontally [melodically] or vertically [harmonically]." Gracyk continues:

> *Most rock music is simple and repetitive and predictable. . . .*
> *we should be bored by sustained attention when rehearing*
> *recordings of such repetitive, predictable music. What's left to*
> *discover during the hundredth listening to the Kingsmen's*
> *"Louie Louie"?*
>
> *What is needed is a plausible account of how "Louie*
> *Louie" can retain its impact when the record is played over*
> *and over. The answer must be that song structure is often an*
> *incidental framing device for something further, a "coathanger"*
> *upon which other qualities are hung.*

Gracyk's name for those "other qualities" is *timbre*, usefully defined by the *American Heritage Dictionary* as "the quality of a sound that distinguishes it from other sounds of the same pitch and volume." Strikingly, however, while most people can remember the different sounds of a trumpet and a clarinet, even trained musicians cannot store a particular timbre's details:

> *[A]uditory memories seem to be restricted to* species *of*
> *timbre. We can* hear *minute differences between similar*
> *timbres while listening, but those nuances begin to be*
> *forgotten about a second after the sounds cease.*

Thus, as Gracyk explains, if even a knowledgeable listener is presented with samples of the guitar tones from "Green Onions" and "Louie Louie," detached from their contexts, she will prove unreliable in identifying them. We simply cannot store and remember musical nuance. Gracyk pinpoints the result: the more a particular kind of music relies for its effect on timbre, the more it will repay listening; "the local qualities always promise 'the thrill of the unexpected; you never know what you will hear.'" "Louie Louie," in other words, will always seem surprising because we can't quite remember the precise sound of the ramshackle drumming, metallic guitar, and partially buried vocal.

Timbre is the musical equivalent of *photogénie*, or what the *Cahiers du Cinéma* writers called mise-en-scène, a code term for everything they valued about the cinema but were unable to specify. Part of *The Philadelphia Story*'s "timbre" lies in its light, a delicate flickering that plays across the walls of the Lords' rooms, evoking youth and money and summer afternoons long ago in the last century. I can detect this timbre while watching the movie, and I can distinguish it from the light in a similar movie, *The Awful Truth*, when I put the two side by side.

But I cannot quite remember it, and its fragile buoyancy, whose slight shadows suggest offscreen trees, surprises me every time I watch the film.[12]

ac the Nightwatchman

"Mac the nightwatchman is a prince among men," Tracy declares, and Dexter offers even higher praise: "You could marry Mac the nightwatchman, and I'd cheer for you." Despite his minuscule role, undeveloped character, and single brief appearance, Mac seems *The Philadelphia Story*'s most respected character. And yet, neither Philip Barry nor George Cukor appears especially interested in this walk-on part, played with a slight Scottish accent by the uncredited David Clyde. Why, then, does the movie repeatedly refer to him?

Mac is *an alibi*, providing assurance that character, not wealth, determines a person's quality. Although Tracy has contemplated marrying George, though she has entertained having an affair with Mike, she ultimately marries Dexter, thereby defying Ellie Andrews of *It Happened One Night* and, indeed, the whole screwball comedy genre. Tracy's decision represents the genre's retreat from socioeconomic to marital conflicts. Instead of bridging social classes, the union of Tracy and Dexter unashamedly reunites old money with old money. Mac, however, offers the continuing promise of a classless, utopian American society, and thus, he enables *The Philadelphia Story* to avoid the scandal of snobbery. Only Mac's "princeliness," the means of displacement from class to character, permits George to be "beneath" Tracy.

(with Jason Mendro)

M arlin

On one wall of the Lords' pool
house hangs a painting of a
marlin, clearly visible as Mike
changes clothes. While the
painting amounts to simply
another sign of "class," the
more likely decoration, a
photograph, might prove
disruptive, providing a window

to a world beyond the film, a "story" withheld (did Tracy catch it
on her honeymoon with Dexter?). Research project: what is the
effect in the movies of photographs of extradiegetic events?

(with Matt Bernstein)

M atch

After the ball, Tracy wheels Mike around in a lawn chair, leaning
toward him as the cut occurs on his line, "You can't marry that
guy." The transition, roughly accurate, is nevertheless imperfect:
Tracy suddenly appears closer to Mike than in the previous shot's
tail, and her forearms, rather than her hands, now rest on the

chair's frame. Connor makes the problem explicit: "You don't match up." Mike's objection is, of course thematic, another assertion of Kittredge's unsuitability. The formal connotation, almost certainly unintended, will go unnoticed, as the plot's momentum whirls the viewer ahead from shot to shot. Classic Hollywood always understood that absolutely perfect editing was never needed to produce what Noël Burch called "the diegetic effect," the spell of seduction that encourages complete investment in the events onscreen. Star power was always more important than exact continuity. And yet, this "bad match," an anomaly in *The Philadelphia Story*, is like a tiny tear in a fabric, a hole through which appears something on the other side, the filmmaking *work*: the repositioned cameras, the reframing, the lighting adjustments, the actors' new positions, and the editor's ever-so-slight indifference.

(*with Brian McCullough*)

Notecards

While waiting with Liz to meet the Lords, Mike catalogs objects and wedding presents on notecards. After running through his research on Kittredge and Seth Lord, he stops at Tracy's card, asking, "What's her leading characteristic?" "I can fill them in right now," he tells Liz. "The young, rich, rapacious American female. There's no other country where she exists." This desire to simplify signification mimics studio era filmmaking, which reduced actors to types for the purposes of narrative economy. As played by Jimmy Stewart, Mike himself is a type, the goodhearted, down-to-earth midwesterner, and by 1940, Katharine Hepburn certainly represented precisely the type of character *The Philadelphia Story* asks her to play.

And yet, the movie's goal is to complicate all initial judg-ments: Mike's about the rich, Tracy's about both Kittredge and

Dexter, and the viewer's about Katharine Hepburn. Thus, *The Philadelphia Story* adheres to the structure established by Jane Austen, whose violently prejudiced heroines (Elizabeth Bennet, Emma Woodhouse) must learn to recognize the ideal qualities of their equally proud suitors (Darcy, Knightley). (See *The Philadelphia Story*: Grant.) Mike's notecards, however, also suggest a modern sense of identity as a collection of fragments, always available for reformulation. More immediately, they offer an image of the filmmaking process itself, a discontinuous gathering of details awaiting a provisional arrangement.

(with Kate Casey-Sawicki)

Not Wounded, Sire, but Dead"

With Dexter and George already on the terrace, Tracy arrives in her bathrobe, carried by Mike.

> **Dexter**: *She's not hurt?*
>
> **Mike**: *No, no.*
>
> **Tracy** [**drunkenly**]: *Not wounded, Sire—but dead.*

Tracy's line, also appearing in Barry's play, is an abbreviated version of a passage from Robert Browning's "Incident of the French Camp":

> *"You're wounded!" "Nay," his soldier's pride*
> *Touched to the quick, he said:*
> *"I'm killed, Sire!" And his Chief beside,*
> *Smiling the boy fell dead.*

Tracy's ability to cite Victorian poetry, even in garbled form, amounts to a class marker. In American culture, precisely the *uselessness* of literature renders it an appropriate field of study only for those who don't need money. The Morrill Act of 1862, which founded the land-grant public colleges, had mandated that "the leading object shall be, without excluding other scientific or classical studies, to teach such branches of learning as are related to agriculture and the mechanic arts." That effectively left the liberal arts to the private schools, where Barry (Yale), scriptwriter Donald Ogden Stewart (Yale), James Stewart (Princeton), and Hepburn (Bryn Mawr) had all been educated. Neither George Kittredge nor Jay Gatsby could have borrowed Browning's line. Tom Buchanan might have. For *The Philadelphia Story*'s viewers, the key word is "Sire," whose anachronistic connotations signal "a quotation," delivered ironically. Hollywood humor has never depended on its audience's completely understanding every joke. Thus, in *Manhattan*, Woody Allen would get a laugh by describing someone as "the winner of the Zelda Fitzgerald Emotional Maturity Award" because, as a student who had never heard of Zelda Fitzgerald once explained to me, "the name just sounds funny."[13]

 melet

Tracy's first words in *The Philadelphia Story* amount to a simple question: "How do you spell *omelet?*" Her mother doesn't know (offering *ommelet*), and neither does Tracy: "I thought there was another *l.*" This latter joke is a sophisticated variant (you have to know how to spell *omelet* to get it) of a contemporary Jack Benny radio routine: after Rochester worried that he had misspelled *Happy Birthday* on Jack's cake, Benny consolingly advised, "That's OK, you can always add a *p.*" "Add one?" Rochester moaned. "I've gotta take one out."

    The word *omelet*, of course, and the gift for which Tracy is thanking someone (an omelet plate) are both what Barthes's *S/Z* refers to as "reference codes," signifiers activating culturally shared knowledge derived from the realm of "the already read": books, advertisements, magazines, newspapers, radio broadcasts, the movies themselves. In 1940, *omelet* signified not merely wealth, but old money comfortable with European cuisine. Only in the early 1960s, more than 20 years after *The Philadelphia Story*, would Julia Child introduce mainstream Americans to French cooking; significantly, her show's initial episode, the first cooking program ever televised, would demonstrate how to make an omelet. Thus, *The Philadelphia Story*'s reference, like any detail whose meaning has shifted, confirms *S/Z*'s point that every moment involves "a vast dissolve" of fading and emerging codes. The movies provide an archaeological record of those superimpositions.[14]

(with Chris Soldt)

"Over the Rainbow"

The movie version of *The Philadelphia Story* interpolates two songs not present in Barry's play: Connor's "Over the Rainbow" and Dinah's "Lydia the Tattooed Lady," the latter replacing something called "Pepper Sauce Woman." Both songs, written by Harold Arlen and E. Y. Harburg, had appeared the previous year in MGM movies: "Lydia" in the Marx Brothers' *At the Circus*, "Rainbow" in *The Wizard of Oz*. By recycling songs it already owned, MGM could save money while simultaneously promoting its own product. In fact, however, this retroactive product placement was less important than it now seems. Prior to the late 1950s, when television began to revive even Hollywood's most disposable products, all but the rarest extravaganzas (e.g., *Gone with the Wind*) vanished after their initial exhibition at first-run and neighborhood theaters. Thus, while MGM might have had some interest in promoting *The Wizard of Oz*, which would reappear at seven-year intervals, it would have cared very little about *At the Circus*, which had come and gone.

But the songs achieve a different, more-valuable effect: when Dinah belts out "Lydia the Tattooed Lady," when Mike croaks "Over the Rainbow," the viewer infers that, last year, these characters must have seen *At the Circus* and *The Wizard of Oz*. Dinah and Mike, in other words, don't inhabit a nonexistent, made-up universe; they live in the same world we do, and like us, they go to the movies.

(with Joseph Magrisso)

P A55

As Mike and Tracy leave the suburban library, they pass a car with the license plate *PA55*, an object that demonstrates Hollywood's use of marginal details. While the *PA* indicates "Pennsylvania," and thus contributes to the movie's verisimilitude, the *55* is

random: *changing the number would have no effect on the film*. Indeed, the number's realistic effect depends precisely on its meaning-lessness. Any obviously significant number (e.g., 1940, 1776, Hepburn's age) would undermine its status. The realism of these "futile," "useless" details, in other words, derives from the assumption of reality's inscrutability. As Barthes observed about what he called "the reality effect": "The pure and simple 'represen-tation' of the 'real' . . . thus appears as a resistance to meaning; this resistance confirms the great mythic opposition of the *true-to-life* (the lifelike) and the *intelligible*." *The Philadelphia Story*'s charac-ters rarely engage with any parts of the set (Dinah's piano and Tracy's swimming pool are the great exceptions). Hence these questions: What elements of that set, like *55*, could be changed without affecting the movie? Are movies with a greater number of fungible details more "realistic"?[15]

(*with Matt Bernstein and Michael Kinney*)

Patron Lady Bountiful"

Having discovered Mike's writing at the local library, Tracy questions him:

> *Tracy*: *When you can do a thing like that book, how can you possibly do anything else?*
>
> *Mike*: *Well, you may not believe this, but there are people in this world that must earn their living.*
>
> *Tracy*: *Of course, but people buy books, don't they?*
>
> *Mike*: *Not as long as there's a library around. You know that book of mine represents two solid years' work. And it netted Connor something under $600.*
>
> *Tracy*: *But that shouldn't be! . . . What about your Miss Imbrie?*
>
> *Mike*: *Well, Miss Imbrie is in somewhat the same fix. She's a born painter, and might be a very important one. But Miss Imbrie must eat. And she also prefers a roof over her head to being constantly out in the rain and snow.*

Tracy responds by offering Mike her "most wonderful little house in Unionville," which he curtly rejects: "You see, the idea of artists depending upon a patron Lady Bountiful has more or less gone out." In fact, however, it hasn't: Seth Lord's "interest in the arts" has extended to his "putting up $100,000 to display the shapely legs of his mistress," Tina Mara.

Nevertheless, the situation of Mike and Liz reflects the one great problem that, since impressionist painting, has dictated the shape of the art world—the problem of *the gap*. As a movement, impressionism arrived at a moment when art (and, by implication, almost any innovative activity) was encountering a new set of circumstances: for the first time, the art world had begun to assume that between the introduction of a new style and its acceptance by the public, a gap would inevitably exist. This problem had its own history. In the French Revolution's wake, the decline of the stable patronage system, which had depended on a small, sophisticated audience ready to commission and purchase art, had produced an entirely new audience for painting—the bourgeoisie, newly come to power (both politically and financially) but less sophisticated, less secure about its own taste. Such an audience (the prototype of the generalist lost in the world of specialization) would inevitably prove conservative. Its taste would always lag behind the increasingly rapid stylistic innovations stimulated by the emerging market economy, hungry for novelty and eager for new technologies.

Mass taste, in other words, must be educated to accept what it does not already know. Unless avant-garde artists remain content with posthumous success (represented as the only "genuine" kind by Balzac's *Lost Illusions*, a principal source of the avant-garde's myth), they must work to reduce the gap between introduction and acceptance of their work. In the meantime, such artists will have to work for *Spy* magazine.

As a capital-intensive, determinedly commercial enterprise, Hollywood filmmaking could never afford to be avant-garde; its investors would never have tolerated the gap. Indeed, the studios expressed impatience with anything but products aimed at the widest audience. In 1941, Darryl Zanuck would reject Jean Renoir's proposal to film Saint-Exupéry's *Wind, Sand, and Stars*, explaining that in America, every movie had to appeal to everyone. Thus, like most mass art, the movies avoided the gap by reproducing variations of familiar forms. And like Sidney Kidd, the studios employed writers who couldn't sell enough books to make a living, or those (like F. Scott Fitzgerald) whose earnings had declined. In fact, Mike Connor is precisely the kind of writer MGM would "buy." Fitzgerald, who must have understood the bargain, had *The Last Tycoon*'s Monroe Stahr (a fictionalized Irving Thalberg) detail its terms:

> *"These are good writers. . . . And we don't have good writers out here."*
> *"Why you can hire anyone!" exclaimed the visitor in surprise.*
> *"Oh, we hire them but when they get out here they're not good writers—so we have to work with the material we have."*
> *"Like what?"*
> *"Anybody that'll accept the system and stay decently sober—we have all sorts of people—disappointed poets, one-hit playwrights, college girls."*

The studios also understood how to manage their product. Barthes's *S/Z*, in many ways a study of postpatronage literature, suggests that at least since Balzac, popular narratives have depended on a contract that "would have us 'throw away' the story once it has been consumed ('devoured') so that we can then move on to another story, buy another book." By keeping even older volumes available for rereading, libraries, as Mike complains to Tracy, break this contract. Until the 1950s, however, Hollywood kept its viewers hungry by removing almost all movies from distribution after their initial brief runs. Thus, a viewer impressed by *The Philadelphia Story*'s "new" Katharine Hepburn would have to move on to *Woman of the Year* and, prevented from rereading, would, as Barthes observed, be "obliged to read the same story everywhere."[16]

(*with Rachael Murphy, Erin Persley, Chris Soldt*)

Q The Quaker Girl

As a child, George Cukor was inspired by Ina Claire's performance in *The Quaker Girl* (1911), a play turning on plot elements strangely similar to *The Philadelphia Story*'s. Disowned by her family for drinking champagne, the "Quaker girl" cavorts with a French princess before having to choose among three different men, one of whom she bribes with love letters. Champagne, "Frenchnicity," three suitors, blackmail—all of these devices will reappear in *The Philadelphia Story*.

(with Kate Casey-Sawicki)

Quaker Spirit

References to Quakerism recur throughout *The Philadelphia Story*. Mrs. Lord has "the old Quaker spirit" when she gamely decides to welcome the *Spy* journalists; Kittredge is the general manager of Quaker Coal, a company in which Seth Lord owns the controlling interest; a librarian surprises Mike with her antique Quaker diction ("What is thee wish?"). These moments, of course, draw on the codes of "Philadelphianess," established by the opening credits' drawing of the Liberty Bell. Their repetition also suggests the paucity of signifiers for Philadelphia, whose skyline offers no immediate trademark as obvious as San Francisco's bridges or New York's skyscrapers. In fact, however, except for Boston, New Orleans, Miami, and Hollywood, almost no other American cities would prove any more capable of ready identification. With homogenization having depleted the store of regional signifiers, cities will have to be *named*, not merely implied.

(with Matt Bernstein and Kate Casey-Sawicki)

Quaker State Coal

Kittredge is the "general manager" of Quaker State Coal, but we never see his house, his land, his car, or indeed *any* physical representation of his wealth. Even his room assignment, the offscreen "gatehouse," separates him from the Lord mansion, emblem of the family's old money. In *S/Z*, Barthes diagnosed this distinction: "The difference between a feudal society and bourgeois society, index and sign, is this: the index has an origin, the sign does not." Compared to the Lords' wealth, George's new money lacks representation. *The Philadelphia Story*, anchored by the main story's opening shot of the Lord house, makes "George Kittredge" into an empty sign, ungrounded, and utterly dependent for its meaning on agreement among its users. Dexter's role is to undermine that agreement, to revise the significance of "George." "Kittredge is no great tower of strength," he warns Tracy. "He's just a tower."[17]

(with Matt Bernstein)

Quick Swim

Early in the film, Dexter takes approximately 3 minutes, 45 seconds, to walk from the Lords' front door to the pool and back to the sitting room. Later, however, Tracy and Mike require only 3 minutes of screen time to run from the terrace to the pool, have a swim, and return—a quick swim, indeed. Of course, screen time cannot be trusted as *actual* time. As Noël Burch points out, the movies rely on temporal ellipses, measurable or indefinite. While cinematic abridgements often prove obvious ("Two Years Later" reads the title card after *The Philadelphia Story*'s prologue), Cukor typically works subtly, alternating between characters and events, while implying that another activity is continuing offscreen. Thus, Dexter's return to the Lord mansion with Liz and their brief conversation with Mac the nightwatchman cover the ellipsis involved in Mike and Tracy's "quick swim."[18]

(*with Caitlin DiCristofalo*)

 R ed

Although Katharine Hepburn's father called her "Redtop," she has been alternately described as having "red," "coppery-reddish," "reddish-brown," or "auburn" hair. Pinpointing the exact shade proves difficult. Hepburn didn't make a color film until 1951's *The African Queen*, when she had reached her mid-40s, and her hair had begun to turn gray. Even the promotional posters for *Holiday* (1938), another Barry-Cukor-Grant-Hepburn production, offer contradictory images of a coppery-reddish and an auburn-haired Hepburn, dueling representations repeated by *The Philadelphia Story*'s ads.

In black-and-white film, we can, of course, distinguish the blonde from the brunette; we can only imagine the redhead. The hair color richest in signification ("passion," "anger," "embarrassment," "fieriness") is lost to *The Philadelphia Story*'s film stock. Thus, the viewer must be encouraged into *seeing red*, a pun suggesting not only Kittredge's furious resentment (necessary to the resolution), but also Tracy's "true nature." Although Dexter refers to Tracy as "Red" throughout *The Philadelphia Story*, only his affectionate "You're my redhead" near the end clearly connects that nickname to hair color: hence the metonymic slide from "redhead" to "Red," a shift from the visual to the linguistic required by black-and-white film. Unable to see *red* hair, the viewer must be told to see *Red*, Tracy Lord, and behind her, Katharine Hepburn herself.

(*with Eric Lachs and Kate Casey-Sawicki*)

Rooms

Although the exterior shot of
the Lord mansion reveals a
house of impressive size, the
movie's action uses only five of
its immediate areas: the south
parlor, a small living room, an
enormous dining room (piled
high with wedding presents), a

family sitting room, and the terrace. Clues encourage us to
imagine other rooms: the presence of the "south parlor," for
example, implies a north, and possibly east and west parlors;
Kittredge's unanswered phone call locates Tracy's bedroom,
offscreen, but close enough for the ring to be heard.

    The film works even more subtly by employing deliberate
spatial uncertainty to suggest a labyrinthian interior of indeterminate size. Liz and Mike's arrival, for example, triggers a sequence

involving a series of rooms
whose relative locations remain
imprecise. The couple enters
the south parlor from the main
hall, using a door that a cut
reveals to be on the parlor's
screen-right wall.

Liz's exploration leads
them to another door, connecting to a living room ("What's
this room?" she asks. "I've lost
my compass"),

from which Connor enters the banquet hall housing the wedding presents. Shamed by a guarding servant, he retreats to the living room, rejoining Liz. At the same moment, Dexter is consulting with Tracy, Mrs. Lord, and Dinah in a family sitting room whose location is unclear.

When Dexter takes Tracy aside to explain Kidd's scheme, they appear to enter the same wedding-presents room previously discovered by Connor. The guard, however, is missing, and the suppression of any full shots of the space makes its identification impossible. The film practices a sleight of hand, distracting us from inconsistencies, indeed *working* them to achieve the effect of a much larger interior than we are ever shown.

(*with Chris Soldt*)

S *py*

Sidney Kidd's *Dime* and *Spy* magazines, with their celebrity photo spreads and "horrible, snide, corkscrew English" ("No hunter of buckshot in the rear is Cagey Crafty Connor"), are obvious parodies of Henry Luce's *Time* and *Life*, whose syntax would again be imitated by *Citizen Kane*'s newsreel. *Dime* goes unmentioned by the movie, but *Spy* (read: *Life*) initiates the plot, prompting a gathering of characters and romantic confusion worthy of Jean Renoir's *La Règle du Jeu*, made only a few months earlier. Nevertheless, *Spy* caused Philip Barry trouble. On the one hand, Kidd's blackmail provides the motivation for introducing Mike and Liz into the Lord household while, at least in the film version, also enabling Dexter's return. But, on the other, integrating that story into the narrative of the Tracy-Dexter reunion was a problem. "As he started the second act," Barbara Leaming reports, "Barry lost track of the original story about a reporter." The movie version of *The Philadelphia Story* betrays Barry's struggle.

1. The scene in Kidd's office, where Mike and Liz receive their instructions, seems borrowed from another studio. Although the actor playing Kidd, Henry Daniell, had worked regularly for MGM during  the 1930s (*Camille, Madame X, Marie Antoinette*), his five films prior to *The Philadelphia Story* had been with Warners (four) and Universal (one). He would go on to play archvillain Dr. Moriarty in Universal's mid-

1940s Sherlock Holmes series. Daniell's menacing suavity is enhanced by the room, with its bare walls, *noir*ish venetian-blind shadows, and distorted geometry: the ceiling appears at least 30 feet high, and a single odd window has been installed 12 feet up one wall. Close inspection reveals that the fireplace is only a drawing. In the early 1940s, Hollywood would largely restrict its use of this decor, with its threatening dimensions, to horror movies and scenes of Nazi interrogations. It looks like nothing else in *The Philadelphia Story*.

2. Henry Daniell resembles a more handsome British version of L. B. Mayer himself.

Thus, as Stanley Cavell and others have pointed out, the *Spy* office scene provides a *mise-en-abyme* of *The Philadelphia Story* itself, with producer Kidd hiring scriptwriter Connor, camera operator Imbrie, and director Haven. This self-reflexivity, however, seems entirely out of keeping with classic Hollywood's programmatic effacement of the filmmaking process.

3. The *Spy* plot turns on Tracy's objection to precisely the kind of publicity on which Hollywood has always depended. As the studios consolidated, photographs

of the movie-star-at-home played an increasingly important role in the creation and marketing of an actor's persona. Hepburn herself would appear on a *Life* cover. Thus, *The Philadelphia Story* asks its viewers to hold two contradictory ideas at the same time: publicity is bad for these characters (Tracy: "So I'm to be examined, undressed, and generally humiliated at fifteen cents a copy"), but good for the people playing them.

4. *The Philadelphia Story*'s famous ending returns to the temporarily abandoned *Spy* plot. As Dexter and Tracy join hands in marriage, Sidney Kidd suddenly photo-

graphs them, and their still images appear in the turning pages of *Spy* magazine.

This development, a kind of visual punch line, provides a concluding figure (the freeze-frame) that will spawn hundreds of imitations (see Truffaut's *Les Quatre Cents Coups*). But by indicating that Kidd has willingly ignored Dexter's counterblackmail, it also effectively *annuls the narrative's solution*, retroactively transforming the *Spy* threat into what Hitchcock famously called a "MacGuffin," a meaningless pretext for setting things in motion.[19]

(*with Michael Kinney*)

wo Years Later

This title card, appearing after the prologue's Tracy-Dexter fight, represents the movie's only obvious concession to the demands of temporal discontinuity. Like almost all classic Hollywood films, *The Philadelphia Story* relies on radical abridgement made legible: its events, if played out in real time, would require far more than the movie's 112 minutes. Here is the basic structure:

Section 1: Prologue

Section 2: Title card "Two Years Later" specifies the ellipsis and introduces the family scenes taking place on the Thursday before the wedding, which the inserted *Philadelphia Chronicle* story sets for Saturday.

Section 3: A punning transition from Uncle Willie's discarded *Spy*, trampled by a horse's hoof, takes us to Kidd's office (identified by the door's explicit sign:

DIME AND SPY

INCORPORATED

SIDNEY KIDD

EDITOR AND PUBLISHER

Dialogue indicates that it is still Thursday. The scene ends with a fade-out, classic Hollywood's signal of a temporal ellipsis.

Section 4: Fade-in to Dexter's car arriving at the Lord house, delivering Mike and Liz. Since Haven has promised Kidd that he will pick them up Friday "at noon" in "North Philadelphia," the movie has omitted

roughly 24 hours, but provided the audience with a verbal cue.

Section 5: After the 22-minute previous section ends with a dissolve from Seth Lord to Liz and Mike arriving at the library, this section will run without explicit abridgement for almost 23 minutes. In fact, as we will see, this part contains the movie's most subtle temporal ellipsis.

Section 6: A dissolve from Tracy, busy downing three glasses of champagne, to Uncle Willie's ball initiates this part. Dialogue in section 5 marked the time as just past 7:30 p.m. Here, Kittredge warns Tracy that "it's after 4" in the morning. Thus, the movie has omitted over eight hours. This long part will end on a medium close-up of Dinah watching from her window.

Section 7: Uncle Willie's hung-over descent down the staircase opens this part, which with only minimal abridgement takes the movie to its conclusion. If the previous section ended near dawn, this one begins around noon on Saturday, since after having brought Uncle Willie to the Lord house, Dinah announces the time as 12:30. The movie has omitted more than six hours.

These transitions enable abridgements at once legible and invisible. They provide the viewer with clear, but discreet, markings, effectively forestalling the question that has always threatened narrative filmmaking: *what time is it now?* While most of the devices are standard Hollywood issue, two sections work in particularly subtle ways. In section 5, Tracy walks to the diving board in bright sunlight, her short shadow indicating early afternoon. Just 3 minutes, 35 seconds, later, after 16 shots without any explicit signs of temporal ellipsis, the sequence ends with Tracy looking at the model boat, the *True Love*, floating in the pool in complete darkness. Two factors prevent this sudden appearance of night from appearing as a disruptively bad match. First, the scene's thematic importance, which reveals Kittredge's profound misunderstanding of Tracy, absorbs our attention: as it develops, it slips free from its point of origin, the daylight diving board shot. Second, and more important, each shot in the sequence is *slightly darker than the one before.* Thus, after Tracy's dive, the cut George reveals him in a more covered light. As Tracy swims to the side in shot 3, the area has apparently lost its sun. The slight lighting mismatch between shots 14 and 15 (when Tracy stands up, George's light seems to have gone out) prepares us for the harsher transition to the final shot 16, which reveals the larger space now plunged into full darkness.

Section 6 proves even more complicated. On the one hand, Dexter's arrival with Liz and the now-typed blackmail letter, only 7 minutes after they had stayed behind to do the job, depends on an unmarked temporal abridgement. And yet, the sequence as a whole turns on an imprecise, but significant, temporal *expansion*. After leaving Uncle Willie's ball sometime well after 4 a.m., Mike has (a) driven to Dexter's house, (b) waked him, (c) discussed Dexter's feelings for Tracy, (d) reached an agreement with Dexter to blackmail Kidd, (e) dictated a multipage document, (f) waited while Dexter talked to Tracy in her car, (g) driven Tracy back to the Lord house, and (h) walked to the terrace to begin dancing with her—*and it is still not dawn. The Philadelphia Story*, in other words, demonstrates the elasticity of cinematic time, which in Hollywood's hands, responds only to narrative pressure.

Typewriter

Looking for the wandering Mike, Liz arrives at Dexter's house in the early morning hours after the ball. "Can you use a typewriter?" Haven asks, quickly shanghaiing her for a typical "woman's job" as secretary. Why can't he simply type the blackmail letter himself? After all, he has managed to take Connor's drunken dictation. At this point, however, the movie confirms the collusion of ideology and narrative. To free Mike for his dalliance with Tracy, the plot must keep Liz behind; an accepted stereotype ("typists are

women") prevents that need, and its solution, from seeming
purely mechanical (the weakness of the "well-made play"). At the
same moment, the narrative's *speed* (things are coming to a head)
averts any objections to the regressive image of "a woman's
place." Thus, the typewriter represents *The Philadelphia Story*'s
economy: by acting in cahoots, the movie's narrative and ideological tactics *render each other invisible*.

(with Rachel Murphy)

Unanswered Telephone

To suggest narrative's interference with what he most valued
about the cinema, its capacity for producing *photogénie*, Jean
Epstein complained, "The telephone rings. All is lost." *The
Philadelphia Story* offers one solution to that problem: don't answer
it. Tracy ignores the ringing in her bedroom. In doing so, however,
she triggers the plot's denouement, thereby confirming that
Hollywood cinema can almost never escape a telephone's
importuning. George will arrive to track Tracy down, and the
resulting confrontations will lead her back to Dexter.

The movie's telephones, however, serve another purpose,
suggesting how much cinematic space can depend on sound.
George's unanswered call connects one offscreen space (the
gatehouse) with another (Tracy's bedroom). Similarly, Connor
discovers that the south parlor's telephone offers connections to
the "living room, sitting room, terrace, pool, stables," thereby
evoking as-yet-unseen places which the movie will eventually
visit. Upon hearing this list, Liz remarks, "That's probably so
they can talk to the horses without having them in the house." A
more accurate comment: "That's so the house can seem bigger
without its having to be all onscreen." The film, in other words,

practices a strict economy, decreasing its diegetic world visually while increasing it aurally. When the remake, *High Society*, does the reverse, with aerial overhead shots of hypertrophied Newport mansions, the dilated settings shrink the characters into insignificance. *The Philadelphia Story*'s mise-en-scène is enclosed. We infer that the Lord house contains many unseen rooms and an overall space much larger than we ever see, but as a result, it feels more like a house in which people actually live.

In fact, *The Philadelphia Story* often relies on samples to hint at the size of the Lords' house and grounds. Thus, leaving Mike and Liz at the front door, Dexter goes to look for Tracy by the pool. The 3 minutes, 30 seconds, that elapse before an offscreen whistle signals his arrival in the sitting room implies the space he has presumably traversed. How far is the gatehouse from the Lord mansion? An 8-minute, 30-second, walk, the time between Kittredge's unanswered telephone call and his arrival on the scene. "I telephoned Tracy," he explains to Dexter, "and her phone didn't answer." (See *The Philadelphia Story*: Framing, Quick Swim, and Rooms; *Grand Hotel*: Telephone.)

(*with Lindsey Averill, Caitlin DiCristofalo, Joseph Magrisso, Erin Persley*)

egetation

With its lush, suburban setting, *The Philadelphia Story* rejects screwball comedy's typical New York world of art deco apartments and streamlined skyscrapers. Instead, the Lord mansion appears in its establishing shot proudly surrounded by trees, lawns,

and shrubbery. Inside, the house is a virtual arboretum, with plants sprouting from corners and flowers floating on every tabletop.

As the film progresses, the vegetation becomes increasingly prominent. Indeed, after Mike and Tracy walk home from the library, through a park she casually identifies as "part of our place," only three brief scenes will take place indoors: Mike's nocturnal visit to Dexter, Dexter's goodnight to Liz, and the final flurry of proposals that leads to the wedding in a room crammed with enormous bouquets. Significantly, no one is ever shown tending to anything; all the flora seem to operate on their own. In other words, the movie ignores physical labor while displaying its picturesque results, precisely the practice of studio filmmaking.

All this vegetation provides *The Philadelphia Story*'s setting with an Edenic air. Stanley Cavell has noted screwball comedy's connections to what Northrop Frye called Shakespeare's "green world" plays, whose prototype is *A Midsummer Night's Dream*. As Cavell has shown, *The Philadelphia Story* echoes that play, as long as one doesn't insist on exact correspondences. Mike, for example, resembles both Quince and Lysander, while Dexter mixes Puck with Oberon. The parallels depend increasingly on the mysterious nocturnal setting, simultaneously sophisticated and pastoral, always implying that the Lord estate lies in the midst of nature, but barely removed from civilization's protocols.

Hepburn famously requested Clark Gable for the Dexter Haven role. Gable's hypermasculinity, however, would have disabled the prologue: Gable shoving Hepburn to the floor would have simply seemed too violent. Grant, on the other hand, can get away with that act because he never appears physically threatening. Like Puck, he operates more by magic (charm) than by direct aggression, and the film gives the impression that once night falls, everyone begins playing on Dexter's terms in a green world.[20]

(with Paul Johnson and Joseph Magrisso)

Weidler

The brief career of Virginia
Weidler, who plays *The
Philadelphia Story*'s precociously
sentient Dinah, suggests the
vagaries of Hollywood stardom. Appearing in movies by
the age of 4, Weidler arrived at
MGM in 1938 when she was 12
and already a veteran of 17
pictures.

She proved a perfect foil for the studio's biggest juvenile,
Mickey Rooney, appearing with him in *Love Is a Headache*, *Out West
with the Hardys*, *Young Tom Edison*, and *Babes on Broadway*. She could
sing (in what is reported to have been a "husky voice"), dance,
and wisecrack, and she always seems alert, intelligent, and funny.
Yet after 1943's *Best Foot Forward* (a musical with a score by *Meet
Me in St. Louis*'s Martin and Blane), she would never make another
film. She was only 16, and at 40, she would be dead of a heart
attack. Luck had been against her. In the studio system, stardom
always depended on a complex calculus of roles and performers.
Although MGM was the company most committed to the kinds of
movies best suited to Weidler, it was also the one most stocked
with young female talent, especially Lana Turner and Judy Garland. Then, near the end of 1940, with Weidler emerging from
prominent roles in four top 10 box-office hits (*Out West with the
Hardys*, *All This, and Heaven Too*, *The Women*, and *The Philadelphia
Story*), MGM would sign Shirley Temple, almost exactly Weidler's
age, and the number-one movie attraction from 1935 to 1938.
Temple would last at MGM for only one picture, and her refusal
to accompany Wallace Beery in 1941's *Barnacle Bill* ensured that
Weidler would have to. She would prove unable to save it and, in

the same year, unable to compete with Garland in *Babes on Broadway*. Virginia Weidler, in other words, was like a centerfielder forced to play on the same team as Joe DiMaggio. She is unforgettable as Dinah.[21]

(*with Rachel Murphy*)

Wristwatch

During Tracy's drunken exploits on the eve of her wedding, Dexter tries to save her embarrassment by pocketing the jewelry she has removed to swim with Connor. When Mike deposits her upstairs, however, he drops his wristwatch on the floor beside her bed, where she finds it the next day ("I nearly stepped on it"). In the midst of a different scene, whose cutting would pivot around a magazine and a coffee cup, Godard would speculate that "maybe an object is what permits us to reconnect, to pass from one subject to the other." In places, *The Philadelphia Story* literally pursues this filmmaking logic. Thus, when Dexter

emerges onto the terrace in the predawn hours, he joins Kittredge, come to investigate why his phone call has gone unanswered. As the men confront each other in standard two-shot, Dexter glances down at an adjacent

table, the point-of-view cut revealing a portable radio, bracelet, engagement ring, champagne bottle, and two wine glasses. In the renewed master shot, Dexter's expression and glance toward the

pool reveal his gradual, ironic understanding of the situation. The table's objects, in other words, connect not only Dexter and George, but also the offscreen Mike and Tracy, who have left their trail. (The sequence also confirms Grant's effectiveness in Kuleshovian acting: when intercut with certain objects, he can convey precise emotions merely by using facial expressions and bodily gestures, a skill exploited by Hitchcock for *North by Northwest*'s crop-dusting scene.)

Connor's wristwatch has an identical function. When Tracy discovers it in her hand the next morning ("Only I wonder what this might be?"), the cut isolating Dinah implies the entire previous evening and

implicitly uses the object to connect all of the main characters.

This tactic, the deployment of a small detail to embody a complex narrative's information, works especially well in the cinema, which endows even the most insignificant objects with a photogenic spell. Hence Louis Aragon's rhapsodic description of what he called the movies' "decor." (See *The Maltese Falcon*: Curtains.)

*The door of a bar that swings and on the window the capital
letters of unreadable and marvelous words . . . the obsessive
beauty of commercial inscriptions, posters, evocative lettering,
really common objects . . . a newspaper or a packet of
cigarettes.*

Or a wristwatch, lost after a late-night swim.[22]

(with Caitlin DiCristofalo and Renee Moilanen)

While X could represent the cinema's rapid vulgarization (*The
Philadelphia Story*'s Tracy Lord became pornography's "Tracy
Lords"), here are other possibilities. The Roman numeral for 10, X
indicates the number of primary characters in *The Philadelphia Story*:

Seth Lord

Margaret Lord

Tracy Lord

Dinah Lord

Uncle Willie

C. K. Dexter Haven

George Kittredge

Mike Connor

Liz Imbrie

Sidney Kidd

Furthermore, as the 24th letter of the alphabet, it equals the number of hours before the wedding, during which time, a series of reversals (X-like crossings) will occur. X stands for the kiss Tracy shares with Mike, while also indicating the erasure of fiancé Kittredge. The algebraic X, the unknown quantity (whom will Tracy marry?), finds its own solution: X marks the spot, as Tracy reunites with eX-husband Dexter, the only character bearing an X in his name.

(with Eric Lachs and Jason Mendro)

 are

This esoteric word, initially an assessment of Dexter's sailboat, the *True Love*, appears twice in *The Philadelphia Story*, the first time suggesting the filmmakers' assumptions that (a) Kittredge must not understand it, and (b) the audience will also require an explanation. "*Yare*, what does that mean?" George asks, standing in for us. Tracy's definition ("quick to the helm, fast, right, everything a boat should be") may suggest her intellectual superiority over George, whom Dexter has described as "beneath" her ("a difference of mind"). But since Tracy has proved incapable of spelling *omelet*, her vocabulary signifies not differences of intelligence but of class. The film could more effectively imply George's intellectual inferiority by demonstrating his ignorance of a common word known to the audience.

Yare, in fact, applies almost exclusively to the description of vessels, a hyperspecialization amounting to diction's version of luxury. This lexical specificity, a kind of excessive verbal expenditure, mirrors *The Philadelphia Story*'s unabashed approval of wealth. Thus, Dexter will recognize *yare* less because of his intelligence than his money, and Tracy will eventually appropriate the term for herself ("Oh, Dexter, I'll be yare now"), thereby promising to become a "responsive" possession.

Influenced by Flaubert, Roland Barthes regarded popular narratives as the propagators of "a nauseating mixture of common opinions, a smothering layer of received ideas." Yare suggests another possibility, the movies as the new *encyclopédie*, the repository of a culture's knowledge about everything under the sun: guns, banking systems, clothes, alcohol, sex, sports, dances, houses, and even yachts.[23]

(with Jason Mendro)

Y_{acht}

With his superfluous, unexplained initials, C. K. Dexter Haven not only has an aristocratic-sounding name, he also builds and sails yachts, a particularly strong emblem of old, eastern money. Dexter, in other words, is a character who both possesses the signifier of wealth and is capable of generating the signifier himself—a good description of the semiotic function of Cary Grant.

Grant appears upper-crust despite his origins as an impoverished Cockney. Thus, he seems completely at home with yachts, estates, servants, and formal dress. This aristocratic persona survives even the revelation of his actual background, so much so, in fact, that when playing a role that approximates it (*None but the Lonely Heart*), he seems miscast. The converse occurs with Bogart, who came from high society but would prove utterly unconvincing as a blue blood (*Sabrina*).

By revealing the unpredictable idiosyncrasies of class (not all aristocrats look alike), photography undermined the cultural codes supporting the nineteenth-century novel. (See *Grand Hotel*: Types; *The Philadelphia Story*: Grant.) The star system, however, perpetuated those codes but severed them from their indexical origins: if aristocratic appearance had once resulted largely from diet and care, it now became merely a sign, arbitrarily distributed throughout any given population. Cary Grant, in other words, simply *looks* like high society, while Humphrey Bogart doesn't. Given this semiotic instability, Hollywood always worked hard to reinforce the connotations on which its stories depended: Haven's "upper classness," therefore, cannot rely entirely on Grant's physiognomy; the character must be surrounded by appropriately coded objects, like yachts. Indeed, by discrediting the very fact of an "aristocratic look," photography (and its extension, the cinema) requires such supporting evidence.

Hollywood only intermittently understood these concepts. It's hard to predict how someone will photograph, and most actors have a certain amount of malleability, allowing them to play different kinds of parts. James Stewart would not have worked for certain roles (Rhett Butler, for example), but he proved capable of both *The Philadelphia Story*'s light romantic lead and *The Naked Spur*'s neurotically cruel antihero, a range that isn't obvious simply from looking at him. The relationship between actor and audience amounts to a language game, in which the performer's appearance becomes part of his available vocabulary, a resource that both enables and limits his ability to communicate. For some actors, looks may constitute their entire lexicon (John Gilbert, Robert Taylor, Tyrone Power). For others, appearance is simply one rhetorical device (albeit a major one) at their disposal.

(with Paul Johnson)

Y o-Yo

Tagalog for *come back*, the yo-yo is one of the oldest (second only to the doll) and most widely used toys in the world. At one time characterized as an aristocratic device that "dispels the fatigue of thinking" (Beaumarchais, *The Marriage of Figaro*), the yo-yo figures in *The*

Philadelphia Story as an upper-class child's own signifier of deep worry concerning the impending marriage of her sister. After the brief prologue, the movie begins with Dinah spinning a dual-colored, Imperial yo-yo and calling out "Tracy, Tracy" as she makes her way through the Lord mansion. With the toy in her hands, she proposes that "the ghost of bridegroom number one" still haunts the house, trying to disrupt the wedding plans. With her double name and spinning yo-yo, Dinah/Diana becomes a seer, predicting the returns of both Dexter as a husband and Hepburn as a star. With each spinning moment of "sleep" and "return," the yo-yo traces the movie's history: the "return" of "bridegroom number one" after a two-year long "sleep," the return of Hepburn and Grant together at MGM (after *Bringing Up Baby*'s flop at RKO), the return of Hepburn to success after being labeled box-office poison only two years before.

(with Kate Casey-Sawicki)

 ingers

With Barry's play as its blueprint, *The Philadelphia Story* relies on a verbal repartee that becomes a means of intimacy. Zingers abound: Liz uses them to bring Mike down to earth, Dinah punctuates family conversations with them, and Dexter deploys them as weapons against Kittredge. "I suppose I should object," George remarks, upon finding Tracy and Dexter together. "That would be most objectionable," replies Dexter, a typical exchange. Barry's dialogue, as Cukor explained to Gavin Lambert, "seemed to be realistic, but it wasn't really. The words always had a kind of rhythm underneath them, and the speech was sometimes quite elaborate." "Can you use a typewriter?" Dexter asks, eager to have a formal copy made of Connor's dirt on Sidney Kidd. "No thanks, I already have one," Liz replies.

The point seems so obvious—*The Philadelphia Story*'s dependence on dialogue—that this anecdote from Cukor comes as a surprise:

When MGM bought the rights to The Philadelphia Story, *they made a recording of a stage performance of the play. The idea was to find out where the laughs came. After the picture was made, we checked it against the recording and the laughs came quite differently. In the theater all the comedy was in Phil Barry's verbal wit, but in the movie a lot of it was visual, reactions, pieces of business, and so on.*

We could list a few of the film's visually comic moments, starting with Dexter's double take after Liz's Gracie Allen retort about the typewriter: the silent, slapstick prologue; Connor holding open his coat to a servant, proving that he hasn't stolen anything; Connor peeking around the stacks at the Quaker librarian; Dexter saving Mike from George's punch by hitting Connor himself; a hung-over Tracy raising her arms to block the sun.

Research question: how much can a movie rely on dialogue and still prove interesting? King Vidor's proposition represents the extreme view: "In the history of films, every great moment that shines in memory is a silent one." *Casablanca* would provide the great counterexample, not *The Philadelphia Story*, whose lines we don't remember, but whose images—of Dexter bobbing and weaving around Tracy, of Connor and Tracy in the moonlight, of Dinah and her yo-yo—remain vivid after well over a half century.[24]

(with Eric Lachs)

The Maltese Falcon

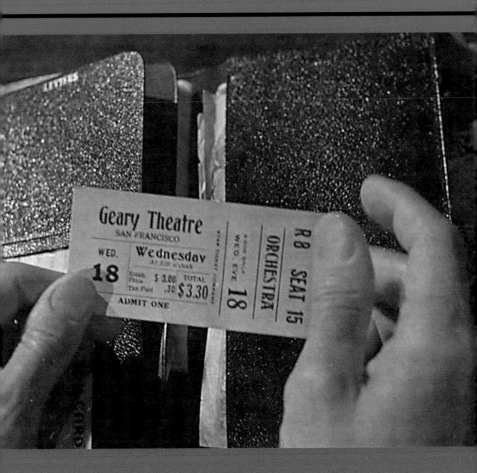

rcher's Murder

Archer's murder at Bush and Stockton is the only scene that does not appear in Dashiell Hammett's novel, John Huston's script, or either of the two previous film versions. (Responding to preview audiences' request for more exposition, Jack Warner had ordered the shot's inclusion.) Although often described as the only moment in *The Maltese Falcon* when the viewer receives information before Spade, in fact it anticipates another: as the detective leaves Gutman's hotel room, his hand shaking from his feigned anger, he enters an elevator without spotting Cairo getting off another. Retroactively, this event will explain what at the time seems utterly gratuitous, Spade's drugging. "Cairo got in touch with me," Gutman will reveal.

> **Gutman**: The Paloma *was his thought. He saw the notice of its arrival in the papers and remembered that he had heard in Hong Kong that Jacobi and Miss O'Shaughnessy were seen together. Well, sir, he saw that and, putting two and two together, guessed the truth. She'd given the bird to Jacobi to bring here for her.*
>
> **Spade**: *And at that juncture, you decided to slip me a mickey, huh?*
>
> **Gutman**: *There was no place for you in our plan, sir.*

The 1931 film version had been less subtle, taking Gutman from a conference with Spade to a connecting room, where Cairo

relayed the information, making the detective redundant. In
Huston's version, Spade's sudden wooziness (represented by an
out-of-focus shot of Gutman) fits Hitchcock's definition of *surprise*:
it resembles an unrevealed bomb that suddenly goes off. Hitchcock
insisted that *suspense* derived from showing the audience the bomb
before its explosion, concluding that "whenever possible the public
must be informed." Huston's refusal to do so indicates that *The
Maltese Falcon* does not depend on suspense; its narrative, like
Brigid's description of Spade, is "wild and unpredictable," neutraliz-
ing any logical calculus. Archer's murder, Brigid's vanishing and
reappearance under yet a third name, Cairo's attempt at burglary,
Wilmer's tailing Spade, Gutman's story about the Falcon, Jacobi's
delivery of the bird, the bum steer, and the final gathering in
Spade's apartment—none of these abrupt turns is foreshadowed or
anticipated. They resemble Flitcraft's falling beams; Spade's success
depends on an agility that keeps him from getting hit.

But as Hitchcock intuited, surprise can confuse an audience
as well as a detective: hence Warner's insistence on greater
narrative clarity, achieved by reshooting Brigid's initially halting,
oblique statements and by adding both the historical prologue
("In 1539 the Knight Templars of Malta . . . ") and the footage of
Archer's murder. The filmmakers' ability to make this latter
insertion transparent suggests a sophisticated system highly
attuned to narrative linearity. In 1903, Edwin S. Porter had also
provided exhibitors of *The Great Train Robbery* with an additional
shot: an unidentified man (outlaw? sheriff?) aiming his gun

directly at the camera and, in the words of Thomas Edison's catalog, "firing point-blank at each individual in the audience." As Noël Burch has shown, exhibitors were free to choose where this shot would appear, although most simply affixed it to the end. In any case, it existed extradiegetically, playing no discernible part in the movie's story. Significantly, the shot of Archer's death—with its revolver intruding into the frame, firing at a victim who faces the camera—is the exact *reverse* of Porter's, with Archer having assumed the place of the audience.[1]

(with Jennifer Simmons)

 ogart

The favorable early line on John Huston derived almost entirely from two sources: James Agee's 1950 *Life* essay, "Undirectable Director," and Lillian Ross's *New Yorker* articles on the making of *The Red Badge of Courage*, published as *Picture* in 1952. Both pieces were essentially puffs, with Agee's so gushing that it would quickly win its author the chance to collaborate with Huston on *The African Queen*:

> *Most of the really good popular art produced anywhere comes from Hollywood, and much of it bears Huston's name. To put it conservatively [?!], there is nobody under fifty at work in movies, here or abroad, who can excel Huston in talent, inventiveness, intransigence, achievement or promise.*

Agee, in other words, was proposing Huston as a better filmmaker than Orson Welles, Anthony Mann, Vincente Minnelli, Nicholas Ray, Otto Preminger, George Stevens, Roberto Rossellini, Marcel Carné, Luchino Visconti, and Vittorio De Sica—all under 50 and already well established. In doing so, Agee anticipated *la politique des auteurs'* two basic themes: the heroic individualism of the director and the priority of shooting over scriptwriting. "Incapable of yesing, apple-polishing or boot-licking," Agee wrote of Huston, in the Occupation-inspired existentialism that would become so dear to the *Cahiers du Cinéma*, "he instantly catches fire in resistance to authority." On the second matter, Agee sounded less jejune; in fact, with its brief against the primacy of scriptwriters, his argument amounted to another version, *avant la lettre*, of the *auteurist* manifesto, François Truffaut's "A Certain Tendency of the French Cinema" (1954):

> *Most movies are like predigested food because they are mere reenactments of something that happened (if ever) back in the scripting stage. At the time of shooting the sense of the present is not strong, and such creative energy as may be on hand is used to give the event finish, in every sense of the word, rather than beginning and life. Huston's work has a unique tension and vitality because the maximum of all contributing creative energies converges at the one moment that counts most in a movie—the continuing moment of committing the story to film.*

Ironically, it would be the *Cahiers* writers who turned the tide against Huston, denounced by Truffaut as "an excellent scriptwriter" but "a second-rate director." "Don't you see," Truffaut insisted to André Bazin, "that all Hawks's films are good, and all Huston's are bad?" Huston's style, declared Eric Rohmer, "has always seemed, despite some lucky finds, to be lacking in invention." "While Huston has had his moments," Jacques Rivette admitted in May 1957, "I can't see why in France we should start by taking him as an example." In the same interview, Rivette proved even more strident, announcing flatly that "Huston is finished." Later that same year, Eric Rohmer completed the dismantling of Huston's reputation by writing a savage critique of the filmmaker's misguided *Moby Dick*, which he described as "useless." By 1968, Huston's stock had fallen so low that Andrew Sarris's influential *The American Cinema* would consign him to the category of "Less than Meets the Eye."

One of Sarris's most famous observations about Huston, that his successes like *The Maltese Falcon* "owe more to casting coups than to directorial acumen," found its own refutation in James Naremore's essay on that movie. Starting from Sarris's dubious premise that "*Falcon*, particularly, is an uncanny matchup of Dashiell Hammett's literary characters with their visual doubles," Naremore showed that, in fact, "Humphrey Bogart is the visual opposite of Hammett's Sam Spade," a tall, bearish "blond satan." (Bogart's New York accent also seems inappropriate for a California detective: an actor has reached stardom when the audience can accept discrepancies between performer and character.) "Huston," Naremore argued, "has gained ascendancy over Hammett," producing a movie that "is more emphatic, more stylized than the book." The economically signifying sets; the deep-focus, low-angled camera; the action's allegorical circumscription; the fetishistic objects arrayed on Spade's desk; the dialogue's regulated speed—all these directorial decisions, Naremore maintained, created a mood in which "[t]he atmosphere is heightened, so that a splash of whiskey in a glass is more important than the sound of gunfire."

Naremore's short essay is the best thing ever written about *The Maltese Falcon*, and even a cursory look at Roy Del Ruth's 1931 version, with its lugubrious pacing and cluttered mise-en-scène, will confirm his insistence on Huston's contributions. And yet, one cannot help imagining how much even that badly directed movie might have been improved by replacing the inept Ricardo Cortez with Humphrey Bogart. Significantly, Bogart is the name evoked by David Thomson for his definition of great movie acting, cited elsewhere in this book. (See *Grand Hotel*: Daniels.)

> *This touches on a vital principle: that it is often preferable to have a movie actor who moves well than one who "understands" the part. A director ought to be able to explain a part, but very few men or women can move well in front of a camera. In* The Big Sleep, *there are numerous shots of*

> *Bogart simply walking across rooms: they draw us to the*
> *resilient alertness of his screen personality as surely as the acid*
> *dialogue. Bogart's lounging freedom captures our hopes.*

"Bogart," André Bazin wrote in his famous eulogy, "is, without doubt, the actor/myth of the war and post-war period. I mean the period between 1940 and 1955." And yet, Bogart had been in the movies for more than 10 years before that, making it hard to think of another major star who found success so late. (William Powell and John Wayne might prove comparable.) Bogart would not become a top-10 box-office star until 1943, and after his 7-year run ended in 1950, he would make that list only once more, largely on the strength of two hits released in late 1954, *The Caine Mutiny* and *Sabrina*. His death on 14 January 1957 increased his stature. In April of that year, the Bogart revival would begin at Harvard's Brattle Theater when *Casablanca* played there for the first time, initiating the Bogart festivals (always including *The Maltese Falcon*, *Casablanca*, and *The Big Sleep*) which would run during each semester's reading periods and exam weeks. Cyrus Harvey, Jr., the Brattle's co-owner and principal programmer, had spent a Fulbright year in Paris discovering Henri Langlois's Cinémathèque Française, whose rich, eccentric programming had schooled the *Cahiers* critics.

As he emerged into stardom in the early 1940s, Bogart did not come trailing clouds of glory. Indeed, had his career continued on its established path, he might well have found himself playing the gunsel Wilmer rather than the hero, Sam Spade. The following list will suggest just how rarely Bogart had played a sympathetic part:

Three on a Match (1932)	villain
Midnight (1934)	villain
The Petrified Forest (1936)	villain
Bullets or Ballots (1936)	villain
Two against the World (1936)	hero
China Clipper (1936)	second lead

Isle of Fury (1936)	hero with a criminal past
Black Legion (1937)	hero gone wrong
The Great O'Malley (1937)	villain
Marked Woman (1937)	unsympathetic hero
Kid Galahad (1937)	villain
San Quentin (1937)	villain
Dead End (1937)	villain
Stand-In (1937)	alcoholic second lead
Swing Your Lady (1938)	conniving hero
Crime School (1938)	hero
Men Are Such Fools (1938)	second lead
The Amazing Dr. Clitterhouse (1938)	villain
Racket Busters (1938)	villain
Angels with Dirty Faces (1938)	villain
King of the Underworld (1939)	villain
The Oklahoma Kid (1939)	villain
Dark Victory (1939)	second lead
You Can't Get Away with Murder (1939)	villain
The Roaring Twenties (1939)	villain
The Return of Doctor X (1939)	villain
Invisible Stripes (1939)	hero gone wrong
Virginia City (1940)	villain
It All Came True (1940)	soft-hearted villain
Brother Orchid (1940)	villain
They Drive by Night (1940)	second lead
High Sierra (1941)	sympathetic villain
The Wagons Roll at Night (1941)	hero gone wrong
The Maltese Falcon (1941)	hero

Even after *Casablanca* clinched his stardom in 1943, Bogart would occasionally return to form, playing murderers, swindlers, cowards, and violent men: *Conflict* (1945), *The Two Mrs. Carrolls* (1947), *The Treasure of the Sierra Madre* (1948), *In a Lonely Place* (1950), *Beat the Devil* (1953), *The Caine Mutiny* (1954), and *The Desperate Hours* (1955).

Bogart's vast repertoire of villainous parts informs *The Maltese Falcon*, making Spade's character more ambiguous and his ultimate decision about Brigid far from a sure thing. "Don't be too sure I'm as crooked as I'm supposed to be," Spade advises Brigid, in words that might also be intended for a viewer aware of Bogart's previous roles. The technical name for this effect is *intertextuality*, a term suggesting how much the meaning of any individual film derives from other movies remembered by the audience. With stars, this phenomenon is particularly acute: when we talk about the cinema, we tend to speak not of roles, but of performers—"and then, Bogart drew his gun," or "Garbo appeared at the door." If we go to the theater to see *Hamlet* played by John Gielgud, we go to the movies to see John Wayne *tout court*. A great stage actor succeeds by disappearing into the role of Hamlet, but even a secondary movie performer, if familiar and typecast, will cause us to forget his character's name. Who does Elisha Cook, Jr., play in *The Big Sleep*? In *Phantom Lady*? Who does William Demarest play in *The Lady Eve*? In *The Palm Beach Story*? "The screen performer is essentially not an actor at all," Stanley Cavell argues, "he *is* the subject of study. . . . After *The Maltese Falcon* we know a new star, only distantly a person." After *The Maltese Falcon*, in other words, we know "Bogart," who has made "Sam Spade" unrepeatable.[2]

(*with Kristin Davy and Eric Garcia*)

C locks

To what extent can a movie *withhold* information without confusing its viewers? Although Glenn Todd has demonstrated that the events in Hammett's novel take place over five days (6–10 December 1928), Huston's film confines the same action to four, with the conclusion in Spade's office occurring at dawn on the fourth day. Since the movie must compress almost 72 hours of story time into 100 minutes, it relies on continual ellipses, whose exact durations often remain uncertain. The movie's temporal demarcations become increasingly ghostly, the result of a calculated untethering of events from normal routine: Spade eats no meals, his newspapers have no dates, and the camera keeps his wall calendar just out of legible range. Even Cairo's theater ticket seems mysteriously incomplete: "Wednesday 18."

Like the film's four principal settings (Spade's office and apartment, Brigid's apartment, Gutman's hotel room), the days begin to seem indistinguishable. And yet, *The Maltese Falcon* distributes specific signals, however parsimoniously, that provide occasional orientation: the clocks on Spade's bedside table (2:05, 3:40)

and Brigid's wall (12:15, 10:15),

his announced appointment times with the D.A. (2:30) and Gutman (5:30). Hence the movie's resemblance to a dream, its time a mixture of extreme precision and deliberate indeterminacy. We can trace this effect as it gets produced.

Day 1

1. Brigid meets Spade and Archer at an unspecified daylight hour.

2. The dissolve to Archer's nighttime murder involves an indefinite ellipsis, rendered somewhat less vague by Brigid's previous information that Thursby would come "after 8 o'clock" the same night.

3. Dissolve to Spade's apartment, where a clock reads 2:05. Nothing indicates the exact amount of time elapsed since Archer's death.

4. Dissolve to murder scene, another ellipsis, this one roughly measurable: Spade has told the caller in number 3 that he can reach this spot "in 15 minutes."

5. Dissolve to phone booth, the same night, but nothing indicates how much time has passed between number 4 and this scene.

6. Superimposition from the drugstore in number 5 to Spade entering his apartment. Another temporal ellipsis, made retroactively measurable by Iva's later confession to Sam that she had telephoned the police from "the drug store across from your place." The bedside table clock now reads 3:40. Police interrogation reveals that at least 30 minutes elapsed between numbers 4 and 5. Scene ends by fading to black.

Day 2

7. Fade-in on newspaper: Spade's office the next day. With no time provided, the temporal ellipsis between the previous scene and this one is uncertain. It will become more specific retroactively.

8. Dissolve from the ashtray with its burning address to Spade arriving at Brigid's apartment. A wall clock reads 12:15.

9. Superimposition to Spade entering his office; the neon signs outside his window are illuminated, and Effie is quitting for the day. No precise time is given, but since Spade will subsequently show up at the Geary Theatre, prompted by Cairo's ticket specifying 8:30, we infer that the time is early evening. Where has Spade been since leaving Brigid's apartment? Fade to black.

10. Nighttime street scene, Spade at Geary Theatre. He takes a cab, loses Wilmer. A temporal ellipsis has occurred.

11. Superimposition to Brigid's apartment, whose clock now reads 10:15.

12. Superimpositions connecting Brigid's apartment to a cab and then to Spade's apartment, where Cairo

and police also will arrive. Spade's clock is turned away from the camera.

Day 3

13. Dissolve from Wilmer watching Spade's apartment to Hotel Belvedere lobby. Indefinite ellipsis from the previous scene, although Spade greets Cairo with a possibly ironic "Good morning."

14. Superimposition to Spade's office, where by telephone he makes an appointment with the D.A. for 2:30.

15. Superimposition to Gutman's hotel, an ellipsis made measurable by Spade's as surance in number 14 that he can be there in 15 minutes. He gives Gutman a deadline: "You've got until 5 o'clock."

16. Superimposition to D.A.'s office, presumably at 2:30 p.m.

17. Superimposition to street scene where Spade tells Wilmer, "I didn't expect you till 5:25." Spade's previous deadline (5 o'clock) seems to have been extended to 5:30.

18. Superimposition to Gutman's hotel. No precise time indicated. With Spade unconscious, the scene ends with fade to black.

19. Spade wakes up. Indefinite ellipsis, but windows indicate that it is now dark outside.

20. Superimposition to *La Paloma* on fire at night. Indefinite ellipsis between number 19 and this scene.

21. Superimposition takes us to Spade's office, where it is still nighttime. After Jacobi's delivery of the Falcon

and Brigid's hysterical call, Spade leaves for the post office.

22. Emerging from the post office, Spade takes a cab to investigate what turns out to be a "bum steer." The imprecise ellipsis acquires some specificity from Spade's questions for the driver ("You got plenty of gas? Do you know where Ancho Street or Avenue is in Burlingame?"), which indicate a trip to an immediate suburb.

23. Dissolve to a phone booth at an unspecified location.

24. Another ellipsis returns Spade to his front door, where he discovers Brigid.

Day 4

25. Once inside Spade's apartment, the movie subtly abridges time until dawn arrives. Note that the movie has withheld inferable exact time since Spade's meeting with Wilmer in number 17 (number 16).

On the one hand, these steps represent a solution to narrative filmmaking's basic problem: how in 90 minutes do you represent events whose actual duration would be much longer? On the other hand, the issue seems more elusive. As primitive cinema's thinly motivated narratives gave way to Hollywood's rigorous continuity, the movies threatened to lose the intensities produced by filmmaking like Feuillade's, whose isolated, haphazard attractions would now require long stretches of banal exposition. Thus, film criticism's ideal goal, *"to penetrate the veil while retaining its hallucinatory quality,"* finds its analogue in classic Hollywood's own project: *to attain coherence without surrendering the cinema's mysterious spell.* To this end, *The Maltese Falcon* pursues a strategy of exploiting filmmaking's inherent discontinuities, the result of shots taken at different places and times. All of the movie's devices—the allegorical names, the unexplained gaps, the insufficient rationales—suggest the replacement of the nineteenth-century novel by the anecdote, understood for the first time less as a narrative's outline than as its perfection. "The ideal screenplay," Huston once told an interviewer, is "closer to poetry than to the novel." The apotheosis of this way of working, in which time becomes inseparable from mood, will be *The Big Sleep*, a film whose sublime delirium would result from Warners' insistent cutting, a demonstration of this rule: when classic Hollywood protocols clash, the 90-minute convention trumps all others.[3]

(*with Jennifer Beckett, Nic Jelley, Mason Laird*)

Curtains

As *The Maltese Falcon* moves from Miles Archer's murder to Spade's receiving the news, a new sequence opens with a medium close-up of the detective's bedside table. A still life of sorts: the ringing, old-fashioned telephone; a hardware-store alarm clock,

signaling masculine austerity, a suspicion of ornament, and an absence of both money and what Hollywood at the time would have called "the feminine touch"; a law book suggesting perhaps

an attempt at self-improvement or, more likely, the constant need to outmaneuver the police. These objects, along with the pipes, tobacco pouch, and cigarette rolling papers, resemble the chess set, cigarette, and champagne glass used to introduce *Casablanca*'s

Rick Blaine. With their ready-made connotations, these semes, as Barthes calls them in *S/Z*, establish a character *without asserting one*. Their "natural" meaning is inferred on-the-fly by a viewer absorbed in the narrative's sudden developments. (See *Grand Hotel*: War Souvenirs)

A commutation test that makes substitutions within an object's own paradigm reveals the calculation. Look first at *Casablanca*'s possibilities:

chess	cigarette	champagne glass
checkers	cigar	beer bottle
solitaire	pipe	shot glass

Compared to chess, checkers would make Rick seem more folksy and less intellectual, while solitaire would convey nihilistic indifference. A cigar connotes "gangsterism," but a pipe implies an academic intellectualism too remote for Rick's pragmatic instincts. As replacements for champagne, beer is too plebeian, whiskey too desperate. Even *one* substitution, however, would decisively modify the character that *Casablanca* asks us to imagine. Imagining them uncovers the process. Thus, to supply Spade's nightstand with a modern white telephone, a jewelry-store clock, or a gun would encourage a reinvention of the detective.

The still life, in other words, has a functional value; every part is motivated. And yet, the image also resembles Louis Aragon's celebration of the cinema's recurring habit of achieving something beyond use value. (See *The Philadelphia Story*: Wristwatch.)

> *All our emotion exists for those dear old American adventure films that speak of daily life and manage to raise to a dramatic level a banknote on which our attention is rivetted [sic], a table with a revolver on it, a bottle that on occasion becomes a weapon, a handkerchief that reveals a crime, a typewriter that's the horizon of a desk.*

The passage amounts to a celebration of the movies' infinite capacity for *fetishism*. As William Pietz has shown, the problem of fetishism first arose in a specific historical context: the trading conducted by Portuguese merchants along the coast of Africa in the sixteenth and seventeenth centuries. Renaissance businessmen, the Portuguese were looking for straightforward economic transactions. Almost immediately, they were frustrated, particularly by what Pietz evocatively calls "the mystery of value." For the Africans, material objects could embody—"simultaneously and sequentially—religious, commercial, aesthetic, and sexual" worth, and the balance among these categories seemed, at least to the Europeans, a matter of "caprice." Especially troubling was the Africans' unpredictable estimate of not only their own objects, but also those of the European traders, which the merchants themselves regarded as "trifles."

Like the Portuguese traders, commercial filmmakers began naively by proposing an uncomplicated deal: a story in exchange for the price of a ticket. Almost immediately, however, they were surprised by their viewers' fascination with individual players. For a brief moment, the industry resisted this unintended consequence of the movies, this admiration for actors which seemed an overestimation of value, a fetishism. Preserving the players' anonymity, after all, had minimized their power and kept them cheap. Inevitably, however, Hollywood came to see this fetishism as a means of making money, and the star system deliberately set out to encourage it. In fact, although continuity cinema's insistence on story often reduced the immediate attraction of its components ("while an image itself could be beautiful, it wasn't to be so beautiful as to draw attention to itself"), inadvertently the movies glamorized everything: faces, clothes, furniture, trains, landscapes. A dining car's white, starched linen (*North by Northwest*), a woman's voice (Margaret Sullavan's in *Three Comrades*), an unusual cigarette lighter (*The Maltese Falcon*)—even the most ordinary objects could become, as Sam Spade puts it in a rare literary allusion, "the stuff that dreams are made of."

Fetishism attends to details that become, in Michel Leiris's description of "crisis moments," "futile and stripped of symbolic value, and if one wishes, *gratuitous*." By interrupting the "rational" trade relations that govern the cinema—objects must "contribute" to the plot—fetishism amounts to a "counternarrative." Hence the tension: the arresting appeal of cinematic details versus the forward momentum of storytelling. *The Maltese Falcon* offers the ideal solution: the fetish object (the Falcon itself) as a plot's *primum mobile*, around which everything turns.

Behind the nightstand, a less obvious detail: a window curtain, fluttering gently in the breeze. This movement seems incongruous. In *The Maltese Falcon*'s four increasingly interchangeable rooms—Spade's apartment, Brigid's apartment, Gutman's hotel room, and Spade's office—where almost all the movie's action occurs, an airless, claustrophobic quality dominates. Although set in downtown San Francisco, the movie and its locales seem sealed off from the world—into these rooms, no street sounds intrude. Outside them, on the sidewalks, only the narratively portentous Wilmer appears, as all traffic, all pedestrians, all shoppers and strollers seem to have vanished. In such missing details of everyday life, particularly in their randomness, Bazin located the cinema's revelatory power. "If I were deprived of the pleasure of seeing *Boudu* again for the rest of my days," Bazin wrote, celebrating the miracle of a summer road's white dust, accidentally raised by an incidental kick, "I would never forget that grass, that dust, and their relationship to the liberty of a tramp."

And yet, as Noël Burch has shown, Hollywood consolidated around a continuity style that eliminated, or carefully controlled, the appearance of such unintended events, redefined as threatening. Following Frederick Taylor and Henry Ford, whose systems eliminated the "styles" of individual workers (and any possibility that such individuality might intrude into the production process), Hollywood developed the continuity script as a means of controlling mavericks like Erich von Stroheim. The early 1930s move onto sound stages went even further in keeping the accidental out of the frame and away from the microphone, regulating the proliferation of meaning in what Burch calls the inherently "refractory" nature of what goes on in front of the camera.

Significantly, all three of Warner Brothers' versions of *The Maltese Falcon* omit the book's famous Flitcraft story, Spade's earlier case of a man gone missing. Having narrowly escaped a near-fatal accident, terrifying in its randomness (a falling beam from a construction site had grazed his cheek before crashing into the sidewalk next to him), Flitcraft had walked away from everything because he had recognized chance's awful role. The movie's suppression of this story matches Hollywood's suppression of the chance events that Bazin treasured—the leaves blowing in the background of Lumière's films, the details that slipped out from under the net of meaning. In *The Maltese Falcon*, the wind does blow, if not leaves, at least the curtains, precisely the kind of detail to which Bazin had pointed as guaranteeing the cinema's realism. This wind, however, achieved on a carefully controlled studio set, is not real; indeed, it is not even random, since a later shot will motivate it: As Spade leans over to kiss Brigid, the fluttering curtains, in a kind of meaningful commentary, will part to reveal Wilmer watching from the street outside.

In a kind of allusion to this scene, Godard would advertise his differences with it, panning his camera away from *Vivre sa Vie*'s

record store scene, with its fictional characters, to the nonfictional randomness of the Parisian boulevards—an homage to the Bazinian aesthetic that had nurtured him.[4] (See *Meet Me in St. Louis*: Curtains.)

 D oorbell

Returning home after visiting the Archer murder scene, Spade takes off his coat and sits on the side of his bed, pouring a drink. A doorbell buzzes insistently from offscreen. Spade looks to his left, apparently toward the sound.

The immediate cut to the door appears to be a point-of-view shot, motivated by Spade's glance. Almost immediately, however, Spade walks into the shot, changing its status.

In an essay on Carl Dreyer, Noël Burch once proposed the possibility of "three distinct camera attitudes":

> [*T*]*he camera can . . . "look through the eyes" of one or the other of the characters; it can make itself "voyeur," in other words behave in such a discreet "distant" way toward what is being filmed as to make us "forget" its presence; the camera can be "author," in other words its "gaze" can be so oriented as to stress the fact that there is someone behind the camera who knows what is going to happen and who, at times, chooses to anticipate the actors' behavior, even to the point of guiding our attention away from the characters.*

Although *The Maltese Falcon*'s camera operates primarily as a "voyeur," it occasionally becomes an "author," disconnecting from the characters to focus on objects whose importance seems both mysterious and symbolic. For example, after receiving a telephone call from Brigid, Spade burns the piece of paper on which Effie has written the address; as he places the page in an ashtray, the camera leaves him, zooming in on his desktop, where we see a folded newspaper, his exotic lighter, and a matchbox with a perfectly legible brand name: "DEPENDABLE."

The camera's "attitude," in other words has shifted in midshot, moving from voyeur to author. While DEPEND-ABLE might hint at Spade's real character (or Effie's), the zoom seems intended less symbolically than rhetorically: it functions as a punctuation mark, the scene's period.

The problems posed by Spade's doorbell, however, seem more profound. By making the doorway shot do double duty as both the object of Spade's gaze *and* a voyeuristic observation of him responding to the buzzer, Huston has rendered the shot unstable, forcing the viewer to revise his first sense of it. Were *The Maltese Falcon* to practice systematically this "principle of uncertainty," it would begin to resemble Dreyer's *Vampyr* or Antonioni's *Blow-up*, whose heroes often appear unpredictably in shots initially attributed to them. Even in *The Maltese Falcon*, however, this isolated redefinition of camera attitude disrupts what Daniel Dayan called "the tutor-code of classical cinema." With the movies, the "succession of images" has always threatened to provoke the question, "Who is showing me these things?" To forestall this challenge, with its potential to disrupt the filmmaking process's invisibility, Hollywood developed the "system of suture," the shot/reverse-shot patterns that assign a movie's views *to the characters themselves*. "Narrative cinema," Dayan concludes, "presents itself as a 'subjective' cinema":

> These films propose images which are subtly designated and
> intuitively perceived as corresponding to the point of view of
> one character or another. The point of view varies. There are
> moments when the image does not represent anyone's point of
> view; but in the classical narrative cinema, these are relatively
> exceptional. Soon enough, the image is reasserted as

*somebody's point of view. In this cinema, the image is only
"objective" or "impersonal" during the interval between its
acting as the actors' glances.*

A "sutured" film like *Casablanca* relies on shot/reverse-shot for over
half of its transitions. In *The Maltese Falcon*, another tightly
organized movie, the shot of Spade's door amounts to a place
where the moviemaking process, with its endless possibilities,
leaks through.[5]

Drugstore

After Archer's murder, Spade
uses an unidentified location's
pay phone to call "Miss
Wonderly" at her hotel, only to
learn that she has checked out
with no forwarding address.
This location will become
retroactively named when Iva
Archer confesses that she had

sent the police to Spade's apartment by telephoning them from
"the drug store across from your place." Armed with this bit of
information, the alert viewer will be able to recognize a drugstore
and a white-coated, barely visible "pharmacist" in the blurred,
shallow-focus, two-second shot that follows Spade from phone
booth to street door.

But why does Spade stop at the drugstore to call Brigid
when his own apartment is just across the street? Because
Hammett's novel says he does? Because the wall phone seems
more visually urgent than a table-top one? Or this: the popular
narrative, as Barthes saw, "is controlled by the principle of non-
contradiction. . . . it is always on the look-out and always, just in
case, preparing its defense against the enemy that may force it to

acknowledge the scandal of some illogicality, some disturbance of 'common sense.'" *The Maltese Falcon* defends itself with *speed*, rushing Spade from murder scene to telephone to apartment, using the rapid dissolves that provide the movie with almost all of its transitions and keep the viewer from asking too many questions. Ultimately, Spade's call and Iva's admission *match*; by confirming each other, they forestall scrutiny of the movie's logic. Spade's unnecessary stop also serves to fill in spaces mentioned elsewhere in the film. "The *readerly* abhors a vacuum," Barthes insisted, using his own term for commercial storytelling; its goal is always "an illusion of continuity." A drugstore immediately "across from" Spade's apartment is too close to leave unseen.[6]

(with Jessica Hanan)

With a nearly famous last name (Thomas Edison, after all, had been one of the movies' inventors), *The Maltese Falcon*'s head cameraman, Arthur Edeson, had a long and distinguished career. In 1919, he had helped found the American Society of Cinematographers, and he quickly developed a reputation as Douglas Fairbanks's preferred director of photography. "*The Maltese Falcon* called for strong, modernistic, eye-arresting camerawork," Edeson recalled, and his compositions, with their deep-focus low angles, resemble those of the more celebrated Gregg Toland, who shot *Citizen Kane* the same year. Edeson would go on to film both *Casablanca* and *The Mask of Dimitrios*, but the complete absence of any mention of him in two standard reference books on John Huston (Lesley Brill's *John Huston's Filmmaking* and Robert Emmet Long's collection *John Huston Interviews*) confirms just how successful *la politique des auteurs* has been in gathering attention to directors. Both *Citizen Kane* and *The Maltese Falcon* were directorial debuts, whose "authors" relied heavily on their cinematographers. Launched by *Cahiers du Cinéma*, *auteurism*, however, would remain a practice of *writing*, forever deploying its

founding analogy of filmmakers to poets and novelists. Although *Cahiers* would champion mise-en-scène against "the tradition of quality's" literary

adaptations and scriptwriters, it would also find mise-en-scene's details difficult to discuss. In "The Third Meaning," Barthes insisted that his equivalent term, "the filmic," "is outside (articulated)

language"; it "disturbs, sterilizes . . . meta-language (criticism)." Indeed, "the filmic is what, in the film, cannot be described. . . . The filmic begins only where language and articulated meta-language cease." (See *The Maltese Falcon*: Threes.) A critical description of Edeson's work would begin, therefore, with a series of juxtapositions, pairing his shots with identical moments from *Dangerous Female* and *Satan Met a Lady*, the two failed versions of *The Maltese Falcon*. The filmic, so difficult to specify in writing, appears in relief against a background of its own inadequate doubles.[7]

(*with Franklin Cason*)

Errors

1. Spade walks into his office with bare fingers, enters an inner room to meet Brigid, and returns to Effie's desk wearing a ring on his right hand and a wedding band on his left.

2. At their first meeting, Cairo tells Spade to contact him "at the Hotel Belvedere, room 635." The next day, however, at the hotel's front desk, Cairo requests, and is given, the key to room 603.

3. After knocking out Cairo, Spade searches his pockets, placing his wallet, cigarette case, and three passports on an adjacent table. But when Spade's hands reach for the wallet, the shot of the table top

shows Cairo's keys, 12 coins (at least 4 with center holes), and a mysterious heart-shaped pill box, none of which the movie has shown Spade removing.

4. The opening shots of Spade's desk show a statue of a dog, screen left, and an eagle trophy, with its head turned screen left. A few shots later, the dog has disappeared, and the statue's head now faces in the opposite direction.

These errors, visible only to train-spotters, nevertheless crack open *The Maltese Falcon*'s hermetic space, revealing an actual world where actors have lives (Bogart was married at the time), continuity girls have short memories (was it 635 or 603?), composition takes precedence over consistency (the elegant spray of coins, with their center holes, a signifier of "foreign-ness"; the disturbing pill box: drugs?), and scenes take more than a day to shoot (and objects disappear or change places overnight). When television's obsessive-compulsive detective Adrian Monk finds himself on a working set, he brings a second take to a halt by pointing out every failure of matching. "It doesn't have to be perfect," the exasperated director tells him. It doesn't, of course, but errors' inconspicuousness depends on a narrative's speed and its actors' fascination.

(with Jennifer Beckett, Jessica Hanan, Mason Laird)

 **litcraft**

"A man named Flitcraft," Spade tells Brigid in the novel, "had left his real-estate office, in Tacoma, to go to luncheon one day and had never returned."

> He did not keep an engagement to play golf after four that afternoon, though he had taken the initiative in making the engagement less than half an hour before he went out to luncheon. His wife and children never saw him again. His wife and he were supposed to be on the best of terms. He had two children, boys, one five and the other three. He owned his house in a Tacoma suburb, a new Packard, and the rest of the appurtenances of successful American living.
>
> Flitcraft had inherited seventy thousand dollars from his father, and, with his success in real estate, was worth something in the neighborhood of two hundred thousand dollars at the time he vanished. His affairs were in order, though there were enough loose ends to indicate that he had not been setting them in order preparatory to vanishing. A deal that would have brought him an attractive profit, for instance, was to have been concluded the day after the one on which he disappeared. There was nothing to suggest that he had more than fifty or sixty dollars in his immediate possession at the time of his going. His habits for months past could be accounted for too thoroughly to justify any suspicion of secret vices, or even of another woman in his life, though either was barely possible.
>
> "He went like that," Spade said, "like a fist when you open your hand."

Spade discovered Flitcraft in Spokane, where, under the name of Pierce, he had acquired a new wife, a baby son, and an automobile business. Spade also got an explanation: while walking to lunch on the day of his disappearance, Flitcraft had narrowly escaped being killed by a beam falling from a construction site. It had struck the sidewalk next to him. With his bland faith in the order of the world suddenly exposed as naive ("He felt like somebody had taken the lid off life and let him look at the works"), Flitcraft had tried to adapt by acting as randomly as the beam that had nearly crushed him. "Life could be ended for him at random by a falling beam: he would change his life at random by simply going away." He had drifted for a while from San Francisco back to the Northwest, until settling down to the same kind of life he had abandoned. "He adjusted himself to beams falling," Spade summarized, "and then no more of them fell, and he adjusted himself to them not falling."

This famous story, omitted from all three film versions of *The Maltese Falcon*, represents Hammett's propensity for anecdotes:

> A man whom I was shadowing went out into the country for a walk one Sunday afternoon and lost his bearings completely. I had to direct him back to the city.

> I knew an operative who while looking for pickpockets at the Havre de Grace racetrack had his wallet stolen.

> I once was falsely accused of perjury and had to perjure myself to escape arrest.

> I know a deputy sheriff in Montana who, approaching the cabin of a homesteader for whose arrest he had a warrant, was confronted by the homesteader with a rifle in his hands. The deputy sheriff drew his revolver and tried to shoot over the homesteader's head to frighten him. The range was long and a strong wind was blowing. The bullet knocked the rifle from the homesteader's hands. As time went by the deputy

sheriff came to accept as the truth the reputation for expertness that this incident gave him, and he not only let his friends enter him in a shooting contest, but wagered everything he owned upon his skill. When the contest was held he missed the target completely with all six shots.

The chief of police of a southern city once gave me a description of a man, complete even to a mole on his neck, but neglected to mention that he had only one arm.

I know a man who once stole a Ferris wheel.

Even at novel length, however, Hammett remains cryptic. All of *The Maltese Falcon*'s principal characters lack pasts: the narrative supplies no information about Spade's background; and Gutman, Cairo, Brigid, and Wilmer possess histories only in relation to their pursuit of the Falcon. Even their names seem more allegorical than novelistic: Gutman ("the Fatman"), Miss Wonderly (with her obvious fabrications provoking "wondering" about her identity), Miss LeBlanc (the self as blank slate, forever renewable), Archer (killed with the weapon rendering him obsolete), Brigid O'Shaughnessy (her first name rhyming with "frigid" and using the last name of the San Francisco official who conceived the Golden Gate Bridge), Joel Cairo (the city at the juncture of three continents), Spade (who "digs" for information, calls things by their right names, and avoids sexual temptation).

The Maltese Falcon itself could be rewritten as a series of anecdotes:

A woman asked me to tail a man who had supposedly run off with her sister. Because the woman was good-looking, my partner took the job; he was shot that night. When I called the woman at her hotel room, she had checked out without leaving any forwarding address.

A foreigner offered me $5,000 to "recover" a stolen statue of a bird. After I had agreed, he drew a gun and started to search my office. I knocked him out and frisked him, discovering that he was carrying passports from three different countries.

I once knew an enormously fat man who told me about a sixteenth-century jewel-encrusted statue of a falcon. He wanted me to help him find it. I found it for him, but when he examined it, the statue proved a fake.

Hammett's anecdotes, including the Flitcraft story, often turn on chance, the great enemy of classic detective fiction, whose commitment to rational deduction requires a chain of intentions waiting to be recovered. (Borges's "Death and the Compass" exposes this convention by describing a detective's fatal refusal to accept a murder's randomness.) Traditional detective stories, with their emphasis on ratiocination and long-winded explanations, inevitably proved troubling for the cinema. More visually appealing was the hard-boiled school, whose detectives got results from physical action and sheer luck. In *The Maltese Falcon*, Sam Spade rarely "figures things out": he provokes the other characters into revelations.

Why are some anecdotes better told than filmed? In *Une Femme est Une Femme*, Godard has Alfred (Jean-Paul Belmondo) tell a story about chance:

> *A girl was in love with two fellows at the same time. She sent*
> *them both express letters, arranging to meet one of them at*
> *the Gare du Nord, and the other two hours later at the Port*

d'Italie. She put the letters in the post, and right after she'd posted them . . . Pow, she realizes she's got the envelopes wrong. That the letter starting "My darling Paul" is in Pierre's envelope and vice versa. Well, she's quite frantic. She rushes over to the first bloke, the letter still hasn't arrived. The girl says to the fellow, "Listen, darling, you're going to receive an express letter; don't believe what it says." He asks for an explanation, and she's forced to tell him the whole story. In the end, he kicks her out for good. So the girl says to herself, "I've lost one of them, but I can still keep the other one." So she goes right across Paris and rushes over to the second fellow. The letter was already there. The second fellow doesn't seem at all angry, quite the contrary. So the girl says to him, "You're a kind-hearted guy, you've forgiven me." He looks very surprised, but doesn't say anything. So she tells the whole story over again, because she thinks he's just keeping quiet to humiliate her before he really forgives her. Suddenly, the second fellow shows her the letter and kicks her out. Only then the girl discovers that she'd put them in the right envelopes after all.

When Godard turned this anecdote into a short film ("Montparnasse-Levallois," part of *Paris vu par . . .*), the result was surprisingly uninteresting, like an elegant equation banalized by the conversion of its X's and Y's into specific commodities. Why are some stories better told than dramatized? If "Flitcraft" amounts to a mathematical proof—an abstract, inexorable demonstration of Hammett's world view—*The Maltese Falcon* resembles an algorithm, a practical step-by-step procedure for solving a problem crucial to Hammett's career: how to write a novel. "Flitcraft" cannot survive its realization; *The Maltese Falcon* thrives on it.[8]

(with Stuart Fensom, Ashley Hendricks, Nic Jelley, Naomi Zell)

G olden Gate Bridge

Huston's version of *The Maltese Falcon* immediately establishes its setting by superimposing "SAN FRANCISCO" over stock footage of the Bay and Golden Gate bridges. Popular narratives, as Barthes saw, are "marked by the excessive fear of failing to communicate  meaning"; hence, they rely on "a certain redundancy, a kind of semantic prattle." Studio Hollywood will always assume the viewer's ignorance of even unmistakable landmarks: The Eiffel Tower must come equipped with an explicit marker, "PARIS." And yet, commercial filmmaking also practices a certain laconic economy, dependent on the audience's knowledge of stereotypes. When she worked as an advisor to the film crew adapting her book *The Return of Martin Guerre*, historian Natalie Davis tried to ensure authenticity by cramming the mise-en-scène with medieval details. The director explained, however, that they were unnecessary since Hollywood worked on the "camel principle": if you want to suggest Egypt, you simply put a camel in the corner of a frame, and the audience does the rest. (See *Grand Hotel: Blue Danube.*)

If the Hollywood studios were striving to become a modern, fully rationalized industry, the great symbol of this techno-utopian modernism was the bridge, at once a literal feat of engineering and a suggestive rhetorical figure ("we need to bridge our differences"). Like Hart Crane's, every bridge represented a connection to the future, a means of crossing from one moment (the premodern) into another (the brave, new world). As early as 1910, the erector set had become the most popular Christmas gift for boys, and the myth of the engineer had seized the American mind. By the 1930s, eastern cities like New York and Boston had their own engineering triumphs. In San Francisco, however, the Golden Gate Bridge, suggested as early as 1872, remained only an idea until the city engineer initiated plans that were finally funded in 1928. The bridge opened in the spring of 1937, seven years after the first appearance of Hammett's novel, but only four years before Huston's film version. Thus, *The Maltese Falcon*'s opening shots may have actually required the apparently redundant SAN FRANCISCO, since viewers might have proved unable to identify something so new.

Hammett was living in San Francisco when the city engineer's proposal for the Golden Gate was widely debated. The engineer's name was M. M. O'Shaughnessy, and Hammett appears to have combined his last name with his project's goal for his femme fatale, Brigid ("bridge it") O'Shaughnessy. In fact, Brigid connects ("bridges") the heroines of 1930s melodrama, tormented and long-suffering, with the more independent women of film noir, self-interested and treacherous. Although the bridge served as modernism's most powerful symbol, the *collapse* of a bridge became the privileged image of this world view's limits: see *Alexander's Bridge* (1912), Willa Cather's novel that uses the collapse of the Quebec Bridge to suggest the affinity between ideologies of progress and the flight of Icarus. Brigid O'Shaughnessy—liar, thief, seducer, betrayer, murderer—is ultimately a bridge in ruins.[9]

(*with Rob Lehman, Renee Moilanen, Brandon Osmond*)

 onolulu

"Mother and Father are in Honolulu," Brigid tells Spade, explaining the urgency of finding her supposedly missing sister. "It would kill them; I've got to find her before they get back home." In Hammett's novel, "Mama and Papa are in Europe." As with *The Philadelphia Story*'s transfer of Junius from London to Buenos Aires, intervening events have forced the revision: the outbreak of World War II, otherwise unmentioned by the movie, excludes European vacations. (Ironically, by relocating Brigid's "parents" to Honolulu, *The Maltese Falcon*, opening just two months before Pearl Harbor, inadvertently puts them in a new harm's way.) The address change assumes that both audience and characters must inhabit the same immediate present, despite the novel's 1929 publication. Thus, the movie must be fine-tuned to avoid any "dated" references that would challenge verisimilitude. The result is an asymptotic process attempting to align the diegetic and actual worlds, as if two axes were coming together. But the decision to leave untouched most of Hammett's hard-boiled slang, surely as outmoded as the idea of a European vacation, makes *The Maltese Falcon*, even in 1941, seem less realistic than stylized, an artifact just slightly removed from a world that now prohibits going to Europe.[10] (See *The Philadelphia Story*: Buenos Aires.)

Horses

The paintings and statues of horses that decorate Spade's apartment and Gutman's hotel room suggest the movie's interest in morally ambiguous characterization: while the vaguely British hunt-club pictures evoke aristocratic codes ("The sport of kings!"), they also recall the sleaziness of American racetrack betting. Certainly, the film works to create suspense about Spade's true character, trading on Bogart's track record as a villain and on Sydney Greenstreet's unfamiliarity; he initially seems jovially Falstaffian, a role he had played on the English stage.

But the horses raise another, more general issue. Given a set for shooting, how do filmmakers choose to decorate it? (1) at random?—apparently the method behind the *Falcon*'s two earlier versions; (2) to suit the story and characters?—the tactic of the "well-made film"; (3) at the director's whim?—both Huston and Bogart liked horses and horse racing. The less the horses "match" *The Maltese Falcon*'s characters, the more inappropriate they would seem, and the more they would violate Hollywood's goal of an invisible style, subservient to plot. But the horses' *visibility*, by signaling Huston's presence, would become precisely the kind of *auteurist* marker famously denounced by Pauline Kael. Citing (and ridiculing) Andrew Sarris's propositions that the *auteur* theory celebrated "the distinguishable personality of the director," which appears in "the tension between a director's personality and his material," Kael summed up the opposition:

> *Their ideal* auteur *is the man who signs a long-term contract, directs any script that's handed to him, and expresses himself by shoving bits of style up the crevasses of the plots. If his "style" is in conflict with the story or subject matter, so much the better—more chance for tension.*

In *The Maltese Falcon*, the horses represent the limits of Huston's first-picture daring, the decorating choice of an *auteur avant la lettre* who wants to get to direct another movie.[11]

(with Ashley Bowen)

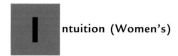ntuition (Women's)

> **Spade** [*hoping Effie will let Brigid stay at her place*]:
> *What does your woman's intuition tell you about her?*
>
> **Effie**: *She's all right. Oh, maybe it's her own fault for being in whatever the trouble is, but she's all right, if that's what you mean.*

Brigid, of course, will prove to be anything but "all right"; the movie's plot will reveal her as a liar, seducer, betrayer, thief, and murderer, thereby discrediting Effie's woman's intuition, a staple of popular fiction. Barthes's *S/Z* suggests just how unexpected this move is. Commercial narratives, Barthes proposed, continually refer to conventional wisdom, deployed as the guarantor of a story's verisimilitude. Balzac's *Sarrasine*, for example, casually describes one character in terms of unquestioned stereotypes ("dark as a Spaniard, dull as a banker") and its hero with the romantic clichés of artistic impetuosity. To the extent that such collective wisdom underwrites a story's realism, it cannot be challenged. How does *The Maltese Falcon* get away with doing so?

Two answers suggest themselves. First, whether as Hammett's novel or Huston's film, *The Maltese Falcon* is not "realistic" in Barthes's sense: with its exotic characters, restricted settings, and outlandish quest, it resembles other storytelling forms reliant on paradox—fable, allegory, anecdote. Thus, the narrative can refute the popular assumption about women's intuition because the story's appeal depends not on its proximity to a recognizable everyday world, but on its *remoteness* from it. Second, the detective story amounts to a special branch of fiction, one that encourages the practice of mistrust. Effie's intuition resembles Henri Bergson's "analysis," "the operation that reduces the object to elements already known, that is, to elements common both to it and other objects." Effie sees Brigid in received categories—the wronged woman, the surprise witness, the woman in trouble—stereotypes the *policier* deploys to *conceal* the truth. As opposed to an analysis that looks at things "from the outside," Bergson proposed his own definition of intuition: "the kind of *intellectual sympathy* by which one places oneself within an object in order to coincide with what is unique in it and consequently inexpressible." While this formulation would explain Effie's failure (she sees Brigid as typical rather than specific), it also suggests a difference between novel and film. On the page, Hammett's Brigid *is* a type (the femme fatale), just not the one Effie intuits. On the screen, however, *Brigid is Mary Astor*, a particular woman, whose voice, hair, complexion, carriage, eyes, and inflection simultaneously suggest multiple possibilities: matron, sophisticate, innocent, liar. Astor, like any other screen performer, is "unique . . . and consequently inexpressible," and as such, she can never quite be reduced to any one thing. Reading her as Brigid will require Bergson's intuition rather than Effie's.

With its haste to move from particular to category, Effie's intuition resembles the semiotician's, which "reduces the object . . . to elements common both to it and other objects." As a complement to this way of thinking about the cinema, Dudley Andrew has proposed reviving "the neglected tradition of phenomenology in film theory," which would amount to a renewal of Bergsonian intuition. "Grammars, lexicons, and structural studies can only remove us from the cinema," Andrew argues; "life itself tells us that experience is dearer and more trustworthy than schemes by which we seek to know and change it." A phenomenological approach to film studies would take up the task of "describing the peculiar way meaning is experienced in cinema" and "come to terms with a surplus value unaccounted for by recourse to a sign of signification": the particular way, for example, Brigid thanks Effie for agreeing to put her up for a few days—"Oh, that's very kind of you."[12]

(with Rashna Wadia)

Journeys

This chart, with its blank spaces, suggests *The Maltese Falcon*'s mixture of precision and incompleteness. The prologue's scroll ("In 1539 the Knight Templars of Malta paid tribute to Charles V of Spain by sending him a golden falcon . . .") and Gutman's history lesson track the peregrinations of both statue and pursuers. But about biographical details not crucial to its immediate narrative, the film remains discreet. When was Gutman born? Where was Brigid before Istanbul? What is Cairo's real nationality? How did Gutman find Wilmer, whom Spade identifies as a New Yorker?

When Victorian fiction's full-disclosure character introductions gave way to modernism's elliptical impressionism, readers learned to accept a new condition: judgments must be made even in the absence of sufficient information. Ford Madox Ford described this situation:

> *Supposing that your name is John, and that you have a friend called James, and for private reasons of his own James takes you into his billiard room and tries to shoot you with a rifle.*
>
> *Now when that happens to you nothing in the outside world says to you, in so many words, "That Man is going to shoot me." What happens to you is roughly this. You are taken by a friend into a room. You perceive the greenish light thrown upwards from the billiard table. . . . Your friend talks. You answer. You are thinking of what he says; of what you are to answer. You perceive other objects; you perceive that some of the cues are not in the rack, and that the last game ended at 100 to 64. James says something else. You notice that his voice is rather high. You answer. You notice that you are saying to yourself, "I must keep my temper!" You also notice that the clock has stopped at 3:17.*

	The Falcon	Brigid	Gutman	Cairo	Wilmer
?	the East				
1539	Malta				
1713	Sicily				
1840	Paris				
?	London				
1923	found in Paris	Paris			
1940	Istanbul	Istanbul	Istanbul	Istanbul	New York
	?	Hong Kong	Hong Kong		
	?	San Francisco	San Francisco	San Francisco	
		Tahatchapi	prison	prison	prison

This is the world of *The Maltese Falcon*. "I've no earthly reason to think I can trust you," Spade tells Brigid, making the calculations required by this new, permanent uncertainty, "but a lot more money would have been one more item on your side of the scales."[13]

(*with Naomi Zell*)

K itchen

Twice in *The Maltese Falcon*, Spade's apartment "kitchen" changes status from its existence as merely an undefined door to an imaginary room. In the first instance, Spade's conversation with Brigid continues even as he slips through the door and offscreen. His emergence with a coffee pot (the narratively appropriate synecdoche) encourages the viewer to "fill in" the unseen area, supplying it with the appliances and utensils that name it "kitchen."

The second case proves more complex. Having extracted Gutman's agreement to make Wilmer "the fall guy," Spade sends

Brigid to "the kitchen" for coffee. As she goes through the door, the camera pans away to Gutman, who, eager to sow dissension, declares that the envelope containing 10 thousand-dollar bills is now missing one. Although Spade quickly forces him to admit to

palming it, Gutman's accusation, timed with Brigid's exit offscreen, suggests that events are happening *unseen by Spade*. In fact, they have been throughout the movie: the murders of Archer, Thursby, and Jacobi; the *La Paloma* fire; the search of Miss O'Shaughnessy's apartment; Brigid's treachery.

(with Nic Jelley)

K<small>LVW</small>

Among the neon lights visible from Spade's office window appears a radio station's call letters. The fact that KLVW has apparently never operated in California (it currently broadcasts from Texas) confirms that in the cinema, visually appeal-

ing details have no responsibility vis-à-vis the actual world. When art director Cedric Gibbons once complained about a Parisian love scene set beside a moonlit ocean, Thalberg implicitly relied on this rule: "We can't cater to a handful of people who know Paris. Audiences only see about ten percent of what's on the screen, anyway, and if they're watching your background instead of my actors, the scene will be useless. Whatever you put there, they'll believe that's how it is."

Warner Brothers may have been reluctant to promote an actual station: in the 1930s and 1940s, after all, radio would prove the movies' greatest rival. Detective shows were especially popular. On any given day in 1941, one could tune to ABC, NBC, or CBS and hear stories like *The Maltese Falcon*: *I Love a Mystery* (1939–1952), *The Adventures of Ellery Queen* (1939–1948), *The Adventures of Charlie Chan* (1932–1948), *The Detective Mysteries* (1929–1959), *The Adventures of the Thin Man* (1941–1950), *Inner Sanctum Mysteries* (1941–1952), and *Sherlock Holmes* (1930–1956). By 1946, *The Adventures of Sam Spade* (with Howard Duff in Bogart's role) would begin on ABC, verifying Marshall McLuhan's axiom that "the content of a new medium is always an old one."

In fact, the Hollywood studios regularly turned out radio versions of their own hits, often with original casts. Thus, Bogart, Astor, Greenstreet, and Lorre all appeared on a 20 September 1943 *Hollywood Playhouse* broadcast of *The Maltese Falcon*. These radio plays, abridged sketches of their sources, indicate which narrative events Hollywood considered essential. They also resemble early films like Edwin S. Porter's *Uncle Tom's Cabin* (1903) in that *they presume prior knowledge of the story being told*. In the radio broadcast, for example, Spade refers to Joel Cairo long before the audience is introduced to him. Noël Burch has described Hollywood's evolution:

> In the context of the system prevalent today (*and this has been true for more than sixty years now*), *a screen adaptation of even a very well-known work must "make as though" that*

work had no previous existence outside the film. The "digest"
that is made of it must hold water on its own: a typical
Hollywood adaptation, even of the Bible, will identify and
establish all its characters and situations as though
introducing them for the first time, *in accordance with*
the canons of the enclosed, autarchic world of the bourgeois
novel, where the story (and history, for that matter) exists
only in so far as it is invented by the text. A film like Uncle
Tom's Cabin, *which "tells" a novel several hundred pages*
long in some twenty tableaux and in ten minutes, was
predicated upon the knowledge of the audience, who were left
to fill in enormous narrative gaps for themselves.

Can we imagine a 10-minute film of *The Maltese Falcon*, one
dependent on prior knowledge of the story? This exercise might help
to identify a movie's hot spots, the places, in Truffaut's terms, where
it *pulses*. "The difficult work is the preparation," Howard Hawks once
confessed, "finding the story, deciding how to tell it, what to show
and what not to show." Making *The Big Sleep*, Hawks discovered
something else: "[Y]ou don't really have to have an explanation for
things. As long as you make good scenes you have a good picture—it
doesn't matter if it isn't much of a story." In some ways, *The Big Sleep*
functions like a radio version of Raymond Chandler's novel, predicated on its viewers' preexisting knowledg of a story presented only in
tableaux. As Hawks told his cameramen, "If you make two good
scenes for me, you can make two mediocre ones and one bad one.
All I'm interested in is the good one."[14]

(*with Brad Bishop and Kristin Davy*)

Kuleshov Effect

When Wilmer wakes up from Spade's punch to learn that he has
become the fall guy, Huston structures the moment as a point-of-
view series.

Medium close-up of Wilmer looking up; cut to MCU of Gutman looking down.

MCU of Wilmer looking screen left; cut to MCU of Cairo looking down.

MCU of Wilmer looking screen left, wide-eyed; cut to MCU of Spade looking screen right.

MCU of Wilmer looking screen right; cut to MCU of Brigid looking screen left.

Although the shots of Wilmer contain background drapes identifiable from earlier establishing shots, those of the other characters eliminate almost every trace of decor. The resulting images, abstract and free-floating (the one of Bogart looks like a studio portrait), resemble close-ups from Soviet films, where individual shots were conceptualized as "words," playing only a small part in a sequence's "sentence." "Everyone who has had in his hands a piece of film to be edited," Eisenstein wrote, "knows by experience how neutral it remains, even though part of a planned sequence, until it is joined with another piece, when it suddenly acquires and conveys a sharper and quite different meaning." The short-hand term for this attitude toward filmmaking is the "Kuleshov effect," named for that director's experiment demonstrating that different emotions would be attributed to an actor's *unchanged* features when his close-up was intercut with shots of different objects. This approach devalues acting, insisting that expressive value results, as Richard Dyer writes, from "signs *other than* performance signs." Note, however, that Huston does not fully trust this way of working; he has had Elisha Cook, Jr., modify his expression for each look. Doing so enables him to take advantage of studio Hollywood's great resource, its stable of wonderfully idiosyncratic performers, while avoiding the Soviet cinema's persistent defect, its reduction of human interaction to the calculus of juxtapositions.[15]

(*with Renee Moilanen*)

 *a Paloma*

"Do you know who he is?" Effie asks Spade, referring to the man who has delivered the Falcon to them before dying at their feet. "Yeah, he's Captain Jacobi, master of the *La Paloma*." Hammett's novel had explicitly rejected the redundancy:

> *"What about Miss O'Shaughnessy?" she [Effie] demanded.*
> *"I missed her too," he [Spade] replied, "but she had been there."*
> *"On the* La Paloma*?"*
> *"The La* is a lousy combination*," he said.*
> *"Stop it. Be nice, Sam. Tell me."*

Hence the novel's consistency:

> *"Who—do you know who he is?"*
> *He grinned wolfishly. "Uh-uh," he said, "but I'd guess he was Captain Jacobi, master of* La Paloma.*"*

With his grammatical meticulousness, Spade anticipates Godard's Michel Poiccard, *Breathless*'s petty hoodlum, who will continually correct his American girlfriend's grammar. Since this incongruity makes for nonstereotypical characterization, why does Huston's movie drop it? Perhaps because when transferred to film, Spade's fastidiousness would signal less intellectual superiority than "unmasculine" fussiness (the stock figure: the emasculated grammarian). *"The novelistic real is not operable,"* Barthes declared in *S/Z*: "suffice it to imagine the disorder the most orderly narrative would create were its descriptions taken at face value, converted into operative programs and simply *executed*." To an American audience, the movie's "master of the *La Paloma*," however incorrect, *sounds* better than "master of *La Paloma*," the equivalent of Spade's initiating a phone call with "it's I." Barthes warned about "the inevitable destruction of novels when they are transferred from writing to film, from a system of meaning to an order of the operable." The *La Paloma* example confirms that with even the most "realistic" novelists (Hemingway, Hammett), the dialogue is often more stylized than the movies can bear.[16]

altese Cross

The Maltese Falcon inadvertently deploys the iconography of Nazism, almost certainly familiar to an audience in 1941, when Hitler's European conquests had reached their peak. The eagle statue on Spade's desk, its head turned to the left, had been a widely circulated image of Germany's ruling party, and the globe on Spade's office cabinet refers obliquely to the world events dominating newsreels. In Bogart's next major success, *Casablanca*, maps of Africa will give way to a spinning globe that stops on Europe, and the

Germans' uniforms will display bird figures pinned to officers' caps and lapels. Below the bird insignia will hang the swastika, a version of the Maltese cross, the device perfected by German inventor Oskar Messter, enabling film projectors to create the illusion of continuous motion. Hence, yet another of the movie's *mise-en-abymes*: the Maltese cross system deployed to project *The Maltese Falcon*'s narrative of betrayals, lies, double crosses.[17]

(*with Franklin Cason and Eric Garcia*)

Mustache

Because *The Maltese Falcon*'s suspense depends on keeping Spade's ultimate decision about Brigid unpredictable, the story must establish Archer as unsavory and expendable. Seymour Chatman has shown that verbal narratives' *assertions* of descriptive details can easily include evaluative words dictating the reader's sense of a character. In Hammett's opening scene, for example, Archer appears "as many years past forty as Spade was past thirty. . . . His voice was heavy, coarse." Confronted with Miss Wonderly, he becomes a stock figure, the middle-aged lecher: "His little brown eyes ran their bold appraising gaze from her lowered face to her feet and up to her face again. Then he looked at Spade and made a silent whistling mouth of appreciation." This exact gesture recurs in Huston's film, where its details are merely *presented*, unaccompanied by instructions about their significance. The cinematic Archer may be coarse, but viewers will have to make that inference for themselves. Thus the movie, deprived of literature's resources, will rely on visual codes, whose meaning, while never as fixed as an explicit adjective like "coarse," can *pressure* the viewer toward an intended meaning. Huston's positioning of Archer suggests his type: sitting on the edge

of Spade's desk, he leans forward to leer at Miss Wonderly. The most important code defining "Archer" is, however, Jerome Cowan, the character actor who plays him. Only two years older than Bogart, Cowan appeared in 132 movies, typically in comic parts. By *The Maltese Falcon*, he had already been in 39 films, never as a star. Thus, the audience would not be surprised by his sudden disappearance from the movie. He is also the only character with a mustache. At some point in the late 1930s, somewhere between *The Thin Man* (1934) and *The Maltese Falcon* (1941), the pencil mustache shifts from being the signifier of urban sophistication (William Powell) to that of a lounge lizard's lechery (Jerome Cowan). Thus, precisely because the cinema *lacks* literature's assertive power, its history amounts to a record of cultural taste, the vagaries of style, the ceaseless dissolve of fashion.[18]

(with Nic Jelley)

ewspapers

Like so many Warner Brothers movies, often advertised as "torn from the headlines," *The Maltese Falcon* uses newspapers to advance its plot:

1. The close-up of the *San Francisco Post-Dispatch* front page, with its headline "THURSBY, ARCHER MURDERS LINKED!" provides the transition between the Dundy-Polhaus interrogation of Spade and his arrival at his office the next day.

2. The rolled-up newspaper Spade carries as he enters his office appears again in the close-up of his desk, next to Brigid's burning address.

3. Brigid tells Spade that Thursby "never went to sleep without covering the floor around his bed with crumpled newspapers, so that nobody could come silently into his room." "Well," Spade replies, "you picked a nice sort of playmate."

4. "Is there, Mr. Spade," Cairo asks, "as the newspapers imply, a certain relationship between that, uh, unfortunate happening [Archer's murder] and, uh, the death a little later of the man Thursby?"

5. In the Hotel Belvedere's lobby, Wilmer sits reading the sports section of a newspaper.

6. Describing his long search for the Falcon, Gutman tells Spade, "On the train, I opened a

paper, *The Times*, and read that Charilaos's establishment had been burglarized and him murdered."

7. In the newspaper Spade finds in Gutman's hotel room, "The

Shipping News" announces *La Paloma*'s arrival that day.

8. Jacobi delivers the Falcon wrapped in Hong Kong newspapers, confirming the stories of both Brigid and Gutman as to the bird's previous whereabouts.

In the cinema, what's the difference between a real and a fictional object? Indeed, as Dai Vaughan asks, what constitutes "a fictional object"?

> *Imagine two stills from a feature film—a Western, let us say. The first, showing a moment of high drama as the baddies descend upon the stagecoach, bears the caption: "Is this a fictitious event?" The second, which shows a greasy saddle hanging from a peg in a stable: "Is this a fictitious object?"*

At first glance, we may distinguish between the *San Francisco Post-Dispatch*, invented for *The Maltese Falcon*, and the apparently real newspaper perused by Wilmer in the Hotel Belvedere's lobby. This latter object contains a story about the San Francisco Seals, the Pacific Coast League team for which all three DiMaggio brothers had played. The page's lower right even includes a headline with the DiMaggio name, although by 1941, the brothers were all in the major leagues. (Note the bad match involving the paper: When Spade spots Wilmer, the first shot of the gunsel shows him reading the

other half of an illustrated page that a reverse-shot will complete—
a catcher tagging someone at home plate. But when Wilmer
lowers his paper after Spade's approach, he seems to have been
studying a page entirely without pictures. Racetrack results?)

Would replacing this paper with a fictional one change
anything about the scene?

Walter Benjamin once observed:

> *A clock that is working will always be a disturbance on the*
> *stage. There it cannot be permitted its function of measuring*
> *time. Even in a naturalistic play, astronomical time would*
> *clash with theatrical time. Under these circumstances it is*
> *highly revealing that the film can, whenever appropriate, use*
> *time as measured by a clock. From this more than from many*
> *touches it may be clearly recognized that under certain*
> *circumstances each and every prop in a film may assume*
> *important functions.*

In the theater, where both events onstage and their audience
seem to occupy the same "present," a functioning clock that fails to
coincide with actual time may break the spell. The narrative cinema,
on the other hand, resembles the novel: while devoid of tenses, it
appears at some remove, as if in a "past" initiated by "once upon a
time." (Historically associated with live television, video loses this
distance, becoming closer to theater.) Thus, *The Maltese Falcon* can
accommodate an actual newspaper, even one whose "time" will

become increasingly out of sync with its viewers' as the movie ages. The movies, in other words, even when new, are always *history*.

And yet, does a real newspaper, brought to the viewer's attention, interfere with the boundaries that reassuringly separate the film's events from the actual world? What happens if the audience tries to *read* the paper, as it might do with a different kind of movie, one devoted precisely to testing the boundaries between fiction and documentary? "I confess," Eric Rohmer once wrote after seeing Rossellini's *Voyage in Italy*:

> that as I watched the film my thoughts went off in directions
> far from those of the plot itself, like someone who goes into
> the cinema to kill time between appointments and, with his
> mind more on his own concerns than those of the film, is
> surprised to discover himself trying to read the time on a
> watch that one of the actors on the screen is wearing.[19]

(*with Jessica Hanan and Jennifer Simmons*)

 1001

Brigid's apartment number evokes *The Thousand and One Nights* and their heroine, Scheherazade, who invents stories to stay alive. Like *The Maltese Falcon*, *The Arabian Nights* begin with a betrayal, the

cuckolding of King Shahryar by his servants. Determined to prevent further infidelities, the king settles on a plan:

> [I]t became [his] custom to take every night the daughter of a
> merchant or a commoner, spend the night with her, then have
> her put to death the next morning. He continued to do this

*until all the girls perished, their mothers mourned, and there
arose a clamor among the fathers and mothers.*

To put an end to this slaughter, Scheherazade insists that
she herself be given to the king. After the wedding night love-
making, she begins a story about a traveling merchant, who finds
himself sitting under a walnut tree eating bread and dates.
Suddenly, an enormous demon appears before him, vowing
revenge for his son's death, caused by a date pit the merchant
has innocently tossed aside. The merchant pleads for mercy; the
demon is unyielding; he raises his sword to strike. . . . And
Scheherazade halts the story, promising the king to continue it
another night. Eager to learn the merchant's fate, he agrees. The
tale resumes: granted a year to see his family a final time, the
merchant eventually returns to the scene, keeping his vow to the
demon and accepting his fate. But under the same walnut tree,
he now finds only an old man leading a deer by a leash. . . . And
the second night ends. Withholding conclusions, nesting stories
within stories, always halting at the most decisive moments,
Scheherazade survives for 1001 nights until the king, presumably
exhausted by this feat of narrative virtuosity, spares her life.

Like Scheherazade's tales, Brigid's lies to Spade are serial
and linked:

1. I'm here in San Francisco looking for my sister
who's run off with a man named Floyd Thursby.

2. That story wasn't true, but I need your help. I met
Thursby in the Orient, but he betrayed me and shot
Archer. His enemies are after me.

3. I know Joel Cairo, but I don't know what he's
after.

4. Well, actually he and the Fatman are after a statue
of a falcon, but I don't know why it's so important.

They offered me money to get it, so Thursby and I did, but I only saw it once.

5. Thursby was betraying me; I wanted him shadowed to find out why.

6. Thursby killed Archer, but I never planned on that happening.

7. I killed Archer, but I didn't mean to.

8. I'm in love with you.

"You *are* a liar," Spade tells her, almost admiringly. "I am," Brigid admits. "I've always been a liar."

At another level, *The Maltese Falcon* itself operates as a series of connecting stories that postpone, stall, digress. The tale of a woman looking for her sister turns into the one about a murdered detective, which becomes the story about the shooting of a man the original woman wanted followed, which gets dropped while Spade tries to figure out the identity of a perfumed Levantine, until he gets tailed by a gun-carrying tough, who works for a fat man who wants to find a jewel-encrusted statue of a bird, who drugs the hero, who miraculously ends up with the statue, which he hides. The problem for a popular narrative, Barthes observed, "is to *maintain* the enigma. . . . it must set up *delays* (obstacles, stoppages, deviations)." *The Maltese Falcon* practices all of the tactics Barthes identified:

> "the *snare* (a kind of deliberate evasion of the truth)"
> ***Brigid***: *Mr. Spade, you don't think I had anything to do with the death of Mr. Archer?*
> ***Spade***: *Did you?*
> ***Brigid***: *No.*
> ***Spade***: *That's good.*

"the *equivocation* (a mixture of truth and snare)"
Spade: *I've got to have some sort of line on your Floyd Thursby.*
Brigid: *I met him in the Orient. We came here from Hong Kong last week. He promised to help me. He took advantage of my dependence on him to betray me.*

"the *partial answer*"
Spade: *Say, what's this bird, this falcon, that everybody's all steamed up about? . . .*
Brigid: *It's a black figure, as you know, smooth and shiny, of a bird, a hawk or falcon, about that high. . . .*
Spade: *What makes it so important?*
Brigid: *I don't know. They wouldn't tell me.*

"the *suspended answer*"
Brigid: *Suppose I wouldn't tell you anything about it at all? What would you do, something wild and unpredictable?*

"*jamming* (acknowledgment of insolubility)"
Spade [to the police]: *I've never seen Thursby dead or alive.*

For both Scheherazade and *The Maltese Falcon*, storytelling becomes "a matter of survival," a means of holding off a conclusion Barthes defined as "both liberating and catastrophic . . . bring[ing] about the utter end of the discourse." The solution of Archer's death will kill the story; it must, therefore, be withheld as long as possible. The movie's way of doing so resembles Scheherazade's: each story will involve an encounter with a stranger (Cairo, Wilmer, Gutman) who will in turn have his own tale to tell. Geoffrey O'Brien once described *The Thousand and One Nights*' stories in words that apply exactly to *The Maltese Falcon*'s:

They are about the world as a mine field of possibilities, the joys and catastrophes of chance, the utter unpredictability of what finally is seen as inevitable. Above all they are about terror: the terror of opening a door, the terror of falling under the spell of a pair of eyes glimpsed momentarily, the terror of extraordinary good fortune. They do not, in fairy-tale fashion, guarantee a happy ending. Sometimes the lovers are united, sometimes they perish horribly. . . . It is not good pitted against evil, but the ordinary invaded by the unexpected.

As an enterprise, of course, studio Hollywood found itself in Scheherazade's place, condemned to the ceaseless invention of stories that would keep the audiences returning week after week to the theater chains, themselves as cruelly insatiable as King Shahryar. "Looking back on Hollywood," Joan Fontaine once confessed, "I realize that the one outstanding quality it possesses is *fear*. Fear stalks the sound stages, the publicity departments, the executive offices." The fear is that when a character like Sam Spade opens a door numbered 1001, nothing will happen. The fear is that there will be no more stories.[20]

Outside

The Maltese Falcon contains only seven brief moments that take place outside the movie's claustrophobic offices, apartments, and hotel rooms: (1) the opening views of San Francisco Bay, (2) Archer's murder at Bush and Stockton, (3) Spade's arrival at that site, (4) Spade's being tailed by Wilmer before eventually losing him, (5) Wilmer collecting Spade for his meeting with Gutman, (6) the *La Paloma* fire, and (7) the bum steer that leads Spade to a vacant lot. In fact, with the exception of the establishing looks at the bay and one stock shot of a freighter, none of these scenes actually occurs anywhere but on a Warners soundstage: Even the images of *La Paloma* reveal a ceiling.

Since the coming of sound, Hollywood filmmaking had largely moved indoors, furthering its control of the filmmaking process at the expense of the possibilities afforded by accident and surprise. In 1941, while Huston was confining *The Maltese Falcon* to the Warners lot, John Ford allowed parts of *How Green Was My Valley* to occur on location. As Maureen O'Hara walked out of the church on her wedding day, a sudden gust of wind caught her veil, billowing it in the air as it trailed behind her. The actor playing her husband reached out to catch it.

Ford, the movie's scriptwriter, Philip Dunne, later said, had just experienced "one of the greatest strokes of luck a director ever had. . . . My God, what a shot!" "It was just a piece of luck for us," Dunne admitted. "I tried to reproduce it when I directed *10 North Frederick*, and then I realized it was a mistake to try. You can't reproduce those accidents."

With filmmaking, there is "instability at every point," and changing anything resembles "giving an extra shuffle to an already-shuffled pack of cards. You know it will change your luck, but you don't know whether for better or worse." The quotation comes from James Gleick's *Chaos: Making a New Science*, one of the first books to make *chaos theory* a term that now circulates in what Sherry Turkle has called the discourse of "superficial knowledge." Like the weather, chaos theory's first object of study, filmmaking's outcome resists prediction. Thus, despite classic Hollywood's determined efforts to rationalize production and its devotion to Taylorist efficiency, no one has ever been able to *guarantee* a hit or make a star. "Nobody knows anything," says Art De Vany, an industrial economist who has studied filmmaking. "None of them know what they are doing. There is no formula, no way of predicting how a film will do."

De Vany's work attends primarily to the cinema-as-investment. We should recall, however, that François Truffaut would launch *La Nouvelle Vague* by insisting that only the director, the person *on the set*, can really take advantage of filmmaking's contingencies. In arguing for this *disponibilité*, Truffaut would follow his mentor, André Bazin, who had consistently championed a cinema that regards accidents like O'Hara's blown veil as opportunities. John Huston's specialty, the shooting script, invented in 1920s Hollywood precisely to police directors like von Stroheim, had become what it was intended to be all along: a straitjacket.

But even Truffaut's corrective is slightly off. Talking about moviemaking only in terms of directors resembles analyzing battles only in terms of generals. Writing about the First Minnesota regiment's efforts on Gettysburg's second day, when its 82% casualty rate bought the Union army the 10 minutes it needed to save Little Round Top, Kent Gramm has argued that despite all the plans of Lee, Longstreet, Hancock, and Meade, "sometimes it simply comes down to a fight." That fight, Gramm goes on, is "subject to accident or intention or chance or absurdity," and "the essence of war is one step beyond the whole duty of generals, as it is one step beyond the knowledge of planners and analysts." Filmmaking, of course, isn't a battle (well, sometimes it is), but it often lies beyond the control of its generals, the producers, writers, and directors at the top of the command chain. Sometimes, it simply comes down to the wind blowing a veil.

By keeping *The Maltese Falcon* inside, Huston avoids the fight, but he also misses the wind. Even his "outside" scenes bespeak a first-time director's insistence on control. Spade walks down a busy street where even the marginal details excessively signify (a

theater marquee advertises *The Great Lie*, Astor's Oscar-winning
movie).

Nevertheless, we ignore everything but the detective and his
shadow, Wilmer, attending only to the narratively relevant
events.

Research project: How does the viewer know what is and
what is not relevant on his first viewing of a film? Does this ability
depend on prior training by the movies? Godard once asked
something like this question:

> *Suppose we were to go back to a shot from* Nanook, *for
> example, or from any other film, say Hitchcock's* Vertigo,
> *which is considered to be a fiction film with no relation to
> documentary. If it is projected in front of you all of a sudden,
> pow, at 10:00 in the morning, just as you're coming in, and
> you see Kim Novak walking down the street—O.K., a woman
> walking down the street—first it will take you two or three
> seconds to realize you're watching a film . . . or to recognize
> Kim Novak even if you're a movie fan. And if, during these
> first three or four seconds, you were yourself to be filmed with
> a small video camera looking at Kim Novak, it would be
> possible to detect the moment when fiction begins.*

Or suppose, like Spade, you were to find yourself in San
Francisco, and like Jimmy Stewart, you were to mistake a woman

leaving an apartment building for Kim Novak, until you realized you were looking at Effie Perine. That moment occurs in *Vertigo*, when an uncredited appearance by Lee Patrick, *The Maltese Falcon*'s Effie, grown matronly and *haute-bourgeoise*, refers us to another

place, another story, another time, *outside* Hitchcock's film.[21]

(*with Mason Laird and Rashna Wadia*)

assports

Discovered by Spade, Joel Cairo's three passports—Greek, French, and British—suggest the character's connections to nineteenth-century fiction, when the burgeoning European metropolises of London and Paris had begun to render every identity suspect (see Balzac and Dickens). Cairo, of course, is a crook, and his proliferating passports merely fill in that portrait. Determining his origins, however, would prove no more difficult than locating Peter Lorre's. Born Laszlo Löwenstein in Hungary, Lorre had quickly embarked on wanderings that reflected both the scrambled frontiers of between-the-wars Europe and an artistic cosmopolitanism born out of necessity. After Viennese training and a Zurich debut, Lorre had worked in the Swiss, Austrian, and German theaters. His appearance in Brecht's *Mann ist Mann* had brought him to the attention of Fritz Lang, who cast him in *M* (1931), his most famous role. Hitler's coming to power scattered that community, and *The Maltese Falcon*'s passports indicate Lorre's initial trail: first to Paris, where he appeared in *Du Haut en Bas* (1933); then to England, to find prominent roles in Hitchcock's *The Man Who Knew Too Much* (1934) and *Secret Agent* (1936); finally to America, where he worked steadily until his death in 1964.

The great chronicler of the European diaspora of the 1920s and 1930s was Eric Ambler, whose novels inevitably turn on the mysteries of passports, borders, identities. *A Coffin for Dimitrios* (1939) is the prototype, a *Citizen Kane*–style review of a man's past, clouded by lost trails and deliberate obfuscations. "Dimitrios Makropoulos," a police agent reads from a dossier. "Born 1889 in Larissa, Greece. Found abandoned. Parents unknown. Mother believed Rumanian. Registered as Greek subject and adopted by Greek family. Criminal record with Greek authorities. Details unobtainable." Warner Brothers owned the rights to Ambler's novel, and it would reach the screen in 1944 as *The Mask of Dimitrios*, with Lorre in a starring role. The director of that film, the Rumanian Jean Negulesco, had been originally scheduled for *The Maltese Falcon*. He had even begun work on a shooting script, but when he returned from making an army short, he discovered that Huston had gotten the job. A year later, Negulesco reported, Huston apologized:

> *I'm sorry, but no mention was ever made of you or that you had been assigned to do a job on it. I'll tell you what, kid. Tonight I'll make you a present. There is a book the studio*

owns, as good as the Falcon *if not better,* A Coffin for
Dimitrios, *by Eric Ambler. You ask for it. . . . Just do the
book page by page.*

Huston's judgment was right: Ambler's novel *is* better than
The Maltese Falcon. Its relative failure as a movie, however, is
instructive, confirming the proposition that the less a film involves
obvious visual excitement, the more its success will depend on
casting. *King Kong* represents one extreme, a film originating from
commissioned sketches of a giant gorilla for which a connecting
plot had to be invented. *Kong* negotiates its way from one visual
set piece to another, minimizing the importance of any of its
actors. Like *A Coffin for Dimitrios, The Maltese Falcon* represents the
opposite pole, a story where almost all significant action and
violence occur offscreen. Both movies amount primarily to *talk,*
and making that talk interesting requires both an imaginative
director and a compelling cast. Although both Lorre and Sydney
Greenstreet appear in *The Mask of Dimitrios,* that film miscasts
Lorre as the mild-mannered investigative writer and wastes the
title role on Zachary Scott. The two failed earlier versions of
Hammett's novel make one thing clear: *The Maltese Falcon* needs
Humphrey Bogart.[22]

(*with Franklin Cason, Paul Johnson, Akila McDaniel*)

P_{ipe}

Although Spade smokes
nothing but cigarettes
throughout *The Maltese Falcon,*
the shot of his nightstand
reveals a pipe resting in an
ashtray beside a rack of other
pipes. This characterizing
detail (Spade as secret

intellectual?) contradicts almost every other signifier the film
associates with him, indicating a more complex character than
otherwise implied. This effect suggests that Hollywood cinema's
determined effort at seamless matching may prove counterpro-
ductive: our sense of a realistic character thrives on fragmentary
information, mixed signals. Buñuel's *That Obscure Object of Desire*
offers the extreme version of this tactic, using two different
actresses (one blonde, one brunette) to play the same character,
a blatant mismatch rarely noticed by first-time viewers accustomed to "healing" the cinema's gaps, errors, fault lines. Indeed,
narrative filmmaking depends on the presumption of continuity,
and that presumption will survive even the surprising appearance
of Spade's pipes.

(with Mason Laird)

P**oster**

At Archer's murder scene, the
wall behind Spade and Tom
Polhaus shows a weather-
beaten poster for *Swing Your
Lady*, an actual 1938 Humphrey
Bogart musical (?!), widely
regarded as his worst film. The
sign, of course, functions as the
kind of insider joke that
prompted Huston and Bogart to make 1954's *Beat the Devil*, a
parody of movies like *The Maltese Falcon*. It also plays with notions of
"the trap," for just as *Swing Your Lady* stands for the kind of trap into
which the late 1930s Bogart (as actor) had fallen, it also provides a
clue to the movie's enigma: Archer has not been killed at random,
but led into a trap by Brigid, who may "swing" for her crime.

But the poster raises other questions, too. What, for
example, is the status of a real object in a fictional world? If we

imagine the hermetically sealed space of *The Maltese Falcon* as one large theatrical set, the *Swing Your Lady* poster seems like a door in the stage's rear wall, suddenly flung open to reveal the actual world. The very lack of attention accorded the poster achieves another effect. As Barthes points out, when real historical characters (or objects) get introduced into a fiction *obliquely*, in passing, "their modesty, like a lock between two levels of water, equalizes novel and history." After *The Maltese Falcon*'s success, Warners would exploit such "locks," casting Bogart in a series of World War II adventures (*Across the Pacific, Casablanca, Action in the North Atlantic, Sahara, Passage to Marseilles, To Have and Have Not*), the first of which, 1942's *Across the Pacific*, concerns the Panama Canal.[23]

(*with Ashley Bowen*)

Quay

How does a set-bound film stage the burning of a large freighter? In *The Maltese Falcon*, a dissolve takes us from the "Shipping News" notice of *La Paloma*'s arrival to a medium shot of a fireman scaling a ladder toward what seems a burning ship. The cut to grainy

stock footage of a smaller boat (a documentary image roughly docked to the quay of the movie's narrative) calls attention to the artificial nature of what follows: a mastless vessel rising to a visible ceiling, attended to by men wearing uniforms labeled "Los Angeles Fire Department." Just as the movie will reveal the

Falcon as a fake, this sequence momentarily ruptures the narrative's spell, exposing it as the result of studio artifice.

(with Jennifer Simmons)

Questions (Irrational Enlargement)

Why didn't Archer's wife love him?

What did Archer do on the night he was murdered before he kept his date to follow Brigid?

How does Spade always know when Brigid is lying?

What is Gutman's *exact* weight?

What used to be on the empty lot where Spade goes on the bum steer?

What did Gutman's "agents" do to Kemidov to "persuade" him to give up the Falcon?

What was the *next* object stored in the baggage claim *after* the Falcon?

What happened to the letter posted immediately *after* Spade's letter?

What happened on Effie's trip to deliver the Falcon to Spade's apartment?

When did "Mr. Wells's history" become an opaque phrase?

What previous occupation has made Gutman so adept with calculations?

Where was Iva on the night of her husband's death?

Where is the real Maltese Falcon?

(with Mason Laird and Naomi Zell)

 **ed Herrings**

While *The Maltese Falcon*'s plot offers numerous false trails, red herrings that lead nowhere, Effie plays a decisive role in two of them. "Suppose I told you," she remarks to Spade the day after Archer's murder, "that your Iva hadn't been home many minutes when I arrived to break the news at three o'clock this morning?" Spade quickly dismisses Effie's suggestion: "You're a detective, darling, but she didn't kill him." But how can he be so casually sure? Given Iva's infatuation with Spade, Effie's revelation provides her with not only the motive but also the opportunity to have killed her husband. This possibility, of course, will come to nothing, and indeed the movie will simply abandon it, never providing any explanation for Iva's whereabouts on that night. Effie will again mislead Spade when her "woman's intuition" tells her that Brigid is "all right"; she will prove anything but.

Effie's contributions, in other words, work to divert the viewer's attention from the truth, which if revealed too soon would bring the movie to an end. Effie's wrong turns merely resemble the intentional lies and countless stories the characters tell each other. In almost every scene, in fact, at least one character is lying. *The Maltese Falcon*'s larger narrative contains smaller plots. Within them lie still smaller narratives involving histories withheld and fabrications offered in their place. Thus, each unit of the story—Effie's suspicions of Iva, for example—functions *holographically*: extracted from the movie and held under the microscope of close reading, each retains the shape and structure of the whole. Taken together, these subnarratives insinuate that the plot's prime mover, the Falcon itself, is as insubstantial and imaginary as the fabrications of the characters pursuing it. Or as insubstantial and imaginary as a fictional world created on film.

(with Bryan Hoben)

Ronson Touch-Tip Lighter

"The *Black Mask* detective
genre," James Naremore
argues, "is among the most
fetishistic of fictions. . . . it
fascinates us with all kinds of
objects":

> [*I*]*n Huston's film, for*
> *example, we have the leather*
> *swivel chair in Bogart's*
> *office, his roll-your-own cigarettes, the gadget on his desk*
> *from which he can withdraw lighted matches, the little neon*
> *signs outside his window that glow KLVW or DRINK.*

Spade's gadget is a Ronson Touch-Tip, a luxury art deco
lighter that would also appear, 10 years later, in *Strangers on a
Train*. With its visual appeal, the device serves double duty as both
fetish object and revenue source: for several years, Warners
received money from Ronson for product placement. Thus,
Spade's desk also displays a Ronson cigarette box, and Gutman's
room has a Ronson Touch-Tip Turret. Hollywood's *economy* is at
work here: just as the Falcon itself serves as both fetish *and*
narrative *donnée*, the lighter must function as more than just
something to look at. How would we define the kind of cinema
satisfied simply by the Ronson's *photogénie*?[24]

(with Jennifer Beckett and Mason Laird)

Rooms

Most of *The Maltese Falcon* takes place in the rooms of Spade,
Brigid, and Gutman, each decorated to suggest its occupant's
character: Spade's austerely masculine apartment finds its
antonyms in Miss O'Shaughnessy's well-furnished sitting room

and Gutman's floral, baroque hotel room, apparently stocked with his own *objets*. Yet despite the different decors, the three rooms have the same floor plan, with a fireplace, vertical windows, and identically located front doors.

Hence an imaginary research project concerning art direction: would reassigning these spaces have any narrative impact?

(*with Eric Garcia and Naomi Zell*)

 pade's Bed

In the movies, subtle, unexplained alterations in established decors suggest that reality itself is being rearranged every time the camera turns away. Hitchcock's *North by Northwest* shows how this unsettling effect can be deliberately produced: returning with the police to the house where he has been held down and plied with alcohol, Roger Thornhill (Cary Grant) finds that bourbon stains have mysteriously vanished from a sofa, and a liquor cabinet has become a bookcase. In *The Maltese Falcon*, such changes are smaller, probably uncalculated, but insidiously disturbing. Spade's bed, for example, from which he receives the call about Archer's murder and where he sits to entertain the police, is missing from all subsequent scenes set in his apartment.

And when the detective first brings Brigid to his rooms, the pale, rectangular outline of a missing picture appears on the wall to the right of his fireplace.

What object has been re-moved? How might it have changed our sense of Spade's character?

The disappearing frame represents a double-cross. On the one hand, the filmmakers clearly intended it to be the kind of highly specific, but insignificant, detail that Barthes described as essential to "the reality effect." It makes Spade's room seem real *precisely to the extent that it remains meaningless*. On the other hand, two earlier scenes in Spade's apartment have shown nothing at all hanging at this spot; thus, the sudden absence becomes simply a careless match, probably the result of nonsequential shooting.

The missing bed, however, seems a more complicated case. Certainly, it indicates a *theatrical* approach to set design, where an object's appearance results from a director's calculation rather than a camera's automatism. Chekhov's dictum, that a rifle over a mantle in act 1 must go off by act 3, would eventually find its repudiation in Rossellini's advice: "Things are there. . . . why manipulate them?" After the coming of sound encouraged studio-bound production, however, classical Hollywood thought of sets as miniature narratives, perfectly corresponding to the stories that everything about its filmmaking process was designed to serve. Since the two subsequent scenes in Spade's apartment (Brigid's confrontation with Cairo and the climactic sorting-out) don't require a bed, it can be dismissed without a second thought.

And yet, with its enigmatic objects (Spade's lighter, Cairo's heart-shaped pill box, the black bird itself) and unexplained events (where *was* Iva Archer the night Miles was killed?), *The Maltese Falcon* continuously works to swing the weight of its narrative from detection to atmosphere. In this context, the transformations to Spade's apartment register more viscerally: when Spade meets there with Brigid and Cairo, not only has the bed vanished, but the room itself seems larger and the furniture rearranged, with a small settee now occupying the bed's previous position. Thus, a disappearing bed, lost and unaccounted for, becomes important to the film's effect, a suggestion of a more profound disturbance. In words that uncannily coincide with *The Maltese Falcon*'s world, where rooms expand and contract without explanation, Nietzsche once diagnosed the unraveling of a morality that had sustained Western civilization for centuries: "The image of things still shifts and shuffles continually, and perhaps even more so and faster from now on than ever before."[25]

(*with Kristin Davy, Nic Jelley, Charles Meyer, Jennifer Simmons, Naomi Zell*)

 T **hrees**

The Maltese Falcon was Hammett's third novel.

For *The Maltese Falcon*, Hammett returned to third-person narration.

Three film versions: *The Maltese Falcon* (1931; also known as *Dangerous Female*), *Satan Met a Lady* (1936), and *The Maltese Falcon* (1941).

Mary Astor and Humphrey Bogart were both divorced three times.

Astor and Bogart were both on third marriages at the time of filming.

The Huston family has three generations of Oscar winners: Walter, John, and Angelica.

The film contains three gay characters: Gutman, Cairo, Wilmer.

Cairo has three passports: Greek, French, and British.

Cairo's theater ticket cost $3.30.

After *High Sierra* and *All through the Night*, *The Maltese Falcon* was the third occasion when Bogart benefited from George Raft's refusal of a role.

Huston's budget: $381,000.

The story describes three murders (Archer, Thursby, Jacoby).

Astor's character goes by three names: Wonderly, LeBlanc, and O'Shaughnessy.

Warners' unsuccessful attempt in 1939 to make a third version of *The Maltese Falcon* was to be called *The Clock Struck Three*.

This list results from the kind of revved-up hermeneutics that resembles Salvador Dali's "paranoiac-critical activity." While academic film studies' rapid expansion, with its attendant publishing demands, has furthered such scrutiny, it once seemed less common with the cinema, perhaps because before VHS and DVD players, the movies wouldn't sit still. Not only did almost all feature films vanish after their initial runs, their relentless unfolding, so different from the literary experience (which proceeds at the *reader's* pace), effectively disabled analysis. "Resistance to the cinema," Barthes declared in his autobiography, "the signifier itself is always, by nature, continuous here, whatever the rhetoric of frames and shots; without remission, a continuum of images . . . statutory impossibility of the fragment." The film buff was a fetishist, not a conspiracy theorist: he wanted to own Dorothy's red slippers, not formulate their "intertextual significance."

When Barthes got around to writing about the movies, he avoided the problem by using stills, the cinema's "immobiliza-tion." Conveniently for this entry on threes, those stills prompted his description of "the third meaning" (which "cannot be grasped in the projected film"), a property of images exceeding their informa-tional and symbolic levels. If a single image from Eisenstein's *Ivan the Terrible* contained (1) the representation of a woman (information) and (2) the sign of grief (symbol), it also offered something else not reducible to language: the fall of her kerchief, her eyebrows' curve, the slope of her mouth. Barthes called that "something else" by several names: "the obtuse meaning," "the third mean-ing," "the filmic." (See *The Maltese Falcon*: Edeson)

> *The filmic is what, in the film, cannot be described, it is the representation that cannot be represented. The filmic begins only where language and articulated meta-language cease. Everything we can say about* Ivan *or* Potemkin *can be said about a written text (which would be called* Ivan the Terrible *or* The Battleship Potemkin. . . . *hence the filmic is precisely here, at this point where articulated language is no more than approximative and where another language begins (a language whose "science" cannot therefore be linguistics, soon discarded like a booster rocket).*

The filmic, third meaning, *photogénie*, the *Cahiers du Cinéma*'s mise-en-scène—these are equivalent terms, struggling to define the best cinema's elusive essence. "It is not surprising," Barthes acknowledged, "that the filmic (despite the incalculable quantity of films in the world) should still be rare." It should not be surprising, therefore, that it took Warner Brothers three tries to succeed with *The Maltese Falcon*. If we posit the 1931 version as the "informational" presentation of Hammett's story (the facts, characters, and situations are all there) and *Satan Met a Lady* as the "symbolic" account (the same events and people have become comically allegorical), then the success of Huston's *Maltese Falcon* derives from its "third meanings," the photogenic appeal of Bogart's *louche* resourcefulness, of Greenstreet's rolling Shakespearean rhythm, of Astor's perpetually surprised features, of the sets' austere elegance, of the unexpected contents of Cairo's pocket.[26]

(*with Kristin Davy and Jennifer Simmons*)

U mbrella

In rainy San Francisco, only Joel Cairo carries an umbrella, which he erotically caresses as he flirts with Spade. The umbrella's dainty handle and polished sheen, Cairo's white gloves and bow tie, his prissy

manners and dainty stature— the signs converge to suggest the stereotyped homosexual, a figure banned from explicit representation by the Hays Office. Huston's film quickly covers its traces: When Spade emerges from his office after his encounter with Cairo, the wet sidewalks retroactively justify the umbrella, providing an alibi for the previous scene's codes, naturalized by "the weather."

(with Jessica Hanan and Renee Moilanen)

alue

Brigid's initial fee, paid to Spade: $200

Cash that Spade takes from Brigid's purse: almost $400

Cairo's offer for the Falcon's "recovery": $5,000

Brigid's next offer to Spade: "What else is there I can buy you with?"

Gutman's offer to Spade: $50,000 or one-quarter of the proceeds, perhaps $250,000

Gutman's "coin of the realm" offer: $10,000

Huston's budget for *The Maltese Falcon*: $381,000

Actual cost of *The Maltese Falcon*: $327,182

The Falcon statuette used in the film, sold at Christie's, 1994: $398,500

These values, a brief history of fetishism and its production, suggest Hollywood's success in stimulating desire for the *referential grail*. In his famous essay "The Work of Art in the Age of Mechanical Reproduction," Walter Benjamin argued that the new media, especially photography and film, had annulled the traditional distinction between *original* and *copy*: Asking for "the original copy" of a snapshot dead-ends in an oxymoron. And yet, Benjamin was wrong to predict that mechanical reproducibility would destroy "cult value." If in the cinema, an "original" does not exist (where are *The Maltese Falcon*'s hotels and apartments and streets? like all sets, struck after their usefulness has ended), that condition has encouraged an even greater longing for it. The movies were always designed for *exchange value*, that ungrounded worth existing only in circulation and desire. *The Maltese Falcon* itself represents this situation, converting its viewers into seekers for the unattainable.[27]

(with Rashna Wadia)

 **W**ebley-Forsby

"A Webley-Forsby 45-automatic, eight-shot," Spade replies, responding to Polhaus's request to identify Archer's murder weapon. "They don't make them any more." In fact, they never did. Even under its actual name, Webley-*Fosbery* produced only .38-caliber eight-shot revolvers. Hammett, who got both the name and the caliber correct, almost certainly underestimated this gun's rarity: some reports suggest that as few as 40 were manufactured. By making Spade able to recognize an impossibly rare weapon that he would have almost certainly never seen, Hammett was endowing his hero with the kind of specialized knowledge championed by Sherlock Holmes. But why does Huston's film depart from Hammett's text? On the one hand, "Forsby" sounds like "Thursby," a near-rhyme linking Archer's murder weapon to his suspected killer. On the other, *The Maltese Falcon*'s effect depends far less on precise verisimilitude than on convincing *presentation*. If Spade's description of the gun *sounds* right, the audience will accept it. Would it also accept the following uncanny coincidence? The revolver's original manufacturer, an Englishman named Philip Webley, started the business in 1856 for one reason: His brother and business partner, James Webley, had been shot dead. A nonexistent weapon, a fictional narrative, an actual crime: "The marvelous—," Paul Hammond writes, "the contamination of reality by the imaginary—is the crux of surrealism." And of the cinema.[28]

(*with Ashley Hendricks, Nic Jelley, Kory Krinsky, Mason Laird, Rashna Wadia*)

W ells's History

"These are facts, historical facts," Gutman asserts, having begun his tale of the Falcon's past; "not school book history, not Mr. Wells's history, but history nevertheless." Gutman, of course, is referring to H. G. Wells, whose enormous *The Outline of History* (1920) and its abridgement, *A Short History of the World* (1922), became bestsellers purporting to offer encyclopedic summaries of civilization. Much earlier, Thucydides had seemed equally confident: he insisted that he could begin his account of world history with the Peloponnesian Wars because nothing important had happened before then. The new historicists have suggested, however, that the most significant things, the ways that people actually live, get neglected by the *grands récits* and require new modes of "encounter with the singular, the specific, and the individual." Catherine Gallagher and Stephen Greenblatt's "method of Luminous Detail," for example, involves the use of archival anecdotes "of strangeness or opacity," intended "to arouse the bafflement, the intense curiosity and interest, that necessitates the interpretation of cultures." An anecdote like the one about the Maltese Falcon?

At stake here is the issue of *coverage*, the problem confronting every ambitious history. How much can any account describe? As Seymour Chatman has shown, written description is inevitably selective, while "[f]ilm narrative possesses a plenitude of visual details, an excessive particularity compared to the verbal version." Thus, if it were possible to write down *every single thing* that appears in Huston's version of *The Maltese Falcon*, the result would prove far longer than Hammett's 200 pages. The film, in other words, both abridges *and expands* its written source, providing a more exhaustive history. In doing so, it confirms Irving Thalberg's remark, cited elsewhere in this book: "In the future, the movies will be the best record of how we once lived."

A contemporary viewer will likely mistake "Wells" for "Welles," the Orson Welles whose own accounts of Charles Foster Kane and the Ambersons amount to counternarratives that resist Hollywood's "history as usual." As if to further the confusion, Orson Welles's initial fame derived from his radio play of H. G. Wells's *The War of the Worlds*, designed to resemble a breaking-news report. The mass panic caused by Welles's show resulted not only from its perfect mimicry of the news (the harried announcers, abruptly cut off; the crackling static), but also from its audience's late tuning in (many people had been listening to *Edgar Bergen and Charlie McCarthy*). This latter factor seems peculiar to film, radio, and television. When, if ever, do we begin reading in the middle of a novel? Yet we often tune into a program already in progress, understanding and accepting the irretrievability of the missing scenes. Like Welles's listeners, Spade enters the Falcon story *in medias res*: like them, he must learn to accept that story *as a story*, and not as something historically true.[29]

(with Renee Moilanen)

 **X** enophobia

Foreign references in The Maltese Falcon

Malta

Spain

Honolulu

the Orient

Sicily

Hong Kong

Istanbul

Greece

France

Great Britain

Jerusalem

Paris

London

Russia

Tasmania

Germany

The Maltese Falcon relies on a mise-en-scène stripped down to the objects that "count." Unlike many films, it does not offer what Seymour Chatman finds typical of the cinema, "a plenitude of visual details, an excessive particularity," a "visual 'over-specification.'" Instead, Huston's film often resembles a cartoon: everything appears suffused with meaning, ready to further the narrative. Even the most insignificant objects seem deliberate: the statues and paintings of horses, a heart-shaped pill box (contents unknown), a movie poster (*Swing Your Lady*), the title on a marquee (*The Great Lie*), a partially dated theater ticket. This quasi-allegorical world, simultaneously remote and familiar, becomes, in Spade's valediction, "the stuff that dreams are made of."

The movie's villains personify this disorientation. Their names signify an often indeterminate foreignness: Kasper Gutman (with his English accent and German first name), Joel Cairo (a Middle Eastern capital, but a name without specific ethnicity), Brigid O'Shaughnessy (a Celtic reminder of Irish immigration). Since almost all of the film's foreign references derive from these characters, *The Maltese Falcon* seems to reflect the dominant sentiment of American isolationism: *anything foreign is suspect.* William Luhr has attributed this tone to the era's xenophobia:

> The Maltese Falcon *joins with many films of its era from different genres in demonstrating a distrust of things foreign. Non–U.S. characters, places, and things tend to be exotic at best, and often perverse, sexually overcharged, and dangerous. The Falcon itself is foreign—Maltese. Gutman, Cairo, and O'Shaughnessy have tracked it in their evil and murderous travels through foreign lands before winding up in San Francisco and encountering Spade. The very overlay of foreign cities and countries, given the cultural climate of the 1940s, compounds the evil of their murderous deeds.*

While right enough, this statement seems too simple. The movie's foreign references, after all, come straight from Hammett's original, published in 1929 when American isolationism played only a small role in national politics. In fact, the film's attitude toward foreignness, especially what used to be called the Levant, depends on a disposition less localized than early 1940s xenophobia. Edward Said famously named this discourse "Orientalism," Western civilization's habit of projecting its least desirable traits onto "the East." Another category is also operative. The homosexuality of Cairo, Gutman, and Wilmer; the sexual frigidity of Brigid (with her rhyming name); Gutman's baroque diction and fastidious manners; Cairo's perfumed handkerchief and heart-shaped pill box—these things all suggest *dandyism.* Stanley Cavell has proposed the dandy as a Hollywood archetype, identifying its most important incarnations in the western hero and the detective, especially William Powell (in *The Thin Man* series) and

Humphrey Bogart (in *The Maltese Falcon*). But in Baudelaire's
original formulation, dandyism appeared as "an institution beyond
the laws," a practice of "opposition and revolt" against bourgeois
conformity. Roland Barthes connected dandyism to the pleasures of
perversity, arguing that "in a given situation—of pessimism and
rejection—it is the intellectual class as a whole which, if it does not
become militant, is virtually a dandy." To the extent that classical
Hollywood's enterprise depended on the recruitment of the middle-
class audience, the movies' antibourgeois dandies would often
appear threatening. But what Baudelaire called the dandy's
"elegance and originality," his "joy of astonishing others," his
"burning need to create . . . a personal originality"—all seem
definitions of *photogénie*. When Joel Cairo fondles his umbrella and
purrs, "May a stranger offer condolences for your partner's unfortunate death?"; when Kasper Gutman replies to Spade's objection to
being underpaid with, "This is genuine coin of the realm. With a
dollar of this you can buy ten dollars of talk," we are watching
moments of villainy, foreignness, dandyism, and cinema.[30]

(with Jessica Hanan, Renee Moilanen, Kate Casey-Sawicki)

 Yells

The Maltese Falcon's abstract, hermetic quality derives partially from
its minimal evocation of offscreen space, as if its plot were a
chemistry experiment dependent on the reduction of variables.
The avoidance of location shooting, the suppression of sounds
coming from the edges of the story space (like the street and office
noises in Godard's *Masculine-Feminine*), the strict adherence of the
camera to the main characters—these choices produce a self-
contained world that rarely refers beyond itself. Some scenes, of
course, will suggest space outside the camera's purview: the shot
of Archer's murder, for example, keeps the killer usefully out of

frame. In other places, the activating device proves equally obvious: "[O]ff-screen sound," Noël Burch reminds us, "*always* brings off-screen space into play." Thus, in the opening scene, an opening door's faint click calls attention to an offscreen area, made retroactively visible when first Effie and then Archer enter Spade's office.

Three piercing yells prompt the film's most decisive uses of offscreen space:

1. Cairo's yell for help from Spade's offscreen living room, which brings Dundy and Polhaus into the apartment.

2. Effie's scream as Jacobi falls dead at Spade's feet.

3. Brigid's feigned cry for help, coming over the telephone and causing Spade's "bum steer" trip to the Burlingame vacant lot.

Burch designates four methods for suggesting offscreen space: offscreen sound, figures entering or exiting the frame, figures gazing past the frame's perimeter, and figures' body parts extending beyond the frame. In the three yelling sequences, Huston uses all four of these methods.

1. Cairo's yell: Background music begins to swell as Brigid slaps Cairo. During a medium shot (MS) of Spade slapping Cairo, we hear *offscreen knocking*. All three characters *look offscreen left*. Brigid: "Who's that?" Pan left following Spade to sliding doors. Cut to Spade emerging from sliding doors; pan left with Spade to front door, revealing previously offscreen space of hallway. Background music stops. Reframe to medium close-up (MCU) of Spade, Dundy, and Polhaus. Series of shots/reverse-shots during their

conversation. As Dundy and Polhaus start to leave, we hear *offscreen fighting sounds* and then *Cairo's yell for help.* Spade, Dundy, and Polhaus *look offscreen right.* Slight track backward to MS and a pan right following Dundy to sliding doors. Cut to MS of Dundy emerging on the other side into the apartment; pan right following him as he, Polhaus, and Spade gather with Brigid and Cairo in medium long shot (MLS).

2. Effie's scream: MS of Effie and Spade; we hear *offscreen rustling noise.* Effie and Spade *look offscreen left.* As background music swells (it will continue throughout this sequence), pan left to MS of office door where *Jacobi enters from offscreen,* beyond the immediate set. Reframe while Jacobi stumbles. Effie, *offscreen, screams.* Slight pan right in MS as Spade *enters from frame right.* Cut to MCU of floor between Jacobi and Spade's feet; the Falcon *drops from offscreen above frame.* Slight tilt up to reframe MS as Jacobi collapses onto the couch and Spade comes to him. Effie *exits to offscreen* behind immediate set. Cut to MS of Spade and Jacobi; *offscreen door-locking sounds.* Cut to MS of Effie *reentering frame* through office door, approaching Spade and Jacobi.

3. Brigid's cry for help: MCU of the Falcon on the floor. Spade's arms *enter frame from offscreen above.* Tilt up to MCU on the Falcon as he lifts it. Pan right following the Falcon to the desk, accompanied by *offscreen sound of Effie talking.* Tilt up to MS of Effie and Spade at the desk with the Falcon between them. Cut to MS of the two. Cut to reverse MS of Effie as *offscreen telephone rings.* Effie picks up the phone; we hear *sound of Brigid's garbled talking* and then *a piercing yell.* Cut to MS of Effie and Spade. Effie *exits frame left* and then *returns from frame left* with Spade's coat. Pan follows Spade to the door, and he *exits frame through the door.*

With the exception of Brigid's yell (which we will later learn she has staged from her apartment), each of these imaginary offscreen spaces will be rendered retroactively concrete. (Like most movies, *The Maltese Falcon* runs on the carefully regulated fluctuations of the unseen and the visible.) Effie's yell, however, the most haunting of the three, seems particularly interesting: Huston does not immediately return to her with a shot that would isolate the sound's source. As more *disembodied*, Effie's scream also seems involved in other work.

The Maltese Falcon provides numerous clues to Effie's ambiguous sexuality and incomplete "femininity." She lives with her mother, rolls a cigarette like a tough, and accepts Spade's compliment, "You're a good man, sister." Effie's physical appearance emphasizes her mannish features: the squared jaw, short hair, and sparse make-up. Yet despite this ambiguity, her reactions to Jacobi's death—the scream, the near-faint—adhere to the cultural stereotypes of feminine squeamishness. (The same codes, evoked by Cairo's offscreen yell for help, confirm his effeminacy.) Yet because Effie cries from offscreen, the viewer can never definitively connect her to that sound; in fact, the scream sounds entirely out of place, as if lifted from another soundtrack. Effie's yell, therefore, remains an abstract feminine code (danger + scream = woman) rather than the response of a particular person. Thus, this "proof" of womanhood is deceptive; we accept Effie's femininity because she exhibits the *cultural codes* of femininity. In fact, Effie could be a man in disguise (Balzac's *Sarrasine* has taught us never to dismiss this possibility). Effie's scream, then, does not substantiate her womanhood any more than her cigarette-rolling ability identifies her as a man. Her gender remains ambiguous. The sound, however, by doing double duty as spatial marker and gender characterization, indicates classic Hollywood's economy. In studio era cinema, as Burch points out, "it was essential that there be no superfluous, 'gratuitous' marks. . . . the bourgeois codes are *thrifty*."[31]

(*with Renee Moilanen and Jennifer Simmons*)

Zero

At *The Maltese Falcon*'s center, recurring nothingness: a worthless forgery, an inconclusive plot, a barren band of rogues, a murderer who calls herself "LeBlanc," but whose "real" name begins with the fatal zero: O'Shaughnessy. Early in his career, Samuel Dashiell Hammett had written under the name "Peter Collinson," a pseudonym derived from "Peter Collins," slang for a nobody. Later in life, he went by "Dash Hammett" (–Hammett?), a nickname suggesting an emptiness incapable of replacement by any letter. What is an "empty" event, one without referent, existing solely for the purposes of being recorded? We call such an event "a movie."[32]

(with Renee Moilanen)

Zigzags

In a 1924 *Black Mask* story, Hammett uses the term "zigzags" to describe the procedure for shadowing a suspect:

> *There are four rules for shadowing: Keep behind your subject as much as possible; never try to hide from him; act in a natural manner, no matter what happens; and never meet his eye.*

Hammett's rules correspond to some of classic Hollywood filmmaking's most important protocols. In *The Maltese Falcon*'s opening scene, for example, Huston's camera "keeps behind" Bogart, filming from over his shoulder as he rises to meet Brigid. By occupying Spade's space while still keeping part of him visible, this position falls somewhere between a frontal view's objectivity and a first-person, *Lady in the Lake*-style subjectivity. Always attending to its principal characters, continuity cinema "never tries to hide" the camera away from its stars, who must remain in plain sight. The invisible style, premised on "a natural manner" of shooting and editing, calls no attention to itself. And, from an early period, continuity rules have forbidden the camera to look directly into the eyes of someone facing it. To "hide or conceal from [the viewer's] knowledge" the camera, to "represent," to "paint the likeness of," to "follow and watch"—these dictionary definitions of *to shadow* also define Hollywood filmmaking. "Last night I was in the Kingdom of Shadows," Maxim Gorky wrote in 1896 after his first encounter with the cinema. "If you only knew how strange it is to be there. . . . It is not life but its shadow, it is not motion but its soundless spectre."

Hammett's zigzags amount to a process of *following* and *watching*, the essence of moviemaking. Walter Benjamin located the origins of this activity in the nineteenth century's burgeoning metropolises, where "every person, the best as well as the most wretched, carries around a secret which would make him hateful to all others if it became known." For Benjamin, this situation's hero was the *flâneur*, whose idleness concealed an acute sensitivity to the marginal signs that betray identity. Because this skill inevitably involved him in danger—"no matter what trail the *flâneur* may follow," Benjamin observed, "every one of them will lead him to a crime"—the *flâneur* evolved into a new urban type: the detective. His expertise became "the smallest details of Parisian life[,] [t]he pedestrians, the shops, the hired coaches, or a man leaning against a window." Or, in *The Maltese Falcon*'s case, a man standing in a doorway, seen from an apartment window—a man who has been shadowing Spade.[33]

(with Jennifer Simmons)

Zonked

Knocking someone unconscious or *being* knocked unconscious are sacred rituals of *film noir* (see *Murder, My Sweet* for one of the genre's most extended riffs on getting zonked). Thus, in *The Maltese Falcon*, Spade knocks out Cairo but later gets drugged by

Gutman. These scenes seem meant as surprises, but they aren't, not even on first viewing. Why, then, does the film's formulaic nature not diminish it? In *S/Z*, Barthes proposed rereading as a way to *increase pleasure*: freed from a plot's tantalizations, the rereader will inevitably interrupt the story he already knows, taking time to inspect details, follow leads, imagine other outcomes. In this new context, narrative provides the background hum against which one can detect other whispers, different pleasures:

> A woman's arm suddenly entering the frame without notice while Spade sits at his desk.

> The self-satisfied grin on Spade's face as he leaves Gutman's apartment, having just delivered a bravura performance of "anger."

> Gutman's "You're the man for me, sir."

> Cairo's "Excuse me, please. I must have expressed myself badly. I did not mean to say that I have the money in my pocket, but that I am ready to get it for you on a few minutes' notice at any time during banking hours."

> Gutman disrobing after Spade falls unconscious, revealing that he's already dressed.

> The way Cairo steps gingerly over Spade's body.

> Spade's curtains fluttering in the breeze, parting to reveal Wilmer on the street below.

> The silent sequence of Spade losing Wilmer in an apartment building.

Each of these moments could serve as an example of "the cinematic."

(with Paul Johnson)

Meet Me in St. Louis

rt Director

Vincente Minnelli was one of only two major Hollywood filmmakers who began as art directors (the other was Hitchcock). Having
started in Chicago designing shop windows for Marshall Field's,
Minnelli quickly graduated to New York, where he worked for the
Paramount Theater, moonlighting with Earl Carroll's *Vanities*. For
Carroll, Minnelli displayed his two principal influences: contempo-
rary art deco and the Russian Ballet's lush, decadent orientalism ("a
decidedly Negroid sense of color," Robert Benchley called it in the
New Yorker). In 1933, he became art director of Radio City Music
Hall, which, after an enormously publicized December 1932
opening, had nearly failed. At Radio City, Minnelli produced the
kind of elaborate, sophisticated kitsch that paralleled Busby
Berkeley's simultaneous inventions for Warner Brothers (see *42nd
Street*). By 1934, Minnelli was staging his own monthly Radio City
spectacles: "Coast to Coast," for example, took audiences on
tours of the Riviera, Ascot, Africa, and San Francisco, all con-
cocted from picture books and paintings of places he had never
seen. Two years later, he was directing Broadway musicals,
including some work on a 1936 revival of Florenz Ziegfeld's *Follies*
(in which Bob Hope introduced "I Can't Get Started"). His finale,
1939's *Very Warm for May*, was a famous flop, the last of the
Jerome Kern–Oscar Hammerstein collaborations, wrecked by
changes Minnelli ordered out of town. Even the show's great hit,
"All the Things You Are," couldn't save it.

Why have so few art directors become movie directors?
What happens when one does? Filmmaking proceeds along two
axes, a horizontal movement concerned with sequences and a
vertical effort attending to individual scenes, a division of labor
resembling music's melody and harmony. While producers,
editors, and directors remain responsible for a movie's horizontal

progress, art directors, set designers, and costumers focus on the cinema's more static elements, the mise-en-scène. Art directors harmonize a movie's melody, inflecting it as decisively as a shift from a major to minor chord can transform a melody. But they can neglect a film's movement from scene to scene.

Filmmaking's intensively collaborative nature has always produced contention. While working on *Meet Me in St. Louis*, only his third movie, Minnelli promptly, and irreconcilably, fell out with Cedric Gibbons, Hollywood's most powerful art director. Minnelli, of course, wanted to combine the two roles—and do them both himself. Collaborative disputes, however, are not merely petty. At stake is the most important issue in filmmaking: the ideal site of control. *42nd Street* dramatizes the debate, relocating it to Broadway where a musical, *Pretty Lady*, moves from conception to opening night. Although the movie issued from Hollywood's producer-controlled studio system, *42nd Street* champions the director, Julian Marsh (read: Ziegfeld), while portraying the financial source (Abner Dillon) as a lascivious old fool, the producers (Jones and Barry) as ignorant ciphers, the playwright as a prissy fussbudget, and the star (Dorothy Brock) as a fungible prima donna.

Academic film studies results from the eruption of this question about control's ideal site. We call that event *auteurism*, launched by Truffaut's 1954 manifesto, "A Certain Tendency of the French Cinema," which viciously attacked the French filmmaking dominated by scriptwriters. "When they hand in their scenario," Truffaut wrote, "the film is done: the *metteur-en-scène*, in their eyes, is the gentleman who adds the pictures to it." But scriptwriters have gotten in their licks, too. When Andrew Sarris asked Billy Wilder about his cowritten *Midnight* (1939), a film made by a former art director, Mitchell Leisen, Wilder was, in Sarris's words, "unguardedly contemptuous": "He [Leisen] was just a decorator like Minnelli."

Meet Me in St. Louis evinces Minnelli's background: the seasonal greeting cards introducing the movie's chapters (shop windows coming to life), the saturated Technicolor, the elaborate period costumes—all suggest his attention to precisely those horizontal elements of storytelling that are normally the art director's province. Gerald Kaufman describes this method in a passage cited in the introduction to this book:

> He took enormous—and, to fellow-participants, sometimes infuriating—trouble composing the frames so that each one, if frozen, would be a work of art. A former window-dresser [note the dismissive label], he regarded the apt placement of almost unobtrusive objects as essential. One daily report of the filming recorded, "3:20–3:26. Wait for perfume bottle (special container with satin lining asked for by director)."
>
> Minnelli believed that the texture of a movie depended on immense care over details which the audience might not even notice consciously. He said of making Meet Me in St. Louis, "You have to have great discipline in what you do. I spent a great deal of time in research, and finding the right things for it. I feel that a picture that stays with you is made up of a hundred or more hidden things."

Filmmaking, an activity that involves thousands of choices, inevitably comes down to such details. In his famous essay "Entertainment and Utopia," Richard Dyer argued that movies like Meet Me in St. Louis present "what utopia would *feel* like rather than how it would be organized," and that sense results not only from character and plot, but also from "non-representational signs" like color and texture, precisely the domain of art direction. Thus, in Meet Me in St. Louis, a film moving relentlessly toward its Christmas resolution (when Father decides not to move the family

to New York), Minnelli makes the Smith house's dominant colors red and green, thereby providing the feel of Christmas all year 'round.[1]

 **lue Slippers**

Let us imagine two possible ways of filming Esther and Tootie's cakewalk. The first will require the actors to execute a single continuous performance, covered by at least two cameras. Shot 1: a full shot of the two girls dancing, watched by 10 or 11 others, including Lon, sitting on the floor to the right and accompanying them on a mandolin. As the camera pans in his direction to follow the dance, cut to shot 2, a midshot, provided by another camera, showing only Esther, Tootie, and Lon. The girls reach down to the right for their hats and canes, and as they straighten up, cut to shot 3, a return to shot 1's camera set-up. Since both cameras will presumably be running for the entire sequence, the articulation points will require no scrutiny for potential matching problems.

The second filming method will *construct* one sustained performance out of two different ones. Here, the cuts to shots 2 and 3 will depend for their invisibility on the continuous sound-track ("Under the Bamboo Tree"), the 180-degree system, and the careful matching of all of the scene's many elements. This approach will prove more difficult, but it will enable the editor to hide any mistakes in the dance or lip-synching, which can start from scratch with each new shot. Given Margaret O'Brien's age (six during most of the filming), the director will probably welcome the possibilities afforded by this second approach, knowing, however, that he will have to rely on his "continuity girl" to get the matches right.

Did she? Hollywood filmmaking worked hard to keep that question from occurring to us; ideally, we should never be able to

answer it. In this case, however, we know that Minnelli opted for the second method. Although Agnes's slightly changed position between shots 1 and 3 offers one clue, we have a more obvious one: Tootie's slippers, pink and plain in shot 1, have become blue and tasseled in shot 3.

(with Aylon Ben-Ami and Thomas Obed)

 at (Agnes's and Bertrand Russell's)

In the opening kitchen sequence, Agnes sits holding her cat, Lady Babby, preparing to decorate her with a blue ribbon. After three shots (lasting 26 seconds) of Mrs. Smith, Grandpa, and Rose, the camera rediscovers Agnes, completing a bow in the ribbon that now encircles Lady Babby's neck.

In "The Existence of Matter" section of *The Problems of Philosophy*, Bertrand Russell used a similar scene to demonstrate the logical usefulness of assuming physical objects' existence:

If the cat appears at one moment in one part of the room, and at another in another part, it is natural to suppose that it has moved from the one to the other, passing over a series of intermediate positions. But if it is merely a set of sense-data, it cannot have ever been in any place where I did not see it; thus we shall have to suppose that it did not exist at all while I was not looking, but suddenly sprang into being in a new place.

The cinema, however, complicates Russell's logic. Although the viewer can reasonably assume that Agnes has simply put the ribbon on her cat while the camera wasn't looking, both Agnes and Lady Babby are *simultaneously* existing objects (referents) and mere "sense-data" (images). To the extent that they are the latter, they *can* "suddenly spr[i]ng into being in a new place"; see Buster Keaton's *Sherlock Jr.*, where the hero "enters" an ongoing movie, only to have his tangible existence displaced (by rapid cuts) from house to garden to street to cliff to jungle to desert to railroad track to ocean to snow bank to garden again—without even a nod to the intermediate positions. In fact, with the movies, I must inevitably acknowledge that an object or person "did not exist at all while I was not looking"; see Godard's *Breathless*, which represents a complex event (Belmondo's being refused the key to a girlfriend's apartment, stealing it, taking the elevator, entering the flat, washing up in the bathroom, and emerging into the main room) in only two shots, the intermediate positions having been entirely ignored.

Hollywood cinema, however, always encourages us to infer continuous existence. Elaborating on his cat example, Russell offers this argument:

> If the cat exists whether I see it or not, we can understand
> from our own experience how it gets hungry between one meal
> and the next, but if it does not exist when I am not seeing it, it
> seems odd that appetite should grow during non-existence as
> fast as during existence.

In other words, because *Meet Me in St. Louis* fosters the belief that the Smiths exist, even when we are not looking, we can watch them eat.[2]

(with Michael Sarrow)

Christmas Tree (at the Ball)

Just as *Meet Me in St. Louis*'s polycentric opening on Kensington Avenue evokes Lumière, John Truitt's surprise appearance at the Christmas ball resembles the work of Méliès. Esther dances behind the Christmas tree with

Grandpa, but emerges on the other side with John. By choosing an entirely *visual* solution to Esther's datelessness (the movie offers no explanation for John's tuxedo), Minnelli revives devices perfected by silent cinema. While Méliès would almost certainly have effected John's arrival with trick photography (stopping the camera after Esther and Grandpa's disappearance behind the tree, restarting it for John), Minnelli films the event in one shot, thereby rejecting Méliès' "cinematic" method for one more associated with the theater.

(with Jodie Mack)

Curtains

Located at the border between two spaces (real or imaginary), curtains in movies often function evocatively. Near the end of the Halloween sequence, for example, after Esther has returned to the dining room, but before Mr. Smith's arrival, a single white

lace curtain, motionless in all of the scene's other shots, suddenly flutters gently in the background. Making sense of that brief movement requires the viewer to imagine an entire life outside the frame: an outdoors, a lawn, a fall night, a freshening wind. (One might begin this construction by assembling all of the images of 5135 Kensington Avenue, which add up to an incomplete house.)

Minnelli also uses curtains and windows to frame important moments. "The Boy Next Door" sequence, for example, recalls a nearly identical scene in *Love Finds Andy Hardy*, where Garland as Betsy Booth had looked longingly through a window toward another "boy next door" (Andy), whose house, like John Truitt's, sat to the immediate right of her own.

The *Meet Me in St. Louis* number begins "naturally," with Esther's song emerging from her previous conversation with Rose. After strolling past the stairs, Esther moves to the windowsill, and the camera cuts to a vantage point outside the house, framing her on a stage bordered by the curtains and the (unusually large)

window. By retaining the frame while eliminating the theater audience, Minnelli intensifies the sequence's voyeuristic appeal, making the viewer feel as if Judy Garland is putting on a show only for him. Minnelli concludes with a flourish, openly acknowledging the performance's theatrical quality by having Esther draw the curtain across her face, and the imaginary stage. (For another cinematic use of curtains, see *The Maltese Falcon*: Curtains.)

(with Aylon Ben-Ami, Michael Kane, Renee Moilanen)

Dalmatians

The scene of Colonel Darly dropping off Rose begins with a close-up of his two Dalmatians. First possibility: the Dalmatians as signifiers of wealth. Pure-bred, slightly exotic in origin, dutiful, and purchased in matching pairs, the dogs suit a rich "colonel" with a decided

streak of dandyism, the owner represented by his breed (as with Mr. Braukoff and his bulldog, attired in its studded leather collar). Second possibility: the dogs as eccentric ornamentation, of a piece with Grandpa's hats, clocks, and weapons, details that don't so much "mean" as contribute to an atmosphere. In fact, however, Dalmatians, hardy working dogs with boundless energy, often accompanied carriages through busy streets, clearing the way with their barking. The dogs, in other words, actually served a purpose that the filmmakers assumed the audience would remember. When the memory of that purpose fades, the floodgates of interpretation open. This sort of fading occurs continually with *Meet Me in St. Louis*, where cribbage, carriage steps, and corsets all drift toward the realms of the alien and inexplicable, formerly domestic objects made exotic by our forgetting. Thus, nostalgia reveals itself as a patient exoticism, a fantasy of the previously familiar.

(with Spencer Hall)

D~irt~

As Esther tries to comfort Tootie, sobbing amid her beheaded snow people, the movie provides a shot of Mr. Smith watching from an upstairs window. The subsequent reverse-shots of the girls, taken from a greater distance, will now appear as *his* views, as

the perspective acquires a diegetic source (a procedure known as "suturing"). After tucking Agnes back into bed, Mr. Smith starts down the front stairs, passing the landing's newspaper-wrapped grandfather clock and a lightly shaded space on the wall where a painting used to hang. The moment's melancholy will prompt his sudden decision not to move. A careful inspection of the wall, however, reveals that the undersides of the now-removed painting is not, in fact, any lighter. Instead, the area surrounding the frame has been smeared with dirt to make the newly uncovered section appear lighter by contrast.

The "dirt" suggests the Smiths' coal heating and its inevitable carbon residue, a period detail forgotten after the 1904 fair's spectacular light show prompted the switch to electricity. For the movie, of course, Minnelli could not leave the picture up long enough for the underlying wall to become significantly lighter than its surroundings; the set, after all, did not use coal heat. Instead, the filmmakers code for the *effect* of time. The dirt amounts to *Meet Me in St. Louis*'s equivalent of *Citizen Kane*'s "damaged" newsreel.

(*with Michael Kane and Charlotte Taylor*)

D_{og}

Mr. Braukoff's bulldog, like almost any animal in the movies, occupies a strange middle ground between prop and actor. Although the animal comes directly from Sally Benson's story, he does something in the movie never mentioned in the fiction: he instinctively licks the flour off the doorstep. In the highly constructed world of *Meet Me in St. Louis*, this moment reveals the camera's secret automatism, celebrated by the surrealists and André Bazin. As the bulldog gives in to pure impulse, the apparatus simply watches, *recording* the dog's behavior rather than manufacturing it.

(*with Scott Balcerzak*)

ntrance (Mr. Smith's)

As the family sits in the dining room, eating ice cream after the flurry of Halloween adventures (a scene that reveals Garland's left-handedness), Mr. Smith suddenly enters. Although Esther's previous arrival has been announced by the offscreen, right, sound of the front door's closing, neither a door nor footsteps precedes Mr. Smith, whose abrupt appearance from a direction without a previously established door seems uncanny. In fact, this stealthy entrance is narratively motivated. With all immediate crises averted (Tootie's lip has been repaired, Esther and John have overcome their shyness), the movie seems to be ending after running for barely an hour. Mr. Smith's abrupt entrance, however, resembles his only other noticeable arrival, when he halts Rose's and Esther's singing of "Meet Me in St. Louis" and does his unwitting best to ruin Rose's long-distance call. Mr. Smith's entrances, in other words, disrupt utopia, and the unexpectedness of this one implies that something bad is about to happen. It will: Mr. Smith announces the move to New York.

(with Michael Kane)

 air

By bringing the sights of the world to normal people in provincial towns, the 1904 World's Fair (or, as Tootie properly calls it, the Louisiana Purchase Exhibition) functions as a metaphor for Hollywood's idealized image of itself. Certainly the actual fair dealt in the exotic, offering the following:

> the first hot dogs, ice cream cones, iced tea, cotton candy, Dr. Pepper, and peanut butter
>
> a reproduction of the Alps
>
> a tiger skull containing a chronometer
>
> a moving picture theater, giving many people their first view of the cinema

a 12-country Olympics, with an artificial lake where at least three athletes contracted fatal cases of typhoid

a twice-daily staging of the Boer War

a sculpted bear made entirely of prunes

the first air conditioner

a statue of Theodore Roosevelt sculpted in butter

nine Eskimo families and several African pygmies

a shopping mall

an electric broiler that cooked a steak in six minutes

Thomas Eakins's paintings, displayed in the American Pavilion

Meet Me in St. Louis, of course, shows very few of these things, restricted by budget to portraying the fair metonymically, with stereotypically clad types and nationalities (nuns, Arabs, Indian soldiers, blacks, girls in Tyrolean costume), Warren Sheffield's reference to "the French restaurant" and Tootie's to the Galveston

Flood reenactment, Agnes's cotton candy, the marble statues and fountain, and the concluding electric light show. Near the end, Minnelli reverses the movie's opening by zooming *out* from the

Smith family to a larger shot of the fair, returning for the last shot to a medium close-up of Esther and John.

Here is the story of an event not covered by *Meet Me in St. Louis*: just north of the fair lay the Bad Lands, a red-light district where proper ladies never went alone, and men could find gambling, prostitutes, and nickelodeons, the first movie theaters. In the spring of 1904, a promoter named Richard Norris built a 16,000-seat arena and announced that starting on Sunday, 5 June, he would stage bullfights. He signed Spanish bullfighter Don Emanuel Cervera and 35 others to five- and six-month contracts.

Norris decorated his amphitheater with colorful Spanish streamers, and he sent men with megaphones to the nearby trolley lines to lure customers. Although the promoter's advance publicity had provoked local humane societies and women's groups into protests against bullfighting, Norris's opening day attracted 8,000 spectators, each paying a dollar. With police ringing the arena, the event began at 3 p.m. with a parade from a Wild West show, taking a day off from its duties at the fair (closed on Sundays). Its members, Native Americans, had been paid $500 for the parade and a lacrosse demonstration, but the crowd, impatient for the bullfights, booed them out of the amphitheater.

Even when eight matadors entered the arena, the hostile crowd expressed its dissatisfaction, quieting only when "young boys in bright blue shirts" arrived to decorate the area with brightly colored cloth. Precisely as they finished their preparations, however, sheriffs arrived with an injunction ordering the show's cancellation. Norris quickly refused any refunds, prompting half the crowd to leave. The other half grew increasingly angry.

"By 5:30 PM," Elana V. Fox reports, "the remaining crowd of around 2,000 had turned into a mob and began wrecking the amusement company's office, breaking windows and fighting among themselves and [with the] management." Returning to the arena, crowd members released three of the bulls, revealed as "merely mild-mannered, half emaciated steers from the East St. Louis slaughterhouse." Sensing a fraud, the enraged crowd set fire to the arena, whose tar-paper roof quickly went up in flames, which were blown by a suddenly rising wind toward the fair itself. The fair's own fire department extinguished the blaze, but not before Norris's amphitheater had burned to the ground. Norris threatened suit against the humane societies, but evidence of other confidence-man stunts left him without legal remedy.

Four nights later, American matador E. Carlton Bass killed Don Emanuel Cervera, who had attacked him with a knife in an argument. At the trial, which acquitted Bass on the grounds of self-defense, other matadors testified that they had known that Norris's bulls were not the real thing. When they had complained to Norris, however, he had assured them "that there would be no bullfight and that local officials would stop the event" before it began. Starting on 12 June, just one week after the Bad Lands fire, Bass started working in a local vaudeville theater, where he performed mock bullfights as long as the fair stayed open.[3]

(with Erika Bloch, Michael Kane, Nikki Schiwal, Stephanie Taylor)

F lower

The scene of Rose and Esther watching John Truitt with his new pipe demonstrates why most classic Hollywood continuity errors go unnoticed. The sequence occurs in five shots, with transitions following the basic rules of shot/reverse-shot, point-of-view editing:

Shot 1: a tracking shot follows the sisters as they walk out onto their porch, with John standing on the

neighboring lawn, carefully centered between them, while a man across the street mows grass in the background. The girls turn together toward John.

Shot 2: a reverse-angle, medium long shot of the girls sitting on the porch fence, separated by a post, but staring together at John and turning still further in his direction.

Shot 3: a medium shot of John from the sisters' point of view.

Shot 4: a reverse-angle, soft-focus close-up of Esther, staring dreamily.

Shot 5: a return to shot 1's set-up, with John walking out of the image, presumably back to his own front door.

The continuity mistake occurs between shots 4 and 5. In shot 4, Esther sits immediately next to a corner post, idly caressing a flower with her left hand. Shot 5, however, finds her several feet *away* from the post and without the flower.

The faulty match remains undetectable at normal viewing speeds, rendered invisible by the shots' brevity: the entire sequence lasts only 30 seconds, with shots 2, 3, and 4 together accounting for only 9. Other factors are also at work. The shot/reverse-shot pattern, enabling a view unavailable in a previous shot, always summons the viewer's attention to new information. Thus, the transition from shot 4's close-up of Esther to shot 5, by renewing interest in John (missing from shot 4), discourages any notice of Esther's unmatched posture.

But one factor in particular causes the error to go un-detected: in shot 4, *no one is looking at the flower*. That shot is, above all else, an image of Judy Garland, and a star inevitably monopolizes the viewer's gaze, forestalling any drift to peripheral details.

A research question: how important is shot 4's two-second length? How long does a shot have to last before a star's hold on the viewer is released?

(with Michael Kane)

F olsey

George Folsey, *Meet Me in St. Louis*'s cinematographer, worked on over 60 movies, including *Forbidden Planet*, the 1956 science fiction adaptation of *The Tempest*, with a version of Caliban described by Pauline Kael as "a marvelously flamboyant monster out of Freud—pure id." *Meet Me in St. Louis* offers a different Freudian story, the family romance, haunted by the persistent threats of violence, the actual acts of aggression, the spanking that never comes, the incestuous sibling tension, the rage of an impotent father, and the incongruous Halloween scene, replete with its allusions to fascism, cross-dressing, and arbitrary prejudice.

Other titles on Folsey's resume also seem to refer to *Meet Me in St. Louis*: *The Price of Possession* (home ownership as inertia), *What's Wrong with the Women?* (Mr. Smith's question), *The Fear Market* (a title for a hypothetical film containing only the intensities and thwarted perversities of overdetermined scenes), *The Savage* (Tootie), *No Place to Go* ("We're going to stay here till we rot!"), *Glorifying the American Girl* (Minnelli's intentions with Garland), and *The Shining Hour* (the arcadia of turn-of-the-century St. Louis).[4]

(with Spencer Hall)

 # G arland

Judy Garland represents the extreme case of extradiegetic knowledge affecting the response to a star's performance. Almost everyone now encountering *Meet Me in St. Louis* for the first time has some awareness of what happened to her: the calamitous marriages, the persistent addictions, the increasingly mannered performances, the premature death. She had the misfortune to live through the studio system's own cycles: the all-powerful maturity that determined her roles and exacerbated her anxieties, and the abrupt senescence that left her unprotected. Garland's image was unmoored to any central, stable personality: hence the wigs, the fluctuating weight, the constructed features, edited and revised over and over again by a long stream of uncredited contributors.

Despite all of Minnelli's efforts, by *Meet Me in St. Louis*, she has already lost some of the effortless adolescent beauty that made her best role the one she most quickly repudiated: as Betsy Booth in three Andy Hardy movies. There we rediscover the perpetual surprise of Garland, the shy girl becoming the life of the party, the big voice in the little body, the bravura manner always implying a barely concealed sadness.

(with Spencer Hall)

Gaslight

Although *gaslight* has become the name for an entire era, those last decades before electricity, the Smiths' chandelier is a hybrid device, with both gas and electric lights. Thus, it resembles the house's kitchen sink, a similar technological mix of modern faucets and a black hand-pump.

These peripheral details portray the Smiths' world as in transition. We should not, however, make too much of this point. What period of the last 150 years has not been "in transition"? The automobile, sound recording, the cinema, radio, aviation, atomic power, television, video tape, computers—each of these innovations has dramatically transformed the way we live. Thus, at any moment, we inhabit what Roland Barthes called "a vast 'dissolve,'" a complex superimposition of an old world receding and a new one coming into view.

Because gaslights have to be *extinguished*, the Smiths' chandelier occasions one of *Meet Me in St. Louis*'s most romantic scenes: Esther and John moving shyly through a gradually darkening room. Electric lights, on the other hand, just get *switched off*. Walter Benjamin noticed the difference, citing Robert Louis Stevenson's fond description of

> *the rhythm with which lamplighters go through the streets and light one lantern after another. At first this rhythm contrasted with the uniformity of the dusk, but now the contrast is with the brutal shock caused by the spectacle of entire cities suddenly being illuminated by electric light.*

Or the spectacle of entire fair grounds suddenly lit by Edison's generators. The point here is complex: the turn-of-the-century idyll celebrated by *Meet Me in St. Louis* depends on inconvenience and discomfort—on the primitive transportation that isolated regions and made even a city as large as St. Louis feel like a small town; on the absence of ready-made goods that forced family activities, like bottling ketchup; on the limits of early telephones that turned people into writers; on the radically unequal distribution of wealth that made live-in cooks available for $12 a month. *Meet Me in St. Louis* portrays the idyll and minimizes the discomfort. In doing so, of course, it must often resort to lies: at the kitchen sink, Mrs. Smith washes lettuce in tap water, an impossibility in "Summer 1903," as William R. Everdell shows:

Twain loved the Mississippi, except when it came through a
faucet. The drinking water in St. Louis was, he wrote, "too
thick to drink and too thin to plow. . . . every tumblerfull of it
holds nearly an acre of land in solution." Such richness had
undoubtedly played a large part in giving St. Louis its taste for
beer. Nevertheless, for the millions of visitors it expected for
the great Exposition, St. Louis was prepared to provide
something better. On March 21, 1904, a new filtration plant
north of the city came on line, coagulating and settling the
Missouri silt with large doses of ferrous sulfate and milk of
lime, and the first clear drinking water in the history of St.
Louis began to run out of the taps.

When do we begin to forget the inconveniences and
discomforts? Does photography, which for the first time in human
history enabled people to see what their parents had looked like
when they were young, become our memory? Does the cinema,
with its addition of sound? Noting that electric lights get switched
off, Benjamin made the vital connection:

The invention of the match around the middle of the
nineteenth century brought forth a number of innovations
which have one thing in common: one abrupt movement of
the hand triggers a process of many steps. . . . Of the countless
movements of switching, inserting, pressing, and the like, the
"snapping" of the photographer has had the greatest
consequences. A touch of the finger now sufficed to fix an
event for an unlimited period of time. The camera gave the
moment a posthumous shock.

Thus imagine Minnelli's gaslight scene running side by side
with a color home movie of the same activity, made in 1903. Do
we have a name for the differences between them? *History*?[5]

(*with Kate Casey-Sawicki*)

alloween

Some of the Halloween sequence's production history has become common knowledge: how Benson's version had immediately struck Minnelli ("The scene was the reason I wanted to do the picture"); how he labored over its execution, requiring late hours of the children, especially Margaret O'Brien; and finally, how producer Arthur Freed wanted to cut it because "[i]t's the only scene that doesn't have anything to do with the plot." (Freed ran the film

without the Halloween sequence and blithely changed his mind: "It's not the same picture," he admitted. "Let's put it back.") As with Tootie's other big moment, in the snow, the Halloween sequence represents

a shift in register: when the camera comes upon the bonfire, the movie changes tone, becoming suddenly intense and

mysterious. Certain things seem obvious: the scene's resemblance to newsreel images of Nazi book burning, the children's perverse cross-dressing, the unsettling xenophobia directed at Mr. Braukoff. And yet, despite these conventional explanations, the images of the children around the fire and

of Tootie's solitary walk down a suddenly autumnal Kensington Avenue will continue to haunt viewers. The enormous cart wheel protruding from the pile of burning furniture; the stray leaves falling beside the children; the horse and buggy,

alone and unaccounted for; the dust rising from the road, swept by the wind; the shadows of tree limbs on Mr. Braukoff's house; the Tiffany lamp he uses to read—these details accumulate to create less an anecdote than a *mood*.

Gregory Ulmer has argued that the movies are particularly good at this kind of thing. With electronic culture, syllogistic logic gives way to mood, and rational assessment to something like meditation. The Halloween sequence, in other words, does not offer an *argument*. And yet it prompts a series of illuminations—about the Smith family's birth order and childhood fear, about the way night can make even your own neighborhood seem desolate and unfamiliar, about the sudden change of seasons and the neighbors who live down the street. The scene's power arises precisely from the reason Freed wanted it eliminated: having nothing to do with the movie's ostensible plot lines (Rose and Warren Sheffield, the boy next door, the New York move), the Halloween sequence recalls Sherlock Holmes's comment about Lord Baskerville's missing boot: "It is important *because it is inexplicable*." Like a continuity error, the scene amounts to an effect without a cause. (Imagine, for example, how changing Tootie's destination to John Truitt's house would simultaneously connect her adventure to the main story *and banalize it*.) The Halloween sequence also resembles what Freud called a "screen memory," an anecdotal recollection marked by both vivid persistence and apparent irrelevance. Freud thought that such memories held the key to treatment; they amounted to the patient's unconscious in miniature. (Again the conjectural method: the marginal as the way in. But who is the Halloween sequence's "patient"?) Nothing will come of the children's mischief or of Tootie's bravery, but the movie will not quite be able to forget this mood, darker and more fearful than anything before it.[6]

(*with Paul Johnson*)

Hats

With its swarm of activity and confined space, "The Trolley Song" sequence might easily have regressed to the era of *Tom, Tom, the Piper's Son* (1905), where the combination of excessive detail and a polycentric mise-en-scène produced illegibility. Noël Burch describes primitive cinema's effect:

> The panoramic tableau *of the most characteristic early films offers two basic traits. . . . First there is the relative rareness of any of the indexes of individualization/differentia-tion. . . . Secondly, there is the tendency to confront the spectator's gaze with an entire surface* to scan. At times the gaze is directed along a relatively controlled trajectory (but one which generally took in most of the screen's surface). At other times the gaze is undirected, due to the absence of most of the ordering procedures—strategies of isolation or signalization—which . . . would gradually make it possible to normalize the behaviour of the spectator's eye. . . . As we know, the first step in overcoming this "handicap" was the dissection of the tableau into successive fragments (closer shots), each governed by a single signifier, so that each frame

*would be immediately decipherable (at least in accordance
with certain norms of legibility)* at first viewing.

The trolley scene challenges Hollywood's centering procedures; Esther, after all, is surrounded by swirling color and
movement, as well as a group of undifferentiated characters.
Nevertheless, it looks nothing like a turn-of-the-century film.
Minnelli starts by "dissect[ing] . . . the tableau into successive
fragments," breaking the 4 minute, 56 second, sequence into 14
shots, each carefully centered.

Shot 1 begins with a close-up of the trolley's "Skinker
Road" sign being replaced by "Special to Fair Grounds."
The camera pulls back to a crowded tableau, but the
motivated pan to the right follows four boys pulling
the trolley cable to the rear.

Shot 2 offers a medium shot of Esther, gradually
surrounded (and even obscured) by a flurry of arriving

boys and girls. They part to reveal her, perfectly
centered in the frame.

Shot 3: a close-up of Esther looking for John Truitt.

Shot 4 returns to shot 2, and the camera pans left to
follow people boarding the trolley, leaving Esther
offscreen, right.

Shot 5: a medium shot of Esther, now isolated, with
only a few background figures (differentiated by being

much older). As in shot 4, a left pan follows her as she boards the trolley.

Shot 6: medium shot of the trolley's crowded front. Because this image contains no narratively recognizable characters, it might appear less controlled. It is, however, still an *arranged* shot, with the trolley's roof, sides, and fence framing the riders, while the conductor's uniform provides an organizing focus.

Shot 7 begins on a close-up of a skirt moving up the steps; it passes out of the frame to reveal Esther, framed by the trolley's protective bars. The camera pans left, keeping her centered as she moves through the packed car.

Shot 8: a centered medium shot of Esther at the trolley's rear; the camera pans right as she starts up the steps.

Shot 9's medium shot completes Esther's climb, begun in shot 8. The camera pans right, following Esther through the crowd, keeping her centered. She sits between two girls, but the one screen right promptly moves, allowing Esther more room and separating her from the others.

Shot 10: medium close-up of Esther looking. Camera pulls back to show everyone looking offscreen, left.

Shot 11: close-up of Esther looking excited.

Shot 12: medium shot of John Truitt running to catch
the trolley.

Shot 13: medium shot of Esther, who starts to sing
"The Trolley Song," centered amid three girls with
hats. Three other girls join in, making a ring around
Esther. She stands, and the camera pans left to follow
her. Lasting 1 minute, 58 seconds, this long take
contains most of Garland's famous performance.

Shot 14: beginning on the climactic line "Stop, stop, stop went my heart-strings," cut to a medium close-up of Esther. The camera pulls back to show John Truitt arriving screen right.

The sequence, in other words, deploys the "strategies of isolation" (centering, motivated camera movements) developed by Hollywood cinema to makes its images immediately accessible. It also relies on "individualization" and "differentiation" to corral the spectator's potentially wandering eye. Casting Judy Garland as Esther plays the biggest role in this process. (Imagine the illegibility that might result from staging the same sequence with an unfamiliar actress as Esther.) The presence of a star always serves as a decisive centering device: like Wallace Stevens's "jar in Tennessee," Garland "organizes" everything around her. The decision to leave her hatless also distinguishes her from the other riders, all of whom, male or female, wear hats. It also makes her character seem more modern. In fact, stardom inevitably *modernizes* a part: Errol Flynn's "Robin Hood" seems more contemporary than medieval, and Garland's hatless "Esther" never quite seems turn of the century.[7]

(with Paul Johnson)

Hotel Delmonico

Although the movie locates Rose's suitor, Warren Sheffield, in a phone booth in New York's Hotel Delmonico, the twentieth-century version of that hotel only opened in 1929. MGM, which once located Paris on the ocean, could probably safely assume that few viewers would spot the anachronism. Delmonico, a Wall Street restaurant that gave its name to a steak, had long suggested wealth and sophistication. Presented with a choice of New York hotels (the Waldorf, the Plaza, the Biltmore), the scriptwriters may have chosen "Delmonico" because it *seems* the most associated with an earlier era: *Life with Father*, a model for *Meet Me in St. Louis*, had opened with an 1880s scene set in Delmonico's Restaurant.

(*with Megan Basham*)

 ce

Mr. Neeley's ice wagon represents precisely the kind of syndecdochic detail regularly deployed by Hollywood cinema: like Esther's corset, it is shorthand for an entire era. Nevertheless, the movie's nostalgic image of the horse-drawn cart is ruthlessly ironic. With its electric

light shows, 140 automobiles (driven from as far away as Boston), dishwashers, wireless telegraphy, and mechanized refrigeration ("mechanical refrigeration offers much that is spectacular," proclaimed one ad), the 1904 World's Fair would signal the death throes of Mr. Neeley's world. The year before had already seen the founding of the Ford Motor Company and the publication of Frederick Taylor's *Shop Management*, which proposed a method for scientifically organizing labor. As Tootie sits blithely singing in the back of the wagon, and the last few blocks of ice lie melting under their tarpaulins, this once-familiar routine of everyday life is on the verge of obsolescence. Designed to evoke the gentle quaintness of turn-of-the-century life, Mr. Neeley's wagon and the dissolving ice only suggest its difficulties: the deadly provincialism, the nonexistent sanitation, the claustrophobic, endless summer heat.

(*with Nic Jelley, Michael Kane, Michael Sarrow, Matt Selvagn*)

ockey

Esther's first appearance in *Meet Me in St. Louis* occurs as her buggy pulls up to the Smiths' carriage step, a precisely placed signifier (like the muddy road) of turn-of-the-centuryness. Just to the step's right stands a miniature statue of a black jockey, its right arm extended in greeting. While the carriage step amounts merely to an obsolete utility, nostalgia's idea of a more graceful time (eliding the uncomfortable realities of horse-drawn convey-ances), the lawn jockey represents an obsolete ideology, a tacit racism perpetuated by the movie. Although 1903 St. Louis included 97,000 African Americans, blacks appear in the film only as art (the Smiths' African bust), an unacknowledged source (for Esther and Tootie's cakewalk, a slave dance step), and exotica (the fair's two men wearing Arab headdress). This exclusion of blacks suits the Smiths' self-satisfied provinciality, camouflaged as whimsy: "Wasn't I lucky to have been born in my favorite city?" Tootie sighs to Mr. Neeley. The exposition itself practiced an explicit racism, restricting black attendance to certain "Negro Days" and black employment almost completely. Its organizer,

Frederick J. V. Skiff, intended the fair to provide "a living museum of the differences between races and cultures," including "Anthropology Days," described by William R. Everdell as an "intercultural Olympics," "a way of determining the differing fitnesses of the races." One of the fair's most popular exhibits displayed eight African pygmies, brought back from the Congo by Samuel P. Verner, "a Protestant missionary turned African explorer," commissioned a year before by the fair's "anthropology department." Verner had actually bought one of the pygmies.

When does an ideological disposition become visible? In *S/Z*, Roland Barthes showed that certain stereotypes ("This was woman herself, with her sudden fears, her irrational whims, her instinctive worries, her impetuous boldness, her fussings, and her delicious sensibility"), protected from scrutiny by their collective, anonymous origins, would persist in seeming part of "the natural order." While organized intervention (e.g., feminism) can strip away this disguise, making ideology visible takes time. Thus, although we now notice the black jockey, *Meet Me in St. Louis*'s original (white) audiences almost certainly did not. Hence the movies' status as a kind of archaeological record: *this* is what we once believed. In Hollywood cinema, those beliefs almost never surfaced as explicit formulations; instead, at their most powerful, their most consensual, they appeared merely *as objects*, left behind like a mysterious code, simultaneously mute and eloquent.[8]

(with Spencer Hall, Michael Sarrow, Stephanie Taylor)

etchup

Four scenes about ketchup, taken from the movie's first sequences:

Scene 1

Mrs. Smith [standing over the stove, stirring an enormous pot]: *Best ketchup we ever made, Katie.*

Katie [tasting the ketchup with a spoon]: *Too sweet.*

Mrs. Smith: *Mr. Smith likes it on the sweet side.*

Katie: *All men like it on the sweet side. It's too sweet, Mrs. Smith. [Adds vinegar]*

Scene 2

Lon, Jr. [tasting ketchup]: *Too flat.*

Katie [dismissively]: *You can always put spice in, but you can't take it out.*

Scene 3

Esther [tasting ketchup]: *Too sour?*

Mrs. Smith [triumphantly]: *Just what I told Katie.*

Scene 4

Katie [as Grandpa tastes ketchup]: *Too sweet?*

Mrs. Smith: *Too sour?*

Grandpa: *Too thick! [Starts to add liquid]*

Meet Me in St. Louis portrays ketchup making as a communal, oral practice (the Smiths don't follow a written recipe), whose results issue from trial and error or family tradition. As such, it represents the kind of activity transformed by what Walter Benjamin called "mechanical reproduction," or by what Taylor and Ford termed "standardization." As Benjamin noted, a photograph can be reproduced endlessly, without modification, and Ford's Model T's were identical, made to an exact plan. Soon after *Meet Me in St. Louis*'s time, Heinz ketchup would become the same ketchup, no matter where you bought it. The great celebrant of this kind of mechanical reproduction was Andy Warhol:

> *What's great about this country is that America started the tradition where the richest consumers buy essentially the same things as the poorest. You can be watching TV and see Coca-Cola, and you know the President drinks Coke, Liz Taylor drinks Coke, and just think, you can drink Coke, too. A Coke is a Coke and no amount of money can get you a better Coke than the one the bum on the corner is drinking. All the Cokes are the same and all the Cokes are good. Liz Taylor knows it, the President knows it, the bum knows it, and you know it.*

Although *Meet Me in St. Louis* displays its affection for earlier, less rationalized things like homemade ketchup, the movies themselves, of course, have always been just like Cokes. The print of *Meet Me in St. Louis* screened in Memphis was just as good as the ones shown in New York or London or Paris. They were all the same, and all of them were good. But in 1903, cooking still wasn't like that. What transformed it from an oral, trial-and-error practice to a standardized one? Cookbooks, the Taylorization of rule-of-thumb family methods. (Remember that the wife of Taylor's colleague Frank Gilbreth, whose family is celebrated in *Cheaper by the Dozen*, invented the term "home economics.")

In the "rationalizing" of the family kitchen, one cookbook assumed the decisive role: *Joy of Cooking*. Cookbooks, of course, had existed before, but were not nearly so popular, and *Joy of Cooking* standardized the making of things like ketchup for generations. Still a bestseller, it has been described as "the most important American culinary reference tool of the twentieth century." A book has now appeared (*Stand Facing the Stove*) detailing *Joy of Cooking*'s germination, publication, success, and continuous revisions. From it, we learn the following:

> *Joy of Cooking* appeared in 1931 but only became a bestseller in 1943, just as *Meet Me in St. Louis* was being filmed.

> *Joy of Cooking* had two authors, a mother and daughter (Irma Rombauer and Marion Rombauer Becker). The daughter was born in 1903, the year when *Meet Me in St. Louis* begins. And where were the Rombauers from? St. Louis, of course.[9]

 eaves

What happens when the cinema stages the accidental? As Esther sings "The Boy Next Door," the leaves around her rustle in a studio-manufactured breeze, an homage to the Lumière brothers' *Le Déjeuner de bébé*, whose background foliage had distracted viewers from the intended center of attention, an infant's feeding. But by locating "the third meaning" in details left over *after* the deliberate informational and symbolic messages have been pared away, Roland Barthes proposed the coincidence of the filmic and the *unintentional*. André Bazin, although never cited by Barthes, had made the same argument, celebrating the dust carelessly kicked up by Boudu on a summer road. This tradition diminishes a meticulous craftsman like Minnelli, attentive to every detail. Thus, Barthes's argument strands us without a name for another approach to the movies: if the Lumières' leaves equal "the filmic," what do Minnelli's leaves amount to—"the theatrical"? And, too, where are we now when film's umbilical attachment to the real world, what Bazin called the cinema's "ontology," can be *faked*?[10]

(*with Jody Mack and Michael Sarrow*)

Lockhart, June

The Christmas dance introduces the much-anticipated (and maligned) Lucille Ballard, the New York socialite who enters on the arm of Warren Sheffield and leaves with Lon Smith. June Lockhart, who plays Lucille, predicts the studio system's future. Relatively unsuccessful in film, she will appear regularly in television's *Lassie* (1958–1964), *Lost in Space* (1965–1968), and *Petticoat Junction* (1968–1970), carving out a niche for herself as the *uber*-mom of the new idyll, the televised hometown that will reappear under different names and incarnations: Calverton (*Lassie*), Springfield (*Father Knows Best*), 837 Mill Street (*My Three Sons*), Mayberry (*The Andy Griffith Show*), Central City (*The Many Loves of Dobie Gillis*), Bayport (*The Hardy Boys*). Lockhart would outlast Judy Garland and the studio system, whose monopoly on nostalgia and lost hometowns (Carvel, Bedford Falls) would yield to the pressure of television's lower-cost reveries, stories delivered weekly with predictable plotting and a maximum of convenience. Thus the tension between Lucille Ballard (Lockhart), the representative of television's looming threat, and Esther Smith (Garland), a child of the studio system, becomes clear. Lucille doesn't aim to steal Warren Sheffield from Rose; she intends to steal hometown nostalgia from the movies.

(with Spencer Hall)

eet Me in St. Louis"

"*Meet Me in St. Louis*" (1904)
lyrics by Andrew B. Sterling, music by Kerry Mills

When Louis came home to the flat,
He hung up his coat and his hat.
He gazed all around, but no wifey he found,
So he said, "Where can Flossie be at?"
A note on the table he spied.
He read it just once then he cried.
It ran, "Louis dear, it's too slow for me here,
So I think I will go for a ride."

CHORUS

"Meet me in St. Louis, Louis,
Meet me at the Fair.
Don't tell me the lights are shining
Any place but there.
We will dance the Hoochee Koochee,
I will be your tootsie wootsie,
If you will meet me in St. Louis, Louis,
Meet me at the Fair."

The dresses that hung in the hall
Were gone, she had taken them all.
She took all the rings and the rest of his things,
The picture he missed from the wall.
"What! moving?" the janitor said,
"Your rent is paid three months ahead."
"What good is the flat?" said poor Louis, "Read that."
And the janitor smiled as he read.

CHORUS

The film carefully omits the song's verses, which clash with the movie's values. As sung by the Smiths, "Meet Me in St. Louis" evokes families and home; the missing verses depict infidelity and restlessness. When they resurface on the soundtrack CD (as the ghost in the machine), they seem casually vulgar, blatantly indiscreet. When sung by Garland, the suppressed verses confirm how much the movie depends on disallowing even the most fleeting glimpses of a St. Louis where people live in flats instead of houses and have names like "Flossie" instead of Anna or Rose. The Smiths' perfectly homogeneous world resembles the miniature universe of a child's toy, enclosed in glass. It even snows on Christmas when you turn it upside down.

(with Erika Bloch)

Midwestern Musicals

Show Boat

Oklahoma!

Meet Me in St. Louis

Annie Get Your Gun

State Fair

Bye Bye Birdie

The Music Man

Big River

Although the 1930s Astaire-Rogers films followed Broadway (and especially Cole Porter) by setting the musical in a sophisticated, cosmopolitan milieu, *Oklahoma!* returned it to "Americana," almost always defined by small towns and a mythical Midwest. Oscar Hammerstein II proved crucial to this transformation, cowriting *Show Boat*, *Oklahoma!* and *State Fair*, while coproducing *Annie Get Your Gun*. He almost had a hand in *Meet Me in St. Louis*, but his song "Boys and Girls Like You and Me" (written with Richard Rodgers for *Oklahoma!*) was dropped at the last minute.

(with Thomas Obed)

Mirror

How to make sense of a
photographed mirror? As Esther
and Tootie make their exit after
the cakewalk, a background
mirror reflects a table's objects.
When we look at a mirror, we
are used to seeing our own
reflection; photographing a
mirror, however, *cuts it off* from

our world and restricts its use to the movie's diegesis; the Smiths'
mirror will no longer show us ourselves. In the theater, however,
an actual mirror (like an operating clock) functions simultaneously in the worlds of both fiction and spectator; maintaining
the play's spell, therefore, will require its careful placement so that
audience members don't get distracted watching themselves.
Although mirrors and clocks would seem to belong to a large class
of theatrically treacherous objects, that class is, in fact, far smaller
than would first appear. While most things onstage have the
potential to work for a spectator (e.g., a pen, a coffee pot, a gun, a
telephone), they almost never achieve the doubled status of a
mirror or clock: can we imagine a telephone capable of *simultaneous* use by both character and audience? We need a name for
this small group: *mirror objects*? In effect, Stanley Cavell links
cinematic realism to its elimination of mirror objects, to a
photographed mirror's inability to reproduce us: "Photography
maintains the presentness of the world by accepting our absence
from it. The reality in a photograph is present to me *while I am not
present to it.*"[11]

(*with Jodie Mack*)

Mother

In just 3 years, Mary Astor, *The Maltese Falcon*'s femme fatale, has become the mother in *Meet Me in St. Louis*, a role she would also play in the 1949 version of *Little Women*, another narrative organized around a family's female members. While conventional thematics would attribute these roles to World War II's removal of men from the home, the more interesting questions involve Astor, always hovering between leading lady and character actress. In 1944, Mary Astor was 38, old enough to be the mother of the five Smith children (Mrs. Smith, after all, married at 17). But she had already played Judy Garland's mother 6 years earlier, in 1938's *Listen, Darling*, when she was barely 32. She is clearly not a pure character actress like Marjorie Main (Katie), but her fees indicate that she never quite became a great star. For 1942's *The Palm Beach Story*, for example, she earned roughly the same amount as Rudy Vallee and leading man Joel McCrea, but less than half of Claudette Colbert's $150,000. In 1936, while engaged in a custody battle for her daughter, Astor was surprised by the newspaper publication of what purported to be her diary, a shockingly pornographic document offering a notorious "box score," grading the many men with whom she had supposedly slept. Most of what appeared was probably a forgery, but as Astor wryly summed up the situation, "I had achieved the reputation of being the greatest nympho-courtesan since Pompadour." That only 8 years later she could believably play the proper mother of

Meet Me in St. Louis's Smith family indicates popular culture's amnesia. Hollywood casting always relied on physiology, not biography.[12]

(with Scott Balcerzak and Heather Visser)

Mrs. Wilkins

As Tootie rides the ice wagon on its rounds, the horse stops unexpectedly at a house, prompting Mr. Neeley's explanation: "Robin just can't seem to remember that Mrs. Wilkins has moved." Later, however, as Agnes and Tootie prepare for Halloween, Rose comes into the kitchen to report, "Mama, that was Mrs. Wilkins. She said she'd leave her hammock all folded on the porch, and would the children *please* bring it back when they're through stealing it." Has Mrs. Wilkins moved to another house on Kensington Avenue, or has the movie simply forgotten its earlier mention of her? "Mrs. Wilkins" suggests Hollywood's economy of signs, its estimate of the information needed to convey "a neighborhood." Despite its opening bustle, the film will name only three of the street's residents: the Truitts, the Braukoffs, and Mrs. Wilkins. Of the rest, we will get merely an occasional signal: the mob of children who appear only on Halloween, the man who rides back and forth on an enormous bicycle, the Circle Beer wagon that passes the house just once. The contradictory references to her indicate how much the movie *needs* "Mrs. Wilkins": wanting to imply a social world around the Smiths, but without the time to develop marginal characters, *Meet Me in St. Louis* must make do with an enforced parsimony that encourages forgetfulness. In fact, omitting the second mention of Mrs. Wilkins would have enhanced the film's realism: to say that she "has moved" would imply that *Meet Me in St. Louis*'s characters have lives that *precede* the film.

(with Spencer Hall and Paul Johnson)

Murder

Tootie's obsession with death and violence haunts *Meet Me in
St. Louis*. She buries dolls she has declared dead from "four fatal
diseases"; she insists that she has seen dead bodies in the river;
she "murders" Mr. Braukoff with flour on Halloween; she falsely
accuses John Truitt of trying "to kill" her, when, in fact, she and
Agnes have almost run the trolley off its tracks; and finally, she
hacks her snow family to pieces, sobbing, "I'd rather kill them if
we can't take them with us." Tootie will grow out of this *grand
guignol* and become Sally Benson. (Or maybe not: only the year
before *Meet Me in St. Louis*, Sally Benson had cowritten Hitchcock's
Shadow of a Doubt, in which a serial killer threatens his own small-
town family.) Agnes is already becoming like the older sisters, her
childish sadism unleashed only at the culturally approved moment, Halloween. Tootie will soon follow. In the meantime,
however, her appetite for violence marks her as the perversely
"innocent" eye celebrated by the surrealists. Robert Desnos
summed up surrealism's call to murder the everyday banality and
hypocrisy of bourgeois life:

> *What can I do, wrote Buñuel in* La Révolution surréaliste,
> *against those fervent admirers of novelty, even if a novelty
> outrages their deepest convictions, against a venal or
> hypocritical press, against the idiotic multitude which has
> pronounced as beautiful or poetic what* [Un Chien
> andalou] *in essence is only a desperate and passionate
> appeal to murder?*

To the extent, as Freud posited, that civilization depends on
repression, Tootie remains a holdout. Ignoring conventional
manners, she responds instinctively to events: as Rose waits
anxiously for Warren's phone call, Tootie brightly suggests,
"Maybe he's got himself another girl." With Esther refusing to face
the probable consequences of leaving St. Louis ("Even if I did go

to New York," she tells John, "we could still work something out"), Tootie's weeping attack on her own snow people expresses what the others have refused to acknowledge: moving is a kind of death. *Meet Me in St. Louis* marks the existence and eventual recuperation of the surrealist ethic; it is invigorated by Tootie's murderous logic.[13]

(*with Kate Casey-Sawicki and Michael Sarrow*)

 ames

In *Meet Me in St. Louis*, the original stories' "Waughop" becomes "Braukoff," a homonym for "beerhead." This unsubtle character-ization reveals the calculus of names permeating the movie. Braukoff reduces to "Germanic," "alcoholic," "hostile," metonym-ized in the name's pronunciation: a severe brow punctuated by the staccato, pestilent burst of a cough. In the midst of World War II, his name stamps him indelibly. (Tootie: "I hate you, Mr. Braukoff!") In comparison, the protagonists' surname, the bland and obviously preferable "Smith," conceals the family's Catholi-cism (present in the book) while also referring to it (New York governor Alfred E. Smith, who in 1928 had become the first Catholic presidential candidate). The universal Anglo-American surname, redolent of industry and steadiness, Smith carries no negative connotations.

Meet Me in St. Louis's attention to onomastics does not stop with last names. "Rose" conceals a patriotic overture to a wartime president, *Rose-a-velt*, which when pronounced in a German manner offers a collision of two languages. The world (*Welt*) belongs to both Rose and Roosevelt: thus, the girl's name offers multilingual propaganda in the guise of a homonym. An apparently exotic name, "Alonzo" turns out to have a famously American, manly antecedent: Amos Alonzo Stagg, the father of American football. And "Esther"?

The superficial, Biblical reading will give way here to another, more complex homophone, *ester*, a type of chemical compound including a telling spectrum of utilities: fats, nitroglycerine, and certain perfumes are all *esters*, containing properties easily ascribed to Judy Garland, phobic about fat, explosive in both charm and neuroses, and noncloyingly sweet in the movies.

(with Spencer Hall)

Newspaper

In *Meet Me in St. Louis*'s opening sequence, Mr. Smith arrives home carrying a newspaper, which he takes to read during his hour-long bath. Except for the coming World's Fair, the movie will ignore the outside world, deploying in its stead the stock figures of a nostalgic "past": summer, Halloween, Christmas, family dinners, a boy next door, trolleys, family musicales, tentative courtships, an Irish cook, homemade pies, ice wagons, crushes, snowmen, kisses, first love. What might have been in Mr. Smith's newspaper, that small, barely visible relic from another country?

> a report describing the founding of a new business, the Ford Motor Company, and the production of a new automobile, the Model T

> the U.S. government's attempts to obtain the rights to build (and own) the Panama Canal

> the death of Pope Leo XII (almost certainly noticed by the Catholic Smiths)

> the surprising success of a film called *The Great Train Robbery*

> the Wright brothers' first powered flight, lasting 59 seconds

> the London Congress of the Russian Social Democratic party, during which the party split into two

factions: the Mensheviks and the Bolsheviks (Lenin and Trotsky)

the births of Bob Hope, Bing Crosby, George Orwell, Chill Wills (the ice wagon's Mr. Neeley), and Vincente Minnelli

(with Braden Malnic and Paul Johnson)

New York

Meet Me in St. Louis is at least partially a myth, and as anthropologist Claude Lévi-Strauss has shown, cultures use myths to resolve what in fact are irresolvable dilemmas. The movie develops around the inherent contradiction between family and ambition, confronting Father (and the audience) with an apparently difficult choice: whether or not to leave St. Louis for a promotion in New York. From the start, MGM felt that *Meet Me in St. Louis*'s source, Sally Benson's *New Yorker* stories, lacked what Barthes called "hermeneutic enigmas," those compelling puzzles that make a reader want to know what comes next. In response, the studio invented a love interest for Esther (John Truitt) and greatly expanded the duration of the father's indecision about New York, which Benson had raised and dismissed in only 12 pages.

In the stories, Mr. Smith breaks the news of the move to Mrs. Smith, who then informs the rest of the family. In the movie, however, Mr. Smith announces his relocation to the entire family all at once. The change underlines the narrative cinema's need for speed: the consolidation of the stories' two scenes (Father telling Mother, Mother telling children) into one saves time, helping the film clock in closer to Hollywood's 90-minute standard. It also enables a more compelling mise-en-scène, arranged into a variety of reaction shots of the various family members. The carefully edited group response—a domestic version of *Potemkin*'s Odessa Steps sequence—furthers the family's collective anger at Mr. Smith, filmed here almost entirely in isolation.

Lévi-Strauss demonstrated that myths are structured around concrete oppositions, which function symbolically to organize a culture's thinking about a specific problem. *Meet Me in St. Louis* has as its dominant opposition the contrast between St. Louis and New York:

St. Louis	*New York*
House	Flat/Tenement
Suburb	City
Trolley/Carriage	Subway
Neighbors	Strangers
Family	Career

The film begins as a nostalgic idyll in a past when close family life provided the occasion for all pleasures (parties, family dinners, Halloween, long-distance calls from beaux, singing around the piano, ketchup making) and all pains (above all, the pain of moving). The threat to the Smiths comes disguised as an "opportunity," the chance to move to New York. The movie, in fact, anticipates Vance Packard's *A Nation of Strangers*, with its identification of constant executive relocations as a principal cause of modern anxiety. Minnelli orchestrates *Meet Me in St. Louis*'s opening sequence as a series of homecomings, with each family member entering the Smith house: first John, then Agnes, followed by Esther, Rose, Tootie, and finally Mr. Smith. By film's end, the family has disintegrated: the son has left for college, and two of the girls are now engaged to be married. Thus, the finale shows them *leaving the house* for the fair. New York (and the East in general) represent the future, one that will destroy *Meet Me in St. Louis*'s world.

Charles Eckert once argued that a cultural dilemma appears particularly troubling when a scene's emotional quotient greatly exceeds a story's needs: these spots are white-hot, *overdetermined* (in Freud's term), symptomatic of a problem's insolubility. In *Meet*

Me in St. Louis, the obvious example of this pressure appears when Esther sings "Have Yourself a Merry Little Christmas," one of the most heartbreaking of all Christmas songs, sung under the apparent necessity of choosing an alternative to the domestic values on which the film rests. "Someday soon, we all will be together," Esther sings to Tootie, without being at all sure of it.

But then, of course, magically, the need to choose simply disappears. Father awakens the family just after midnight on Christmas to proclaim that "New York doesn't have the monopoly on opportunity. Why there are plenty of opportunities right here in St. Louis." The film's conclusion, with the family sightseeing at the World's Fair, seems to confirm Father's faith, assuring the audience that nothing has been sacrificed by staying home. With its explosion of technology, the fair has brought the future to St. Louis, making it New York's equal. In fact, however, the movie's "St. Louis" is largely a New York creation. Here is a list of cast and crew members who were either born in New York or started their careers there:

Vincente Minnelli: director	Lucille Bremer: Rose Smith
Irving Brecher: writer	Tom Drake: John Truitt
George J. Folsey: cinematographer	Harry Davenport: Grandpa
Lemuel Ayers: art director	June Lockhart: Lucille Ballard
Charles Walters: dance director	Robert Sully: Warren Sheffield
Irene Sharaff: costume designer	Buddy Gorman: a Clinton Badger

"New York" is also present in Judy Garland, who had played New Yorker Betsy Booth in three Andy Hardy movies, two of which (*Andy Hardy Meets Debutante* and *Life Begins for Andy Hardy*) were set in Manhattan. Born Frances Gumm, Garland owed her stage name to a telephone call from New York. After George Jessel's introduction of "The Gumm Sisters" had drawn laughter from a Chicago World's

Fair audience, he suggested that they change their name, borrowing
one from his friend Robert Garland, *New York World-Telegram* drama
critic, who had called him between shows.

And Sally Benson/Tootie? In real life, the Smith family
moved to New York, where Benson became one of the *New Yorker*'s
most frequently published fiction writers.[14] (See *Meet Me in
St. Louis*: Murder.)

(*with Eleanor Eichenbaum, Paul Johnson, Michael Kane,*

Jessica Espinosa Kirwan, Jodie Mack)

 rioles

> **Esther [*consoling Mr. Smith*]**: *Well, Papa, if losing a case
> depresses you so, why don't you quit practicing law and go
> into another line of business?*
>
> **Mr. Smith**: *That's a good idea. Beginning tomorrow, I intend
> to play first base for the Baltimore Orioles.*

Although a Baltimore team called the Orioles (with John
McGraw and Willie Keeler) competed in the National League
from 1892 through 1899 and in the American League in 1901–
1902, by 1903 the "Baltimore Orioles" no longer existed, having
moved to New York to become the Highlanders (and eventually
the Yankees). Thus, the team anticipated the Smith family's
relocation. The modern Baltimore Orioles would only resume 50
years later when the St. Louis Browns moved to Baltimore in
1953 and revived the name. The allusion, in other words,
provides another example of *Meet Me in St. Louis*'s selective,
intermittent historical accuracy, designed less to reproduce the
real 1903–1904 than the popular memory of it. Like the shampoo that Rose is "bringing from downtown" (although commer-

cial shampoo was not available until the 1920s; in 1903, it was homemade, like ketchup) and the strawberries that accompany the Halloween ice cream (strawberries at the end of October, before refrigeration?), "Baltimore Orioles" is an anachronism, effective because it *sounds* turn of the century. Hence Hollywood's working principle: verisimilitude depends less on history than on "common knowledge," that evolving assemblage of myths, half-truths, lies, and approximations. As long as Custer remains "brave" and the Confederacy "noble," Mr. Smith will be able, however sarcastically, to assert the possibility of playing for the nonexistent Baltimore Orioles of 1903.

(with Charlotte Taylor)

Outside

> *The house seemed very still. Outside, people strolled by and children laughed and screamed.*
> —Sally Benson, *Meet Me in St. Louis*

External shots of 5135 Kensington Avenue reproduce Benson's hubbub: children play in yards and rollerskate on the sidewalks; neighbors pass on sleds, bicycles, cars,

carriages. Shots taken inside the Smith house, however, eliminate the external world almost entirely: street noise disappears, and even the occasional view through a window (as in "The Boy Next Door" number) reveals merely a *painted* landscape of trees and houses.

And yet, only multiple viewings will make the space occupied by the principal characters seem empty. With Hollywood cinema, plot functions as a *search algorithm*, locating the narratively significant elements while suppressing everything else. In *Meet Me in St. Louis*, this process begins immediately, as the opening shots of Kensington Avenue, with their multiple sites of potential significance, narrow to the Smith kitchen, led there by Lon's bicycle. (See *Meet Me in St. Louis*: Street Scene) Since Hollywood convention demands that offscreen interruptions prove significant to a movie's story, *Meet Me in St. Louis* essentially abandons the world outside the Smith house. Doing so, of course, constitutes a choice, a determination about what to show; narrative functions like invisible blinders, focusing the viewer's attention without making him aware that anything has been kept from him. In *2 or 3 Things I Know about Her*, Godard dramatized this problem by showing what his own version of a simple event (a woman visiting her husband's garage) necessarily omitted:

> For example, how to give an account of events? How to show or say that this afternoon, at about 4:10 P.M., Juliette and Marianne came to a garage at the Porte des Ternes where Juliette's husband works. . . . Yes, how to say exactly what happened? To be sure, there is Juliette; there is her husband; there is the garage. But is it really these words and these images that must be used? Are they the only ones? Are there no others? . . .
>
> For example, there are some leaves and, although Juliette doesn't have much in common with a Faulkner heroine, they could, after all, be made as dramatic as those of wild palms. There is also another young woman, about whom we know nothing. We don't even know how to say so in all honesty.

Thus, we might ask, for example, how to show the exact moment on a summer day when Lon Smith arrives home on his bicycle to find his family making ketchup? Here is Minnelli's choice, but is it really the only one? Are there no others? For example, there is Lon, but there is also a woman with a baby carriage, and a couple in a red automobile, and two boys wrestling in the back of a beer wagon. And later in the movie, as Esther

prepares to board the trolley, a smiling, middle-aged man, with a bow tie and a tweed coat and his hands in his pockets, stands on the platform behind her, and we will never know anything about him.[15]

(with Jessica Espinosa Kirwan)

O ver the Banister"

Following *Oklahoma!* and eager to "integrate" its songs into the story line, *Meet Me in St. Louis* provides a narrative "excuse" for all of its musical numbers except "The Trolley Song," a set piece justified by sheer high spirits and turn-of-the-centuryness. Motivations include surrender to a popular fad (the title song), adolescent longing ("The Boy Next Door"), a family party ("Skip to My Lou," "Under the Bamboo Tree"), a first love's shy transparency ("Over the Banister"), and attempts to comfort another family member ("You and I," "Have Yourself a Merry Little Christmas"). Relatively unconnected to the plot, Rodgers and Hammerstein's "Boys and Girls Like You and Me"—also cut from *Oklahoma!*—had to go.

For most of the musical numbers, Minnelli admitted, Judy Garland provided "the much-needed continuing thread in the integration of the songs to the story." In the case of *Meet Me in St. Louis*, the audience *knows* that Judy Garland sings: her stardom derives from that talent. Thus, the audience will readily ascribe this ability to Esther, making it seem "natural" for her to break into song. With this predilection for spontaneous singing already built into Esther's character, the film can seem "realistic" by simply *coaxing* this character trait to the surface. In the "Over the Banister" scene, for example, John Truitt coaxes Esther into the song by simply asking, "How does it go? . . . 'Over the banister leans a face . . . '"[16]

(with Michael Kane)

Pipe

Esther and Rose stare longingly at John Truitt as he stands in his front yard trying a new pipe, an object intended to suggest both his maturity and his masculinity. For *Meet Me in St. Louis*, this latter quality proved to be particularly urgent: Tom Drake, the actor playing Truitt,  never seems convincing as Esther's boyfriend. (Drake, in fact, was gay.) Hence the movie mobilizes several devices (the pipe, basketball) to "heterosexualize" his character. The pipe, however, remains unlit, and is then tossed aside, implying an impotence confirmed by John's subsequent behavior: He does not kiss the eager Esther at her party, he nearly misses the trolley, he cancels their date for the Christmas ball. Even when he finally proposes, he leaves Esther in tears, urging her to choose between him and her family. Truitt's aversion to flame appears most tellingly in the party's turning-out-the-lights sequence (to which the also gay Minnelli devoted four days), where he not only puts out the Smiths' lights but Esther's, too, extinguishing her hopes with a flaccid handshake and hasty departure.

"Voted out of the family" before the story begins, Mr. Smith displays his own impotence amid his female-dominated house-hold. Significantly, his final capitulation occurs as he extinguishes a match, intended for the phallic cigar which he has brought out for the first time. Accepting his fate, and even his death ("We're going to stay here till we rot!"), he puts away the unlit cigar and calls out, "Anna! Anna!" the name of both his wife and Freud's daughter.

(with Spencer Hall, Michael Kane, Renee Moilanen)

 uestions (Irrational Enlargement)

Who lives at 5134 Kensington Avenue?

What case did Mr. Smith lose?

What did Grandpa do for a living?

What happened to Grandma?

What song would the characters sing if they *didn't* live in St. Louis?

When Tootie cuts her lip, the doctor asks, "What is it this time, Tootie?" What was it the last time?

What is Lon's major at Princeton?

What is the unoccupied horse and carriage doing on Kensington Avenue during the Halloween sequence?

What is Mr. Braukoff reading when Tootie knocks on his door?

What was in the bag that Esther accidentally drops from the trolley?

Where did John Truitt find a tuxedo?

Is Grandpa joking, or did he really spend a lot of time "in the great country of China"? If so, why?

What happened to the former head of the New York office of Fenton, Rayburn & Company?

What is the gift that Mr. Smith offers his wife before announcing the move?

Why has Tootie promised not to tell anyone about the whiskey bottles Mr. Braukoff keeps in his basement?

Where are John Truitt's parents?

(with Nikki Schiwal, Daniel Stirk, Stephanie Taylor, Michelle Tomasso)

 Red

the flowers that decorate the title cards

the car that drives down Kensington Avenue in the opening scene the shingles on the Smiths' house

the red-striped shades on the Smiths' house

ketchup

a bench

several hats in Grandpa's room

the buggy that delivers Esther home after tennis

the lawn-jockey's pants

the caps on the stone elves in John's yard

Rose

Rose's hair

a serving jug on the dinner table

a carpet

Esther's dress

the stained-glass window

tomato soup

the flowers on the wallpaper

the bow in a partygoer's hair

a woman on the trolley wears all red

Agnes's Halloween shirt

the bonfire's flames

Esther's skirt, worn when she "beats up" John Truitt

curtains

the strawberries that accompany the ice cream

the sled used by children in the Smiths' front yard

the Christmas wreaths on the Smith house

Katie's winter hat and the frozen long underwear

Agnes's hair ribbon

Tootie's dress as she stands with her snow people

Esther's gown at the dance

While *Meet Me in St. Louis*'s color scheme is occasionally symbolic (the Smith house's seemingly year-round reds and greens; Rose's red hair, a vestige of the stories' indirect references to the family's Irish Catholicism), it is almost never realistic. The movie's bright, hard, painterly colors betray both Minnelli's background (as a window dresser and theatrical set designer) and his obvious intention to create a dreamlike world. Like the Godard of *2 or 3 Things I Know about Her* and *La Chinoise*, Minnelli relies on a "rhyming" palette derived less from real life than from advertising. Thus, the reverse-shot that introduces the musical refrain for "The Boy Next Door" reveals not only a *painted* outdoors, but a series of visual rhymes with Esther's golden hair pin: the goldfish and their bowl's brass stand, a mirror's frame, a door's handle.

(Minnelli's rhymes do not only involve color: Mr. Smith's reference to the "Baltimore Orioles" is doubled by the oriole paintings in Rose and Esther's bedroom.)

The movie, in other words, for all of its tenderness about the past, functions repressively, suppressing what Barthes called the "*futile* details," the insignificant, unplanned things in the corners of the action that produce "the reality effect." Minnelli avoids the contingent, preferring the hyperorganized, fully signifying mise-en-scène of the fairy tale. For the most part, therefore, the movie will not attend to the kind of detail occasionally present in Benson's stories:

> It was cool and quiet in the hall. The front door stood open and a yellow butterfly fluttered outside the screen. The leaves of the honeysuckle vine had opened and there were a few flowers on the vine. The sun, striking the wooden steps, was almost blinding. Katie had turned the hose on the porch earlier in the day, but now it was almost dry, and small pools of water stood only where the steps had sagged in the middle.

The sagging steps, the pools of collecting water, the single butterfly—these are the kinds of details that André Bazin celebrated when the camera automatically recorded them. Their appearance in a film depends on the director's willingness to relinquish at least some control over what appears before him. Minnelli's reluctance to do so suggests a *theatrical* approach to mise-en-scène, where the accidental can only appear as a mistake.[17]

(*with Matt Selvagn and Daniel Stirk*)

Rooms

While certain parts of the Smith house appear regularly (the dining and living rooms, the kitchen, the front hall and main stairs), other areas are subject to only occasional sightings: the lone bathroom, the bedrooms of Grandpa, Agnes and Tootie, Esther and Rose. We never see the parents' bedroom or the basement, sites too charged with sexual meaning or fear to merit inclusion, and the complete absence of Lon's room bespeaks his narrative insignificance.

Although we know that MGM constructed a full-scale model of 5135 Kensington Avenue, all areas of the house seem to shift in relationship to each other, thereby rendering the exact architecture uncertain. Where is the kitchen in relation to the front door? Does the older sisters' bedroom connect to that of Agnes and Tootie? How did Mr. Smith enter the house on Halloween? How many rooms are there on the ground floor?

In 1969, having lost his nerve during a solo race around the world, Donald Crowhurst began to sail aimlessly up and down the coast of South America, forging progress by means of fake radio signals, bounced from different satellites to indicate navigationally significant positions. Like Crowhurst's "voyage," the Smith house is an effect of carefully orchestrated, but frequently contradictory, clues; it is, in other words, despite the presence of its referent, a working *simulation*. Or, in another analogy, it resembles the pulse achieved by certain African music, never itself played, but implied by the different elements surrounding it.

(*with Spencer Hall*)

 t. Louis

Why St. Louis? The easy answer: St. Louis was the setting for *The Kensington Stories*, the movie's source. But the symbolic value of St. Louis also contributes to the movie's effect. Removed from the suspect coasts (New York and Hollywood), near the country's geographic and population centers, and situated on its greatest and most mythic river (see Mark Twain), St. Louis embodies what Roland Barthes would have called "Americanicity." Already the country's fourth-largest city in 1903, St. Louis had become even more prosperous by 1944. "St. Louis," therefore, exists as a sign with a dual purpose. On the one hand, it represents the idealized turn of the century, modernity's innocent childhood. On the other, it confirms American culture's commitment to business: A 1944 viewer, fully aware of St. Louis's success, would recognize that the movie's values (Father's refusal to move, the faith in the fair's celebration of material progress) are good investments—they have paid off in the end.

(with Michael Kane)

Street Scene (Kensington Avenue)

Meet Me in St. Louis's opening follows Hollywood protocols for an introductory establishing shot: an outburst of semiotic noise before the range of attention contracts to a few players, an orientation unencumbered by any significant narrative information. With its polycentric clutter, indecisive camera motivation, and action that overflows the frame, the scene resembles Lumière's *Workers Leaving the Factory*, its "realism" a function of apparent disorder. (Once the sign of documentary, spontaneity when staged becomes part of conventional storytelling: exposition.) An itemization:

1. The sepia title card, labeled "Summer 1903," showing what will retroactively be identified as the Smith house, a three-story Victorian building with ivy-covered

ground-floor walls and striped awnings protruding from five of the second-story windows. An antlered deer statue and wrought-iron lawn furniture in the yard. At the frame's left edge, the profile of a horse and part of a wagon and its driver: As the camera zooms in on this image, the shot becomes a mirror version of Vertov's carriage horse in *The Man with the Movie Camera*, stopped in its tracks by a freeze-frame.

2. As the title card quickens into motion, it assumes its full colors (these transitions, repeated four times and demonstrating the inadequacies of black and white, advertise the movie's use of Technicolor).

3. A single woman walks past a lamppost.

4. The mailman, leaving the Smith house after placing letters in their front-porch box, wipes the back of his neck, signifying "hot day."

5. The camera follows the title-card's wagon, now revealed as a two-horse vehicle labeled "Circle Star Beer" (a sign of "St. Louis"). Two boys wrestle on the beer kegs in back while the driver sits shaded by an umbrella.

6. Two women in long dresses stroll on the sidewalk.

7. A red automobile passes the beer wagon on the left, honking and nearly hitting a bicyclist coming from the opposite direction.

8. On the sidewalk, a man with a wicker basket hurries screen left.

9. A woman pushing a baby carriage passes another woman going in the opposite direction.

10. A two-horse carriage carrying three people comes toward the beer wagon, which the camera still follows.

11. Two boys and a girl rollerskate on the sidewalk.

12. Another boy on the grass.

13. A woman and a girl on the other side of the street.

14. A closed, one-horse carriage approaches from around the bend of the street.

15. A couple in the distance on the other side of the street.

16. As the camera begins to pan left to follow a bicyclist crossing in front of the beer wagon, it reveals another car approaching, ahead of the previously seen one-horse closed carriage.

17. Three children play in a yard.

18. Now detached from the Circle Star beer wagon, the camera follows the bicyclist (retroactively identified as Lon) as he rides into the Smith yard, where a child is playing. Another person approaches. By

moving from right to left, the bicyclist reproduces Lumière's rider, who ends *Workers Leaving the Factory* by riding out of frame, left.

19. Dissolve to Mother and Katie in the Smith kitchen.

This flurry of activity is, of course, anything but the unplanned scene it pretends to be. In this density of detail, everything signifies: the costumes, the vehicles, the children's activities all quickly evoke not only "turn of the century," but an exact moment—the time *after* everyone rode in wagons and *before* everyone rode in cars, the time when a house like the Smiths had both gas and electric lights.

Meet Me in St. Louis is haunted by another movie made two years before, *The Magnificent Ambersons*. Welles's film contains one of the cinema's most melancholy images, the iris shot of Eugene Morgan's prototype motor car clumsily making its way

through the snow toward the Amberson mansion.

Meet Me in St. Louis is a movie that has some difficulty deciding whether to be happy or sad, but the source of its ruefulness seems hard to locate. While *Ambersons* leaves no doubt that the automobile will end an entire way of life, *Meet Me in St. Louis* lacks a similarly obvious thesis. The explicit threat to the Smiths' world, the move to New York, never seems as serious. Hollywood conventions, after all, preclude the possibility of a musical with an unhappy ending. In fact, the sadness at the movie's heart derives from the same source as *The Magnificent Ambersons*': here is a world in the process of fading away. No line of dialogue, no single event, no clever shot declares this decay.

But the opening image of a red motor car, turning down a street in a movie set at the beginning of the twentieth century, in the year that Henry Ford incorporated the Ford Motor Company, reminds us that this world is dying.

(with Aylon Ben-Ami, Paul Johnson, Jodie Mack, Daniel Stirk)

 ennis Racket

Judy Garland enters *Meet Me in St. Louis* carrying a tennis racket, thereby suggesting that her character has a rich offscreen life in places not covered by the movie. We do not quite know how to account for this effect. A photograph seems "real" to the extent that

its people and objects appear to have an existence that *exceeds* the image, both before and after the shutter's click. Thus, candid snapshots often seem more "genuine" than composed portraits. By combining narrative with photography and stringing images into sequences, the cinema complicates the matter. Judy Garland entering the frame carrying a tennis racket, for example, while part of a story, is not the equivalent of the sentence "She entered carrying a tennis racket," a statement with no truth value before its composition. In *Meet Me in St. Louis*, Garland had to be carrying the tennis racket *before* the camera started recording her; thus, the truth value of the image existed prior to the shot. (Note, however, that the image's additional connotation—that Esther was playing tennis before she appeared onscreen—is not true. For one thing, "Esther" doesn't really exist; only Judy Garland does, and she was almost certainly not playing tennis before the filming began.)

Do these facts have any consequences? Literature can certainly refer to events not covered by an immediate narration: Watson's allusions to Sherlock Holmes's "other cases" (like "The Giant Rat of Sumatra," "for which the world is not yet prepared") are an obvious reference to something kept "offscreen." Does realistic characterization depend on such extradiegetic references? Some movies, like *Meet Me in St. Louis*, want to convince us that their characters do things when the audience isn't looking; others, like *The Maltese Falcon*, offer a self-contained world. Except for his affair with Iva Archer, Sam Spade has no implied offscreen life: everything that matters about him happens before our eyes. Is this way of telling stories more "theatrical"? Less "novelistic"? More or less "cinematic"? More or less "realistic"? Esther's tennis racket is the emblem for these questions.

(with Paul Johnson)

Telephone

Meet Me in St. Louis's opening episode revolves around Warren Sheffield's long-distance call to Rose, which sets in motion a series of events: the female conspiracy to alter the sacred dinner hour, Mr. Smith's comic ignorance of the plan, Rose's embarrassment, and her family's response. All of these incidents depend on one thing: the telephone's location in the dining room. The Andy Hardy series had already demonstrated how to profit from this kind of public site: with a coat over his head or crouched whispering in a closet, Andy would often struggle for the privacy he needed to conduct his complicated social life. Thus, the movies prompt a set of research topics: When do middle-class families begin to have more than one telephone? When does the family phone withdraw from the home's most public spaces? When do telephone conversations start to become occasions for privacy?

Cinematic space, of course, proves more flexible. Minnelli's dinner-table choreography functions both invisibly (motivated camera movements and cuts) and symbolically (shots of Rose typically include the portentous telephone looming over her in the background). When Warren's call does arrive, however, the camera assumes a position that would be impossible if the dining room were an actual space. All previous shots of the telephone have shown it affixed to a tapestried wall. Rose approaches to answer the ring,

and the shot changes to show only her. A reaction shot follows of the entire family eavesdropping. Finally, Minnelli provides an image that

contains both Rose talking on the phone and the family listening from the table: the camera has assumed part of the wall's previously estab-lished space.

The conversation between Warren and Rose resembles a barely updated version of something from Flaubert's *Dictionnaire des idées reçues*. Warren's "Here I am in New York, and there you are in St. Louis, and it's just like you're in the next room" amounts to a translation of Flaubert's entry for *railways*: "Enthuse about them, saying: 'I, my dear sir, who am speaking to you now, was at X this morning: I had taken the train to X, transacted my business there, and by X o'clock I was back here.'" But the appearance of Warren's line in the cinema, where distant locations can be edited together and adjoining rooms made to seem miles apart, complicates it beyond even Flaubert's prescience. While continuity principles (Warren faces screen right, Rose faces screen left) create the illusion of a "conversation" from dialogue almost certainly recorded separately, both the cutting and Warren's yelling suggest the great distance between two actors who may well have been standing in adjacent rooms at the same studio.[18]

(*with Erika Bloch and Matt Selvagn*)

Title Cards

Beginning with "June 1903," Sally Benson's *Meet Me in St. Louis* appears in 12 chapters, one for each month of a year ending with "May 1904." Minnelli, however, divides the movie version into four sections, coinciding with the seasons whose imagery marks each section's title card. The change makes sense: while the quarter-note organization would make a book's chapters too long, a 12-sectioned movie would seem too choppy. The seasonal format also coincides with the Smith family's four parts: the younger sisters (Agnes and Tootie), the older sisters (Rose and Esther), the parents (Mr. and Mrs. Smith), and the marginal males (Lon and Grandpa).

The title cards eliminate the less interesting (and more complex) reactions and readjustments that would presumably follow each of the section's endings. The "Autumn 1903" episode, for example, concludes with the family upset about having to move, yet reconciled with Mr. Smith. Additional problems seem inevitable, but the film omits them by skipping ahead to the next season. Thus, the decision's effect is felt, but further arguments are elided and the viewer spared having to see each problem run its course. Restricting itself to incidents, *Meet Me in St. Louis* shares modernism's propensity for *the fragment*. Its motto might come from Nietzsche: "I approach deep problems like cold baths: quickly into them and quickly out again." As Roland Barthes said of himself, the movie seems to like "to write *beginnings*." As each episode threatens to develop into something feared (a 1930s melodrama? an Andy Hardy story? a Victorian novel? an O. Henry punch line, always the *New Yorker*'s bête noire?), the title cards interrupt with Barthes's instruction to himself, "*Cut! Resume the story in another way.*"[19]

(with Michael Kane, Jessica Espinosa Kirwan, Matt Selvagn)

Trolley

At the end of "Summer 1903," Esther and her friends ride the trolley to the fair, still under construction. By leaving their trip unfinished (the young people never arrive at the site), the sequence provides another example of the *delay* that structures the entire film. Warren Sheffield's phone call, the family dinner, Esther's introduction to John Truitt, his declarations of love to her, the explanations for Tootie's cut lip, Father's decision against moving, the fair itself—all these events are stalled, postponed, and drawn out by the narrative as the movie struggles to create dramatic suspense out of its episodic source material, Sally Benson's autobiographical vignettes.

"The Trolley Song" is *Meet Me in St. Louis*'s only number without "realistic" motivation. While "The Boy Next Door" and "Have Yourself a Merry Little Christmas" emerge as extensions of thought or speech, the movie offers no comparable reason for the outbreak of "The Trolley Song" other than one boy's playful tugging on the conductor's bell. Instead, the song has its origins in a cinematic utopia where, as Richard Dyer puts it, "song and dance are 'in the air.'" Unlike the movie's other musical numbers, however, "The Trolley Song" actually offers a miniature story within a story— the progression of Esther's feelings about John. The song begins with all of the trolley's occupants singing, *except* Esther, who skulks to the rear where she leans dejectedly over the railing. When John's offscreen voice appears, Esther, suddenly overcome with love, takes over the singing and dancing, excited and wide-eyed over her beau's arrival. When John sits down next to her, she suddenly stops singing, and the awkwardness between them resumes. While "The Boy Next Door" and "Have Yourself a Merry Little Christmas" amount to freeze-frames of emotion, the mini-narrative of "The Trolley Song" sequence anticipates the music video.

Garland would not have found lyrics like "Zing, zing, zing went my heartstrings" unusual. For her 1935 MGM audition with Arthur Freed, she had chosen "Zing! Went the Strings of My Heart."[20]

(with Nic Jelley, Michael Kane, Stephanie Taylor)

ndergarments

Esther's comic struggles with a corset might prompt some obvious thematic extrapolations: how the two sisters are on the brink of fashion revolution, but they cannot see it coming (in just eight years, Paul Poiret would launch his "Oriental look," abolishing the

petticoat, wide skirt, and corset); how the corset is an emblem of Judy Garland's tragedy (most of her problems originated from the need to appear thinner onscreen). But the sequence also demonstrates some vital points about cinematic performance.

Almost every actor coming to the movies from the theater had to fight overplaying. In 1936, while making only his third picture (*Next Time We Love*), Jimmy Stewart had his career saved by Margaret Sullavan's after-hours coaching in the more economical behavior required by the camera. Four years later, shooting *The Philadelphia Story*, he would still have to hear George Cukor's repeated instruction: "less." Barry King has named the movies' effect on performance as "hypersemioticisation": "The use of close shooting in the cinema invests greater meaning in the actor as a signifying mass, involving [in] the process of signification parts of the actor[']s body, such as the eyes, mouth, and so forth" that would be invisible to a theater spectator. By restricting the camera's view (often to an actor's face), a film director further intensifies the importance of every minute aspect of gesture or appearance.

In *Meet Me in St. Louis*, the aftermath of John Truitt's proposal provides a useful example of hypersemioticization. The scene occurs in two shots, a medium close-up of John and Esther followed by a medium close-up of their faces.

As the scene begins, the camera fades into a medium shot of Garland crying—or, rather, a medium shot of Garland wiping her eyes: presented with the *consequences* of an unseen action, the viewer will infer the event (crying) presumed to have caused them. We soon discover that John has proposed. The gestures multiply: Esther smiles and puts her hands on John's sides, John grabs Esther by the arms and kisses her, they embrace. As they begin to discuss the Smiths' New York move, and Esther's halting speech indicates her growing uncertainty, the camera cuts to a medium close-up that slightly favors Esther's face. The reduced frame enhances the signification of Garland's features and gestures. When John insists, "You do feel it's the right thing to do, don't you?" and then turns away, Esther, freed from having to maintain eye contact, glances at the ground. This minute gesture, unnoticeable in wider framing, becomes intensely significant in close-up, conveying to the viewer more about her uncertain emotions than any other action in the scene.

Hypersemioticization applies even more to stars. As John Ellis observes:

> *Having the audience's attention (and the camera's, and the fiction's), anything that the star does becomes significant. Hence the star is permitted to underact, compared to the supporting cast, and this underacting produces the effect that the star behaves rather than acts.*

According to George Cukor, sometimes behaving is enough:

> *Lewis Milestone used to tell this story: Gary Cooper was playing with Emil Jannings in a silent picture, and Milestone, who was directing it, said to his assistant one day, "Shoot fifty feet of Gary just sitting there." As a matter of fact, Gary wasn't just sitting there, he was asleep, so they shot the footage without waking him up. Then Milestone said loudly, "Wake up!" and Gary did, and they shot this, too. Later Milestone cut Gary waking up into the picture, and when Jannings saw it, he said, "That young man should play Hamlet!"*

Raised in vaudeville and always comfortable in live performance, Judy Garland as a movie star deployed an acting style lying somewhere between silent cinema's blatant over-signification and the emerging "Method" of internalization. The corset scene provides a good example of this hybrid style's effect.

The sequence opens with Rose tightening Esther's corset. Esther struggles with the suffocating fit and walks around the room before gingerly sitting in a chair. All of her actions make her discomfort perfectly clear. The scene's realism derives less from Garland's broad acting than from the situation: Garland is impersonating a girl *overacting* for her sister. After Esther sits down, however, the camera's relative distance (a medium shot) requires Garland to continue working broadly in order to indicate her doubts about Rose's plan. After saying, "We can certainly handle twenty men," she turns to Rose, moving her face to within several inches of her sister's. She raises the pitch of her voice to suggest worry: "I should hope. . . . can you handle ten?" Garland's performance at this point isn't precisely overacting, but it appears to be *because Judy Garland is a star*. By not specifically *under*acting, she seems to be doing the opposite because her stardom adds weight to her every gesture. As Rose, Lucille Bremer often performs broadly: after tightening the corset, she straightens up and puts her hands on her hips to emphasize the line, "Es, it does *wonders* for your figure!" But because Bremer is *not* the center of either the camera's or the audience's attention, she can, indeed *must*, make her gestures more obvious just to have them noticed at all. Thus, the corset appears as the image of stardom's trap: the necessary restrictions on performance, the inescapable dependence on appearance.[21]

(with Erika Bloch, Michael Kane, Stephanie Taylor)

 Value

Compare the following on art's economic specificity:

> Balzac . . . groups a complete history of French Society from which, even in economic details . . . I have learned more than from all the professed historians, economists and statisticians of the period together.
>
> —Friedrich Engels

Nowadays, you can't get a maid for less than twelve dollars a month.

—Esther Smith (1903)[22]

(*with Jessica Espinosa Kirwan*)

V iolinist

Here is a problem: this entry's coauthor argues that by having the actress who plays the violin at the Smiths' party *reappear* in the trolley and ball scenes, Minnelli creates a realistic world where neighbors and friends remain constant. In

fact, however, after repeated viewings, I cannot find the violinist in either of the latter two sequences. Indeed, I can recognize only one of the Smiths' "friends," Quentin, who after the party also has a bit part in the trolley scene. "Time, tide, and trolley wait for no man," he declares officiously. He does not show up for the ball. Neither does T. S. Eliot, a St. Louisian exactly Esther's age.

Because the chorus almost certainly contains other boys or girls who appear in more than one of the three scenes, but also because I cannot identify them, the violinist suggests the difficulty of making background figures *distinguishable*. Quentin stands out as the only male with both glasses and lines; the violinist, directly addressed by Esther ("Eve, it's been ages! And you've brought your violin! How nice"), is also recognizable by her glasses, always Hollywood code for the socially awkward adolescent artist or intellectual. (Surprise: Eve turns out to be a fiddler, playing "Skip to My Lou" as a hoedown.) But the others seem impossibly interchangeable. Thus, if Minnelli had actually wanted to maintain a *noticeably* continuous chorus, he would have had to rely on such obviously distinguishing features as eccentric size, race, or costume. That he did not do so indicates his lack of concern about the issue. The problem, in other words, shifts to the actor: how does a chorus member get noticed when doing so runs counter to the director's intention? Or, in another context, how does a Ford assembly-line worker ever earn a promotion?

(*with Jodie Mack*)

Volume

How does the cinema show someone thinking? One common solution circumvents the problem by moving directly from visible emotion to action, leaving any causal ratiocination to be inferred. But this method's effectiveness depends on the *insignificance* of any interim steps. When those steps are important, the director will need a more creative solution. For example, because MGM regarded the New York decision as *Meet Me in St. Louis*'s central conflict, Minnelli could not resolve it abruptly; his camera had to get inside Mr. Smith's head.

Minnelli uses several methods to represent Mr. Smith's train of thought. First, he deploys Kuleshovian editing, intercutting medium close-ups of Mr. Smith looking from an upstairs window with shots of Esther consoling Tootie, sobbing uncontrollably in the snow. As he leaves the younger girls' bedroom, Mr. Smith stops to tuck in Agnes, thereby signaling that he loves his family and worries about making them unhappy. Next, as Mr. Smith walks down the front stairs, he stops to look at the grandfather clock, wrapped in newspapers, and the empty spaces where pictures used to hang.

This single take amounts to a kind of Kuleshovian mise-en-scène: the emotions we attribute to Mr. Smith derive less from his own expression than from the melancholy setting around him, a *mood of objects*. When Esther enters with a still-whimpering Tootie, Mr. Smith turns his back to the camera and watches for almost 10 seconds as they sulk up the stairs.

As Mr. Smith moves to his chair, music, previously absent from the sequence, appears, initially only in the soft ringing of chimes, but then as an instrumental reprise of "The Trolley Song." Mr. Smith sits down, and the music segues into a halting version of "Meet Me in St. Louis." As Mr. Smith lights a match (off his shoe!), the melody repeats at a louder volume, and the camera begins its slow zoom in on Mr. Smith's face. His eyes widen and dart back and forth; he stares into space as the match burns down and threatens his fingers. The volume rises as the movie's title song plays again. Suddenly, the music stops, Mr. Smith extinguishes the match and jumps from his chair, shouting, "Anna! Anna!" He has decided not to move. The soundtrack's theme, reconnecting Mr. Smith to the movie's opening, has recalled both Mr. Smith and the viewer to utopia.

(with Michael Kane)

 **indow Dressers**

The recurring use of windows as stages for *Meet Me in St. Louis*'s major scenes ("The Boy Next Door," "Have Yourself a Merry Little Christmas") evokes this list of window dressers:

Man Ray

Salvador Dali

Jasper Johns

Robert Rauschenberg

Claes Oldenburg

Andy Warhol

Vincente Minnelli

Although that roster betrays an obvious surrealist connection, the origins of window dressing date back to the mid-nineteenth century and the confluence of the museum, world's fair, and department store. Aristide Bouciaut's Bon Marché, the first department store, opened in Paris in 1852, only a year after London's Crystal Palace Exhibition. Although its rival Le Louvre arrived three years later, this marketing innovation accelerated only when Bouciaut hired M. A. Laplance and Gustave Eiffel to build a store that would occupy an entire block. Eiffel had been involved with the 1867 Exposition; another Parisian fair, the Universal Exposition of 1889, which commissioned the tower bearing his name, would ensure his immortality. That fair would also inspire Frantz Jourdain, the architect of yet another major Parisian store, La Samaritaine, itself influenced by Zola's fictional Au Bonheur des Dames. Zola's famous opening describes the young provincial Denise standing awestruck before the store's windows, "displaying symphonies of window-dressing . . . an orgy of colours."

Like the museum and world expositions, the department store depended on displaying merchandise in a style that Rosalind Williams has called "the chaotic-exotic": "syncretism, anachronism, illogicality, flamboyance, childishness . . . an attempt to express visions of distant places in concrete terms." With its mixture of 1940s slang and Victorian sets, its stuffed rooms and sudden plot turns, its child's perspective on the world, *Meet Me in St. Louis* resembles a series of carefully designed shop windows. In fact, the shop-window aesthetic perfectly suits the cinema. Both are essentially exercises in *miniaturization*, where objects must serve simultaneously as *emblem* and *synecdoche*: Mr. Neeley's ice wagon, for example, stands for "turn-of-the-century America" while also implying a bustling existence beyond Kensington Avenue. Minnelli often designs shots as if they were store windows, using the compressed symmetry enforced by the frame for rhyming compositions: thus, when singing the title song, Esther and Rose are doubled by two busts that both complement and gently mock them. In several scenes, Minnelli also uses mirrors, a standard shop-window device for making a space seem larger.

Richard Schickel once described Minnelli as one of the two most difficult people he had ever interviewed (the other was John Gielgud). "He is not by nature a story-teller," Schickel observed. "Nor does he have an analytical turn of mind. He seems mainly to feel his way toward the solution of creative problems, clued more by visual ideas (and, of course, musical ones) than by any of the signs one might term 'literary.'" Minnelli, Schickel wrote, "keeps a wicker tray into which he tosses clippings—of drawings, paintings, photos—which provide him with the germs of ideas." This randomly generated archive sounds very much like the more extensive one gathered by Joseph Cornell, whose carefully arranged collections of found objects (Cornell's "boxes") occupy the ground somewhere between museum display, shop window, and film shot. Cornell called the boxes "forgotten games," an exact description of *Meet Me in St. Louis*, with its inventory of vanished pastimes: riding on the ice wagon, making ketchup, burning furniture on Halloween (?!). And yet another connection: one of Cornell's most elaborate works, *The Crystal Cage: Portrait of Berenice*, a valise of found materials intended to suggest an imaginary child, contains among its carefully chosen objects the image of Margaret O'Brien as Tootie.

Both *Meet Me in St. Louis* and Cornell's work, mixtures of nostalgia and fetishism, depend on their creator's obsessions. Minnelli detailed his own care with the film:

> *I remembered everything I could of the small town where I was brought up. My aunt used to wear this red tam-o'-shanter [like the one] the maid uses in the winter scene, you know, with the big tassel on top. It is full of things like that. . . . I spent a great deal of time on research and finding the right things for it.*

For Cornell, this kind of order was "spiritual." He believed, as Charles Simic writes, that "somewhere on the island of Manhattan, there are . . . a few objects, dispersed in unknown locations, that rightly belong together despite being seemingly incompatible in appearance." This mystical formulation is, in fact, a recipe for set design, or window dressing, an arrangement of objects, drawn from a studio's inexhaustible supply, that creates a believable place: *these* kitchen curtains with the flowers painted on them, *this* carved wooden breadbox, *this* oriental hall rug, *this* African bust draped with a shawl, *this* stained-glass window on the landing, *this* portrait of a little girl, *this* grandfather clock—"precisely these objects," Thoreau once said about those surrounding him at Walden, "make a world," one that we will call "5135 Kensington Avenue."[23]

(*with Aylon Ben-Ami*)

 (Grandpa's Crossed Sabers)

Although Lucille Ballard greets Grandpa as "Grandpa Prophater" at the dance, finally identifying him as Mrs. Smith's father, the movie omits almost everything else about him.

Benson's stories had given him a historically important hometown
(Harpers Ferry, West Virginia), a military past (as a Civil War veteran
and prisoner in the notorious Andersonville), and a previous career
("At one time he had owned three boats that ran from St. Louis to
New Orleans"). But the stories never explain what appears in the
film, his room's collection of exotic hats and antique weapons (the
sabers, mounted in an X on the wall, near the matched pair of
pistols: "They'll all be safe with me," he cheerily assures Mr. Smith.
"I've got twelve guns in my room"). The fez (French Foreign Legion?),
the Zouave cap (the Civil War?), the Chinese hat (an overseas
mission?), the crossed sabers (souvenirs of a victory or a defeat?)—
these objects offer a set of *potential histories*, any combination of
which would complete the character named "Grandpa Prophater."
The writer, who must *assert* such details, withholds their significance
at the risk of provoking the reader's question: "Why are you keeping
something from me?" In the cinema, however, where objects are
simply *presented* without apparent effort (Hollywood hides its work),
and where what Seymour Chatman calls "a plenitude of visual
details, an excessive particularity" appears "natural," that question is
forestalled. Thus, Grandpa himself remains the X in an equation, an
unknown requiring additional information. Or, in another analogy,
Meet Me in St. Louis seems to underwrite "Grandpa" with something
like Fermat's promissory note accompanying his famous theorem: "I
have discovered a truly marvelous proof of this, which, however, this
margin is not large enough to contain."[24]

(with Spencer Hall)

 ou and I"

The song that serves to reunite the Smith family is not, in fact, an
old tune from the turn-of the century, although it was designed to
sound like one. "You and I" appears to have been written expressly

for *Meet Me in St. Louis* by Nacio Herb Brown (music) and producer Arthur Freed (lyrics), the team responsible for "Singin' in the Rain," a much older song dating back to 1929. For the movie, Freed himself supplied the singing, dubbing for Leon Ames, who mouths the part. What conceals this substitution? First, the human brain's inability to retain a sound's precise timbre ensures that a viewer will only remember the exact register of Mr. Smith's speaking voice for a few seconds: By the time the song begins, the voices of Ames and Freed will have become indistinguishable. Second, and more important, the timbre of a singer's performance often fails to coincide with his speaking voice. With Judy Garland, for example, a distinct "break" occurs when she begins to sing, and someone familiar only with her speaking voice might prove unable to identify her in performance. By 1944, however, this break had begun to sound increasingly old-fashioned. Bing Crosby, the most popular singer of the first half of the twentieth century, was also among the first to make his singing voice an extension of speech. By avoiding the operatic break, which suggests artifice, Crosby's apparently natural style conveyed sincerity and intimacy.

Meet Me in St. Louis's "You and I" sequence has two conflicting goals: the expression of both tradition and sincerity. Since Freed's old-fashioned singing suggests the former, but not the latter, Minnelli must invent business to convey intimacy. He does so by having Mrs. Smith begin the song in a key too high for Freed's voice, forcing him into "errors" that prompt her to start over—generously, understandingly, lovingly—in "your key."[25]

(*with Megan Basham and Charlotte Taylor*)

 oom

Minnelli admitted to modeling *Meet Me in St. Louis* less on the real 1903–1904 city than on Thomas Eakins's paintings. As James

Naremore puts it, "[H]e seems not to have asked himself what turn-of-the-century St. Louis was actually like. Instead, he asked what *art* in the period was like." Nevertheless, the zoom-ins that introduce each of the movie's four sections suggest that Minnelli understood the crucial difference between painting and cinema. Despite their careful geometric arrangements, Eakins's still images accommodate idle scanning, detours to study *The Swimming Hole*'s nearly invisible dog, or the second scull in the distance behind Max Schmitt, the one with Eakins himself. Like so many others, these paintings seem to precede, or follow, a withheld narrative that would have disciplined the viewer's eye, forcing it to attend to certain things at the expense of others. Thus, Minnelli's zooms imply a revision of Chaplin's famous dictum that "life is a tragedy when seen in close-up, but a comedy in long-shot." In fact, the movie depends utterly on the zoom-ins: narrative cannot coexist with the wide view.[26]

(with Jessica Espinosa Kirwan)

Notes

Introduction

1. Minnelli's remark appears in an interview with Richard Schickel, *The Men Who Made the Movies* (New York: Atheneum, 1975), p. 257.

2. Metz's epigram is cited by James Monaco, *How to Read a Film* (New York: Oxford University Press, 1981), p. 130. Metz's remark about no longer loving the cinema appears in his book *The Imaginary Signifier*, trans. Celia Britton et al. (Bloomington: Indiana University Press, 1982), p. 15.

3. cummings's phrase comes from his poem "Buffalo Bill's/defunct." Wallace Stevens's remark appears in a review by Michael Wood, "Out of the Lock-Up," *London Review of Books*, 2 April 1998, p. 17. Walter Benjamin, *The Arcades Project*, trans. Howard Eiland and Kevin McLaughlin (Cambridge, Mass.: Harvard University Press, 1999), p. 846.

4. This story comes from Samuel Marx, *A Gaudy Spree: Literary Hollywood when the West Was Fun* (New York: Franklin Watts, 1987), pp. 75–76.

5. Adorno's remarks originally appeared in a 10 November 1938 letter to Benjamin, reprinted in *Aesthetics and Politics*, trans. Ronald Taylor (London: Verso, 1980), p. 129.

6. Mulvey's 1975 *Screen* manifesto has been reprinted in her book *Visual and Other Pleasures* (Bloomington: Indiana University Press, 1989), p. 16.

7. Michael Taussig, *Shamanism, Colonialism, and the Wild Man: A Study in Terror and Healing* (Chicago: University of Chicago Press, 1987), p. 10. Taussig is citing Frederick Karl, *Joseph Conrad: The Three Lives* (New York: Farrar, Straus and Giroux, 1979), p. 286.

8. Ludwig Wittgenstein, *Culture and Value*, trans. Peter Winch (Chicago: University of Chicago Press, 1980), p. 28e.

9. Cited in Richard Wolin, *Walter Benjamin: An Aesthetic of Redemption* (New York: Columbia University Press, 1982), p. 130.

10. This quintessential Holmes remark appears in "A Case of Identity," in *The Adventures of Sherlock Holmes* (New York: Oxford University Press, 1993), p. 36.

11. Walter Benjamin, *One-Way Street*, trans. Edmund Jephcott and Kingsley Shorter (London: NLB, 1979), p. 91.

12. *Roland Barthes*, trans. Richard Howard (New York: Hill and Wang, 1977), p. 99.

13. Cited in Ray Monk, *Ludwig Wittgenstein: The Duty of Genius* (New York: Penguin, 1990), p. 311.

14. *Roland Barthes*, trans. Richard Howard (New York: Hill and Wang, 1977), p. 74.

15. *The Gay Science*, trans. Walter Kaufmann (New York: Vintage, 1974), p. 343.

16. *Roland Barthes*, trans. Richard Howard (New York: Hill and Wang, 1977), p. 90.

17. *Roland Barthes*, trans. Richard Howard (New York: Hill and Wang, 1977), p. 152.

18. *Culture and Value*, trans. Peter Winch (Chicago: University of Chicago Press, 1980), p. 24e.

19. "Natural History of Massachusetts," in *Thoreau: Collected Essays and Poems* (New York: Library of America, 2001), p. 41.

20. *Culture and Value*, trans. Peter Winch (Chicago: University of Chicago Press, 1980), p. 20e.

21. Roland Barthes, "The Third Meaning," in *The Responsibility of Forms*, trans. Richard Howard (New York: Hill and Wang, 1985), pp. 62, 43.

22. Ginzburg's remarks appear in Jonathan Kandell, "Was the World Made Out of Cheese?" *New York Times Magazine*, 17 November 1991, p. 48.

23. Roland Barthes, *S/Z*, trans. Richard Miller (New York: Hill and Wang, 1974), pp. 12, 21, 13.

24. Gerald Kaufman, *Meet Me in St. Louis* (London: British Film Institute, 1994), p. 40.

25. André Bazin, *Jean Renoir*, trans. W. W. Halsey II and William H. Simon (New York: Delta, 1974), pp. 85–86.

26. *Roland Barthes*, trans. Richard Howard (New York: Hill and Wang, 1977), p. 103.

27. The story, of course, is "The Adventure of the Abbey Grange," in *The Return of Sherlock Holmes* (New York: Oxford University Press, 1993), pp. 268, 276–277.

28. Freud's instructions appear in his essay "Recommendations to Physicians Practicing Psycho-Analysis," in *The Freud Reader*, ed. Peter Gay (New York: Norton, 1989), p. 357. The Kracauer passage

appears in his essay "Photography," in *The Mass Ornament: Weimar Essays* (Cambridge, Mass.: Harvard University Press, 1995), p. 62.

29. I am grateful to Brian Doan for the analogy between Benjamin's captions and film theory's dominant ideas. Benjamin's remarks appear in "A Small History of Photography," in *One-Way Street*, trans. Edmund Jephcott and Kingsley Shorter (London: NLB, 1979), p. 256.

30. D. A. T. Gasking and A. C. Jackson, "Wittgenstein as a Teacher," in *Ludwig Wittgenstein: The Man and His Philosophy*, ed. K. T. Fann (New York: Dell, 1967), p. 51.

31. Ludwig Wittgenstein, *Philosophical Investigations*, trans. G. E. M. Anscombe (Oxford: Blackwell, 1953), §66:

> Consider for example the proceedings that we call "games." I mean board-games, card-games, ball-games, Olympic games, and so on. What is common to them all?—Don't say: "There *must* be something common, or they would not be called 'games'"—but *look and see* whether there is anything common to all.—For if you look at them you will not see something that is common to *all*, but similarities, relationships, and a whole series of them at that. To repeat: don't think, but look!

The advice to "look at them *from close up*" appears in §51.

32. Mallarmé's phrase occurs in "Crisis in Poetry," in his *Selected Poetry and Prose*, ed. Mary Ann Caws (New York: New Directions, 1982), p. 75.

33. Wittgenstein's remark about doing everything twice appears in *Wittgenstein's Lectures, Cambridge 1930–1932*, ed. Desmond Lee (Chicago: University of Chicago Press, 1989), p. 75. The remark appears as the epigraph to Marjorie Perloff's "'But Isn't *the Same* at Least the Same?'" in *The Literary Wittgenstein*, ed. John Gibson and Wolfgang Huemer (New York: Routledge, 2004), p. 34. The tour guide metaphor appears in D. A. T. Gasking and A. C. Jackson, "Wittgenstein as a Teacher," in *Ludwig Wittgenstein: The Man and His Philosophy*, ed. K. T. Fann (New Jersey: Humanities, 1967), p. 51.

34. "The American cinema is a classical art, but why not then admire in it what is most admirable, i.e. not only the talent of this or that

filmmaker, but the genius of the system." André Bazin, "On the *politique des auteurs*" (trans. Peter Graham), in *Cahiers du Cinéma: The 1950s*, ed. Jim Hillier (Cambridge, Mass.: Harvard University Press, 1985), p. 258. Bazin's article originally appeared in *Cahiers du Cinéma* 70 (April 1957). Thomas Schatz borrowed Bazin's phrase for the title of his superb book on classic Hollywood, *The Genius of the System: Hollywood Filmmaking in the Studio Era* (New York: Pantheon, 1988).

35. Pauline Kael, *5001 Nights at the Movies* (New York: Holt, 1991), p. 299.

Grand Hotel

1. Raymond Chandler's remark appears in a 7 May 1948 letter to Frederick Lewis Allen, which can be found in Raymond Chandler, *Later Novels and Other Writings* (New York: Library of America, 1995), p. 1034. The information about Van Dyke's and LeRoy's shooting speeds comes from Thomas Schatz, *The Genius of the System: Hollywood Filmmaking in the Studio Era* (New York: Pantheon, 1988), pp. 54–55, 140–145. J. J. Cohn's praise for Van Dyke's efficiency comes from an interview with me (Hollywood, 1982).
    Information on Cedric Gibbons and the theory of "design intensity" appears in Charles Affron and Mirella Jona Affron, *Sets in Motion: Art Direction and Film Narrative* (New Brunswick, N.J.: Rutgers University Press, 1995), pp. 17, 35–40. See also Christina Wilson, "Cedric Gibbons: Architect of Hollywood's Golden Age," in *Architecture and Film*, ed. Mark Lamster (New York: Princeton Architectural Press, 2000), pp. 101–115, especially pp. 103–109. Gibbons's own remarks about *Grand Hotel*'s sets appear in Miles Kreuger, ed., *Souvenir Programs of Twelve Classic Movies 1927–1941* (New York: Dover, 1977), p. 98.

    I have taken my information about art deco from the following sources: Alastair Duncan, *Art Deco* (New York: Thames and Hudson, 1988), pp. 7–10; Bevis Hillier and Stephen Escrit, *Art Deco Style* (London: Phaidon, 1997); and Lucy Fischer, "Greta Garbo and Silent Cinema: The Actress as Art Deco Icon," *Camera Obscura* 48 (2001): 83–110.

    The information about a map's usefulness appears in Nick Cullather, "Target Malpractice," *Lingua Franca* (October 1999): 14.

Peter Wollen's argument about modernism's competing sides forms the first chapter of his *Raiding the Icebox: Reflections on Twentieth Century Culture* (Bloomington: Indiana University Press, 1993), pp. 1–34. Thalberg's insistence on spending money appears in Schatz's *The Genius of the System*, p. 116.

2. Stanley Cavell, *The World Viewed: Reflections on the Ontology of Film* (Cambridge, Mass.: Harvard University Press, 1979), p. 18. Thalberg's remark about Paris appears in Samuel Marx, *Mayer and Thalberg: The Make-Believe Saints* (Hollywood, Calif.: Samuel French, 1975), pp. 82–83. For Barthes on "Italianicity," see "Rhetoric of the Image," in Roland Barthes, *The Responsibility of Forms*, trans. Richard Howard (New York: Hill and Wang, 1985), p. 23.

3. Schatz's description of MGM appears in his *The Genius of the System: Hollywood Filmmaking in the Studio Era* (New York: Pantheon, 1988), p. 44. Cavell's remarks about intuition and tuition are quoted in William Rothman and Marian Keane, *Reading Cavell's "The World Viewed": A Philosophical Perspective on Film* (Detroit, Mich.: Wayne State University Press, 2000), p. 25. Primitive cinema's best historian is Noël Burch. See his essays "Film's Institutional Mode of Representation and the Soviet Response" and "Porter; or, Ambivalence" in his *In and Out of Synch: The Awakening of a Cine-Dreamer*, trans. Ben Brewster (Aldershot, England: Scolar, 1991), pp. 114–156. For Barthes's notion that certain details provoke "an interrogative reading," see his essay "The Third Meaning," in *The Responsibility of Forms*, trans. Richard Howard (New York: Hill and Wang, 1985), p. 43.

4. For a discussion of Bazin's position, see my essay "How a Film Theory Got Lost," in Ray, *How a Film Theory Got Lost and Other Mysteries in Cultural Studies* (Bloomington: Indiana University Press, 2001), pp. 1–14. See also my essay "The Automatic *Auteur*; or, A Certain Tendency in Film Criticism," in *Directed by Allen Smithee*, ed. Jeremy Braddock and Stephen Hock (Minneapolis: University of Minnesota Press, 2001), pp. 51–75. "The camera shows, and the editing tells" comes from Gilberto Perez's *The Material Ghost: Films and Their Medium* (Baltimore, Md.: Johns Hopkins University Press, 1998), p. 58. Perez cites this epigram as received wisdom, which he disputes, pointing out (in a superb chapter on Jean Renoir) ways in which the camera can tell and the editing can show. However received and disputed, the remark still seems a way into Bazin's ideas about automatism.

Rivette's comment on Preminger comes from Rivette's essay "The Essential," trans. Liz Heron, in *Cahiers du Cinéma: The 1950s: Neo-Realism, Hollywood, New Wave*, ed. Jim Hillier (Cambridge, Mass.: Harvard University Press, 1985), p. 134. The Sarris passage appears in his *Interviews with Film Directors* (New York: Avon, 1967), pp. 399–400. For David Thomson's remark, see his *The New Biographical Dictionary of Film* (New York: Knopf, 2002), p. 36. The observation appears in Thomson's discussion of Fred Astaire.

5. Wollen's phrase appears in his discussion of modernity's two sides: *Raiding the Icebox: Reflections on Twentieth Century Culture* (Bloomington: Indiana University Press, 1993), p. 1. For Fitzgerald's description of MGM's back lot, see *The Love of the Last Tycoon* (New York: Scribner's, 1994), p. 26.

6. Kristin Thompson, *Breaking the Glass Armor: Neoformalist Film Analysis* (Princeton, N.J.: Princeton University Press, 1988), pp. 207–208.

7. Noël Burch, *To the Distant Observer: Form and Meaning in the Japanese Cinema* (Berkeley: University of California Press, 1979), pp. 64–65, 158–159. D. N. Rodowick, *The Crisis of Political Modernism: Criticism and Ideology in Contemporary Film Theory* (Berkeley: University of California Press, 1994).

8. Henry James, *Essays on Literature: American Writers, English Writers* (New York: Library of America, 1984), pp. 1343–1344. Noël Burch's argument appears in scattered essays. See especially his "How We Got into Pictures: Notes Accompanying *Correction Please*," *Afterimage* (U.K.) 8–9 (Spring 1981): 22–38; "Film's Institutional Mode of Representation and the Soviet Response" and "Porter; or, Ambivalence," both in *In and Out of Sync: The Awakening of a Cine-Dreamer*, trans. Ben Brewster (Aldershot, England: Scolar, 1991), pp. 114–156.

9. David Thomson, *The New Biographical Dictionary of Film* (New York: Knopf, 2002), p. 750 (on Ginger Rogers). Christian Keathley, *The Wind in the Trees: Cinéphilia and History* (Bloomington: Indiana University Press, 2006). One of this manuscript's anonymous readers correctly points out that in looking older to today's audiences than she actually was, Garbo is hardly unique. Studio-era actors, working in movies made for older audiences, often cultivated an air of maturity, especially when compared to current stars, whose youth-oriented movies require them to look as young as they can for as long as they can.

10. On the "reference code of the artist," see Roland Barthes, *S/Z*, trans. Richard Miller (New York: Hill and Wang, 1974), pp. 98 (the code of art associated with "excess"), 135. Note that in Grusinskaya's case, the codes of the romantic artist combine with those of "femininity": irrational whimsicality, impetuousness, "instinctive worries" (p. 172).

James Naremore's discussion of the Delsartean system of acting appears in his *Acting in the Cinema* (Berkeley: University of California Press, 1988), pp. 52–67. The Schmidt example appears in Frederick Taylor, *The Principles of Scientific Management* (New York: Norton, 1967), pp. 130, 41–48, 59–64, 83. Robert Kanigel, *The One Best Way: Frederick Winslow Taylor and the Enigma of Efficiency* (New York: Viking, 1997), pp. 316–323, offers a more accurate version of the Schmidt story.

Mamoulian's famous *Queen Christina* instructions to Garbo appear in Andrew Sarris, *"You Ain't Heard Nothin' Yet": The American Talking Film: History and Memory, 1927–1949* (New York: Oxford University Press, 1998), p. 384. Richardson's observation about John Wayne appears in the same book, p. 410.

Walter Benjamin's discussion of film acting appears in his famous essay "The Work of Art in the Age of Mechanical Reproduction," in *Illuminations*, trans. Harry Zohn (New York: Schocken, 1969), pp. 228–234. For James Wong Howe's story about Garbo's 1949 screen test, see Charles Higham, *Hollywood Cameramen* (Bloomington: Indiana University Press, 1970), pp. 91–92.

11. On Garbo's size, see the description in Marcia Landy and Amy Villarejo, *Queen Christina* (London: British Film Institute, 1995), p. 13. Affron's remarks appear in his *Star Acting: Gish, Garbo, Davis* (New York: Dutton, 1977), pp. 135–138. Walker's remark appears in Alexander Walker, *Stardom* (New York: Stein and Day, 1970), p. 146. The Galileo dictum is quoted in Joseph Schwartz and Michael McGuinness, *Einstein for Beginners* (New York: Pantheon, 1979), p. 83. For the formulation of Einstein's problem, see William R. Everdell, *The First Moderns* (Chicago: University of Chicago Press, 1997), p. 237. Daniels's statement appears in Charles Higham, *Hollywood Cameramen* (Bloomington: Indiana University Press, 1970), p. 72.

12. David Thomson, *The New Biographical Dictionary of Film* (New York: Knopf, 2002), p. 324. John O. Thompson, "Screen Acting and the Commutation Test," in *Stardom: Industry of Desire*, ed. Christine Gledhill (New York: Routledge, 1991), pp. 183–197.

13. For information on Vicki Baum and the novel and play versions of *Grand Hotel*, see Lynda J. King, *Best-Sellers by Design: Vicki Baum and the House of Ullstein* (Detroit, Mich.: Wayne State University Press, 1988). On Thalberg, see Roland Flamini, *Thalberg: The Last Tycoon and the World of MGM* (New York: Crown, 1994), pp. 178–181. For a superb study of *Grand Hotel*'s making, see Thomas Schatz, *The Genius of the System: Hollywood Filmmaking in the Studio Era* (New York: Pantheon, 1988), pp. 108–119. On *Gabriel over the White House*, see Matthew Bernstein, *Walter Wanger: Hollywood Independent* (Berkeley: University of California Press, 1994), pp. 82–87. I have taken the information on Hitler's first months in power from Thomas Childers's masterful lectures, *A History of Hitler's Empire* (Springfield, Va.: Teaching Company, 1998) [audio cassettes].

14. On extradiegetic knowledge and camp, see my *The Avant-Garde Finds Andy Hardy* (Cambridge, Mass.: Harvard University Press, 1995), p. 156. Kael's remarks on *Grand Hotel* appear in Pauline Kael, *5001 Nights at the Movies* (New York: Holt, 1991), p. 299. On Garbo's relationship with Barrymore, see Barry Paris, *Garbo* (New York: Knopf, 1995), p. 218. Roland Barthes, *S/Z*, trans. Richard Miller (New York: Hill and Wang, 1974), p. 85.

15. Arno J. Mayer, *The Persistence of the Old Regime* (New York: Pantheon, 1981). For the Grusinskaya quotation, see Vicki Baum, *Grand Hotel* (Mattituck, N.Y.: American Reprint, 1976), p. 111. Walter Benjamin's ideas appear in his essay "The Work of Art in the Age of Mechanical Reproduction," in *Illuminations*, trans. Harry Zohn (New York: Schocken, 1969), pp. 220–221. The argument about rock and roll is taken from my own essay "Tracking," in Ray, *How a Film Theory Got Lost and Other Mysteries in Cultural Studies* (Bloomington: Indiana University Press, 2001), pp. 72, 68–69. For recording's influence on jazz, see Evan Eisenberg, *The Recording Angel: Explorations in Phonography* (New York: McGraw-Hill, 1987), pp. 143–144. The Nazi "official position" on jazz can be found on the Internet. See Dave Dexter, Jr., *Jazz Cavalcade: The Inside Story of Jazz* (New York: Criterion, 1946), or www.shellac.org/wams/index.html and http://jmpdi.blogspot.com/2007/01/jazz-e-banda-deserhada-senpre.com.html.

16. Vicki Baum, *It Was All Quite Different: The Memoirs of Vicki Baum* (New York: Funk and Wagnalls, 1964), pp. 285–286. Susan Sontag, *Illness as Metaphor* (New York: Vintage, 1978), pp. 6–8.

17. For the description of Crawford's oral surgery, see Shaun Considine, *Bette and Joan* (New York: Dutton, 1989), p. 32. Schatz's description of *Grand Hotel* appears in *The Genius of the System*, p. 119. Barthes's characterization of Sarrasine comes from *S/Z*, p. 122. For the Nietzsche passage, see *The Gay Science*, trans. Walter Kaufmann (New York: Vintage, 1974), p. 38.

18. The details about Manchester's growth and living conditions come from Thomas Childers, *Europe and Western Civilization in the Modern Age*, part I, lecture 11 (Chantilly, Va.: Teaching Company, 1998) [audio lectures]. Friedrich Engels, *The Condition of the Working Class in England* (Stanford, Calif.: Stanford University Press, 1958), p. 312.

19. Thalberg's "Ten Commandments" appear in Thomas Schatz, *The Genius of the System: Hollywood Filmmaking in the Studio Era* (New York: Pantheon, 1988), p. 106. For Fitzgerald's "whole equation of pictures," see *The Love of the Last Tycoon* (New York: Scribner's, 1994), p. 3. Siegfried Kracauer's essay "The Mass Ornament," with its discussion of the Tiller Girls, appears in his *The Mass Ornament: Weimar Essays* (Cambridge, Mass.: Harvard University Press, 1995), pp. 75–86. Frederick Taylor's account of training girls to sort ball bearings comes from his *The Principles of Scientific Management* (New York: Norton, 1967), pp. 86–97.

    Noël Burch describes the eyeline match, the crucial element of reverse-angle editing, as "the veritable cornerstone of the Hollywood system," in *To The Distant Observer: Form and Meaning in the Japanese Cinema* (Berkeley: University of California Press, 1979), pp. 65, 158. His discussion of "pillow shots" appears on pp. 155–156, 160–162, 166.

    The idea of "suture" originates with Daniel Dayan's "The Tutor-Code of Classical Cinema," in *Movies and Methods*, ed. Bill Nichols (Berkeley: University of California Press, 1976), pp. 438–451. The data on *Casablanca*'s use of reverse-angle editing is taken from Barry Salt, *Film Style and Technology: History and Analysis* (London: Starword, 1992), p. 237. For Perez's discussions of drama versus narrative, see Gilberto Perez, *The Material Ghost: Films and Their Medium* (Baltimore, Md.: Johns Hopkins University Press, 1998), pp. 50–91, especially pp. 75, 78–79, 81–83.

20. Baum describes seeing "the fading Pavlova" in her *It Was All Quite Different: The Memoirs of Vicki Baum* (New York: Funk and Wagnalls,

1964), p. 286. For information about Pavlova, see Arthur Henry Franks, *Pavlova: A Biography* (Bath, England: Burke, 1956). The photograph of Pavlova as the Dying Swan appears after p. 40 of that book. Cavell's remarks and his quotation of Panofsky appear in Cavell's *The World Viewed: Enlarged Edition* (Cambridge, Mass.: Harvard University Press, 1979), p. 27.

21. Roland Barthes, *S/Z*, trans. Richard Miller (New York: Hill and Wang, 1974), pp. 78–79.

22. *S/Z*, pp. 119–120. On Garbo's appearance and diet, see Alexander Walker, *Stardom* (New York: Stein and Day, 1970), p. 143. The Mayer-Garbo exchange appears in Samuel Marx, *Mayer and Thalberg: The Make-Believe Saints* (Hollywood, Calif.: Samuel French, 1988), p. 65.

23. For a discussion of *photogénie*, see my essay "How a Film Theory Got Lost," in Ray, *How a Film Theory Got Lost and Other Mysteries in Cultural Studies* (Bloomington: Indiana University Press, 2001), pp. 1–14. Epstein's remark about the telephone appears in Richard Abel, ed., *French Film Theory and Criticism*, vol. 1: *1907–1921* (Princeton, N.J.: Princeton University Press, 1988), p. 242.

24. For a longer discussion of the relationship among the *physiologies*, the detective story, and photography, see my essay "Snapshots: The Beginnings of Photography," in Ray, *How a Film Theory Got Lost and Other Mysteries in Cultural Studies* (Bloomington: Indiana University Press, 2001), pp. 15–28. See also the valuable essay by Richard Sieburth, "Same Difference: The French *Physiologies*, 1840–1842," *Notebooks in Cultural Analysis*, no. 1 (1984): 163, 167. Walter Benjamin's remark comes from *Charles Baudelaire: A Lyric Poet in the Age of High Capitalism*, trans. Harry Zohn (London: Verso, 1983), p. 39. The Sherlock Holmes story referred to is "The Red-Headed League," with Holmes's symptomatic observation: "Beyond the obvious facts that he has at some time done manual labor, that he takes snuff, that he is a Freemason, that he has been in China, and that he has done a considerable amount of writing lately, I can deduce nothing else" (*The Adventures of Sherlock Holmes* [New York: Oxford University Press, 1993], p. 51).

For Sophie Calle's project *The Hotel*, see *Sophie Calle: M'as-tu Vue?* (New York: Prestel, 2003), pp. 157–168. Roland Barthes's analysis of *Sarrasine*'s "dark as a Spaniard, dull as a banker" appears in *S/Z*, p. 38.

25. Thomas Doherty, *Pre-Code Hollywood: Sex, Immorality, and Insurrection in American Cinema 1930–1934* (New York: Columbia University Press, 1999), p. 2. On Thalberg's clash with von Stroheim, see Thomas Schatz, *The Genius of the System: Hollywood Filmmaking in the Studio Era* (New York: Pantheon, 1988), pp. 22–25. See also Jonathan Rosenbaum, "Erich von Stroheim," in Richard Roud, ed., *Cinema: A Critical Dictionary*, vol. 2 (New York: Viking, 1980), pp. 973–987. For Thalberg's remark, see Samuel Marx, *Mayer and Thalberg: The Make-Believe Saints* (Hollywood, Calif.: Samuel French, 1975), p. ix.

26. My information on tie-ups and product placement comes from Charles Eckert, "The Carole Lombard in Macy's Window," in *Stardom: Industry of Desire*, ed. Christine Gledhill (New York: Routledge, 1991), pp. 30–39. See Jefferson Cowie, *Capital Moves: RCA's Seventy-Year Quest for Cheap Labor* (Ithaca, N.Y.: Cornell University Press, 1999), pp. 12, 17–19, 24.

27. *S/Z*, pp. 22–23, 67, 191. Albert J. Guerard, *Conrad the Novelist* (Cambridge, Mass.: Harvard University Press, 1966), p. 126.

28. Clarence Brown's remark is quoted by Thomson, *The New Biographical Dictionary of Film*, p. 325.

29. André Bazin, "The Myth of Total Cinema," in *What Is Cinema?* vol. 1, trans. Hugh Gray (Berkeley: University of California Press, 1967), p. 21.

The Philadelphia Story

1. Stanley Cavell, *Pursuits of Happiness: The Hollywood Comedy of Remarriage* (Cambridge, Mass.: Harvard University Press, 1981), pp. 142–145.

2. Walter Benjamin, "The Work of Art in the Age of Mechanical Reproduction," in *Illuminations*, trans. Harry Zohn (New York: Schocken, 1969), pp. 218, 220–221. On "corruptibility," see Jacques Derrida, "Limited Inc[.]," trans. Samuel Weber, *Glyph* 2 (1977): 218. The Derrida passage on "the possibility of disengagement and citational graft" comes from "Signature Event Context," trans. Samuel Weber and Jeffrey Mehlman, *Glyph* 1 (1977): 185.

3. Roland Barthes, *S/Z*, trans. Richard Miller (New York: Hill and Wang, 1974), pp. 88–89, 38, 15–16.

4. For Sarris's rankings of American directors, see his book *The American Cinema: Directors and Directions 1929–1968* (New York: Dutton, 1968). Truffaut ranked Cukor with Lubitsch, Capra, McCarey, and Sturges, the masters of classic era comedy: "that extraordinary man who makes out of every five films, one masterpiece, three other very good ones, and the fifth still interesting." *The Early Film Criticism of François Truffaut*, ed. Wheeler Winston Dixon (Bloomington: Indiana University Press, 1993), pp. 34, 104–108. The *Cinema One* book on Cukor is Carlos Clarens, *Cukor* (London: Secker and Warburg, 1976), p. 61. The first passage on Hawks ("The essential. The truth of the dialogue . . . ") is by Henri Langlois, "The Modernity of Howard Hawks." The second ("Such art demands a basic honesty . . . ") is by Jacques Rivette, "The Genius of Howard Hawks." Both essays appear in *Howard Hawks: American Artist*, ed. Peter Wollen (London: British Film Institute, 1996), pp. 74, 28.

Hawks's remark ("Hell, the first thing you've got to do . . . ") appears in Gerald Mast, *Howard Hawks, Storyteller* (New York: Oxford University Press, 1982), p. 3. Mast's summary of the *auteur*-structuralist findings comes from p. 29. For Sartre's dictum, Hoveyda's reformulation, and Rivette's application, see Jim Hillier, ed., *Cahiers du Cinéma: The 1950s* (Cambridge, Mass.: Harvard University Press, 1985), pp. 9, 76, 104. On Hawks's classicism, see Robin Wood, "Retrospect," in Wollen's *Howard Hawks: American Artist*, p. 172.

For Cukor's dismissal of *Citizen Kane*, see Gavin Lambert, *On Cukor* (New York: Rizzoli, 2000), p. 141. His remarks about Marilyn Monroe appear on p. 135. The performance numbers for Hepburn in the stage version of *The Philadelphia Story* come from Anne Edwards, *Katharine Hepburn: A Remarkable Woman* (New York: St. Martin's Griffin, 2000), p. 174.

For the Walter Benjamin passage, see *Illuminations*, trans. Harry Zohn (New York: Schocken, 1969), pp. 228, 230. On this point, see Barry King's observation:

> [T]he routinised practices in the mainstream cinema tend to shift the frontier of control away from the actor towards the director or, where this is not the same person, those empowered to render the final cut. Equally it is no small matter . . . that the formative

capacities of film (or video) can be used to compensate for a low level of technical ability as an actor, enabling untrained actors to produce convincing on-screen performances. ("Articulating Stardom," in *Stardom: Industry of Desire*, ed. Christine Gledhill [New York: Routledge, 1991], p. 171)

Dorothy Parker's witticism is quoted in Edwards's *Katharine Hepburn*, p. 120. Selznick's memo is cited by James Naremore, *Acting in the Cinema* (Berkeley: University of California Press, 1988), p. 181. Naremore's book uses a close analysis of *Holiday* to provide the definitive study of Hepburn's acting. The description of Hepburn's screen test and Cukor's response to it appear in Edwards's *Katharine Hepburn*, pp. 78–79. Epstein's praise for Hayakawa's movement appears in *French Film Theory and Criticism: 1907–1939*, vol. 1, ed. Richard Abel (Princeton, N.J.: Princeton University Press, 1988), p. 243. Lambert reports Hepburn's remark to Cukor on p. 17 of *On Cukor*.

5. Noël Burch's descriptions of classical Hollywood filmmaking appear in his *To the Distant Observer: Form and Meaning in the Japanese Cinema* (Berkeley: University of California Press, 1979), p. 114, and "Propositions," *Afterimage* [U.K.] 5 (Spring 1974): 50 (with Jorge Dana). Cukor's remarks come from an interview conducted by Peter Bogdanovich in the latter's *Who the Devil Made It* (New York: Knopf, 1997), pp. 445, 449. For Selznick's memo, see *Memos from David O. Selznick*, ed. Rudy Behlmer (New York: Modern Library, 2000), p. 188. Sarris's description of Hepburn's "premature feminism" appears in James Naremore, *Acting in the Cinema* (Berkeley: University of California Press, 1988), p. 175. David Bordwell also refers to film directing as problem solving; see his *Figures Traced in Light: On Cinematic Staging* (Berkeley: University of California Press, 2005), pp. 41–42. Thalberg's dictum, which often recurs in this book, appears in Thomas Schatz's *The Genius of the System: Hollywood Filmmaking in the Studio Era* (New York: Pantheon, 1988), p. 106.

6. For an opposite opinion about verbally smart women in screwball comedy, see Maria DiBattista, *Fast-Talking Dames* (New Haven, Conn.: Yale University Press, 2001).

7. Peter Bogdanovich, *Who the Devil Made It* (New York: Knopf, 1997), p. 451.

8. David Thomson, *The New Biographical Dictionary of Film* (New York: Knopf, 2002), p. 351. For the Mankiewicz letter to Cary Grant and the comparison to Jay Gatsby, see Graham McCann, *Cary Grant: A Class Apart* (New York: Columbia University Press, 1996), pp. 155, 11–12. McCann also makes the point about the difference between Grant's appearance and his background: "It is one of the greatest and most mischievous cultural ironies of the twentieth century that the man who taught the privileged élite how a modern gentleman should look and behave was himself of working-class origin." For information on the *physiologies*, see Richard Sieburth, "Same Difference: The French *Physiologies*, 1840–1842," *Notebooks in Cultural Analysis*, vol. 1 (Durham, N.C.: Duke University Press, 1984), pp. 163–200, especially pp. 164, 167, 180. See also Robert B. Ray, "Snapshots: The Beginnings of Photography," in Ray, *How a Film Theory Got Lost and Other Mysteries in Cultural Studies* (Bloomington: Indiana University Press, 2001), pp. 15–28.

9. Sheridan Morley, *Katharine Hepburn: A Celebration* (New York: Applause, 1984), pp. 75–76. The Nathan description of Barry's working method also appears on these pages. Carlos Clarens's dismissive remark about Barry's play appears in his book, *George Cukor* (London: Secker and Warburg, 1976), p. 62. For Andrew Sarris's famous critique of the movie, see his *"You Ain't Heard Nothin' Yet": The American Talking Film* (New York: Oxford University Press, 1998), p. 451. Cukor's insistence on the camera's truth appears in his interview with Peter Bogdanovich, *Who the Devil Made It* (New York: Knopf, 1997), p. 444. The distinction dividing real person, persona, and role appears in Simon Watney, "Katharine Hepburn and the Cinema of Chastisement," *Screen* 26, no. 5 (September–October 1985): 54.

10. Barry King, "Articulating Stardom," in *Stardom: Industry of Desire*, ed. Christine Gledhill (New York: Routledge, 1991), pp. 168, 170, 176. For Thalberg's dictum, see Thomas Schatz, *The Genius of the System: Hollywood Filmmaking in the Studio Era* (New York: Pantheon, 1988), p. 106. Truffaut's comments appears in *The Early Film Criticism of François Truffaut*, ed. Wheeler Winston Dixon (Bloomington: Indiana University Press, 1993), p. 79.

11. Brendan Gill, "The Dark Advantage," in *States of Grace: Eight Plays by*

Philip Barry, ed. Brendan Gill (New York: Harcourt Brace Jovanovich, 1975), pp. 3–47. Fitzgerald's autobiographical remarks appear on p. 15 of that essay. For Nick Carraway's line, see *The Great Gatsby* (New York: Scribner Classics, 1992), p. 151.

12. Jean Epstein's remarks on *photogénie* appear in Richard Abel, ed., *French Film Theory and Criticism 1907–1939*, vol. 1 (Princeton, N.J.: Princeton University Press, 1988), pp. 315, 246. For Benjamin's remarks on Kafka, see *Illuminations*, trans. Harry Zohn (New York: Schocken, 1969), pp. 144, 143. For the material on timbre, see Theodore Gracyk, *Rhythm and Noise: An Aesthetic of Rock* (Durham, N.C.: Duke University Press, 1996), pp. 57–61.

13. The Morrill Act citation appears in Andrew Delbanco, "Colleges: An Endangered Species?" *New York Review of Books*, 10 March 2005, p. 19.

14. See Roland Barthes, *S/Z*, trans. Richard Miller (New York: Hill and Wang, 1974), pp. 20–21, 205–206.

15. Roland Barthes, "The Reality Effect," in *The Rustle of Language*, trans. Richard Howard (New York: Hill and Wang, 1986), pp. 141–142, 146.

16. F. Scott Fitzgerald, *The Love of the Last Tycoon* (New York: Scribner's, 1994), pp. 57–58. Roland Barthes, *S/Z*, trans. Richard Miller (New York: Hill and Wang, 1974), pp. 15–16.

17. Roland Barthes, *S/Z*, trans. Richard Miller (New York: Hill and Wang, 1974), p. 41.

18. Noël Burch, *Theory of Film Practice*, trans. Helen R. Lane (Princeton, N.J.: Princeton University Press, 1981), pp. 5–7.

19. Barbara Leaming, *Katharine Hepburn* (New York: Crown, 1995), p. 367. Stanley Cavell, *Pursuits of Happiness: The Hollywood Comedy of Remarriage* (Cambridge, Mass.: Harvard University Press, 1981), pp. 139–140. On this same point, see Gary L. Green, "The Author behind the Author: George Cukor and the Adaptation of *The Philadelphia Story*," in *Film and Literature: A Comparative Approach to Adaptation*, ed. Wendell Aycock and Michael Schoenecke (Lubbock: Texas Tech University Press, 1988), pp. 69–79. Hitchcock explains the MacGuffin in François Truffaut, *Hitchcock* (New York: Simon and Schuster, 1984), p. 138.

20. Stanley Cavell, *Pursuits of Happiness: The Hollywood Comedy of Remarriage* (Cambridge, Mass.: Harvard University Press, 1981), pp. 142–145.

21. On Weidler's career and "husky voice," see James Robert Parish and Ronald L. Bowers, *The MGM Stock Company: The Golden Era* (New Rochelle, N.Y.: Arlington House, 1975), pp. 756–759.

22. The Godard movie mentioned is *2 or 3 Things I Know about Her.* "Kuleshovian acting" refers to that Soviet director's famous experiment that demonstrated editing's power to convey emotion: A single shot of an actor's impassive face was intercut with various objects (a soup bowl, a baby, a coffin), and the audience inferred emotion from the juxtapositioning. The Aragon passage appears in Paul Hammond, ed., *The Shadow and Its Shadow: Surrealist Writings on the Cinema* (London: British Film Institute, 1978), p. 28.

23. Roland Barthes, *S/Z*, trans. Richard Miller (New York: Hill and Wang, 1974), p. 206.

24. Gavin Lambert, *On Cukor* (New York: Rizzoli, 2000), pp. 98, 101. Vidor's line appears, without quotation marks, in Joseph Cotten, *Vanity Will Get You Somewhere: An Autobiography* (New York: Avon, 1987), p. 106.

The Maltese Falcon

1. For a discussion of changes ordered by Jack Warner, see John M. Desmond and Peter Hawkes, *Adaptation: Studying Film & Literature* (New York: McGraw-Hill, 2006), pp. 73–79. John Huston started the myth that everything in *The Maltese Falcon* is from Spade's point of view: "the book was told entirely from the standpoint of Sam Spade, and so too is the picture, with Spade in every scene except the murder of his partner. The audience knows no more and no less than he does." Quoted in Rudy Behlmer, "'The Stuff That Dreams Are Made Of': *The Maltese Falcon*," in *The Maltese Falcon*, ed. William Luhr (New Brunswick, N.J.: Rutgers University Press, 1995), p. 117. Hitchcock's distinction between *surprise* and *suspense* appears in François Truffaut, *Hitchcock* (New York: Simon and Schuster, 1984), p. 73. For Noël Burch's discussion of *The Great Train Robbery*'s extra shot, see his essay "Porter; or, Ambivalence," in Burch, *In and Out of Synch: The Awakening of a Cine-Dreamer*, trans. Ben Brewster (Aldershot, England: Scolar, 1991), pp. 147–150.

2. Agee's essay appears in *Agee on Film* (New York: Modern Library, 2000), pp. 413–427; the quoted passages appear on pp. 416, 417, 421. See also Lillian Ross, *Picture* (New York: Rinehart, 1952). For Truffaut's remarks about Huston, see Wheeler Winston Dixon, ed., *The Early Film Criticism of François Truffaut* (Bloomington: Indiana University Press, 1993), p. 101; and Truffaut's *The Films of My Life*, trans. Leonard Mayhew (New York: Simon and Schuster, 1978), p. 14. For Eric Rohmer's dismissal of Huston, see Rohmer's *The Taste for Beauty*, trans. Carol Volk (Cambridge: Cambridge University Press, 1989), pp. 63, 106. Rivette's criticism of Huston appears in *Cahiers du Cinéma: The 1950s*, ed. Jim Hillier (Cambridge, Mass.: Harvard University Press, 1985), p. 41.

   Sarris's treatment of Huston appears in *The American Cinema: Directors and Directions 1929–1968* (New York: Dutton, 1968), pp. 156–158. For James Naremore's essay, see *The Maltese Falcon*, ed. William Luhr (New Brunswick, N.J.: Rutgers University Press, 1995), pp. 149–160, especially pp. 149, 151–152, 154. For David Thomson's definition of great movie acting, see his *The New Biographical Dictionary of Film* (New York: Knopf, 2002), p. 36. Bazin's eulogy for Bogart appears in Hillier, *Cahiers du Cinéma: The 1950s*, pp. 98–101. Cavell's remarks about screen performance appear in his *The World Viewed* (Cambridge, Mass.: Harvard University Press, 1979), pp. 27–28.

3. Glenn Todd's calculations of *The Maltese Falcon*'s exact dates appear in Dashiell Hammett, *The Maltese Falcon* (San Francisco, Calif.: North Point, 1987), pp. 280–281. My analysis of the movie's temporal ellipses derives from Noël Burch's discussion of "Spatial and Temporal Articulations" in his *Theory of Film Practice*, trans. Helen R. Lane (Princeton, N.J.: Princeton University Press, 1981), pp. 4–8. The formulation *to penetrate the veil* appears in Frederick Karl's description of Joseph Conrad's *Heart of Darkness*. It is cited by Michael Taussig as a model for a nonreductive criticism; see Taussig's *Shamanism, Colonialism, and the Wild Man: A Study in Terror and Healing* (Chicago: University of Chicago Press, 1987), p. 10. Huston's remark about screenplay writing appears in *John Huston Interviews*, ed. Robert Emmet Long (Oxford: University Press of Mississippi, 2001), p. 66.

4. The Aragon passage appears in his essay "On Décor," in *The Shadow and Its Shadow: Surrealist Writings on the Cinema*, ed. Paul Hammond (London: British Film Institute, 1978), p. 29. I have taken the

paragraphs on fetishism from my *The Avant-Garde Finds Andy Hardy* (Cambridge, Mass.: Harvard University Press, 1995), pp. 107–109. See also William Pietz, "The Problem of the Fetish: Parts 1, 2, and 3a," *Res* 9 (1985): 5–17; *Res* 13 (1987): 23–45; and *Res* 16 (1988): 105–123. The quoted passages from Pietz appear in *Res* 9:7–9. "While an image itself could be beautiful . . . " is a remark made by Hollywood cinematographer Allen Daviau, which appears in the video trailer for the PBS documentary *American Cinema*. The Leiris passage is cited by Pietz, *Res* 9:12. For Barthes's proposal that the "third meaning" (itself a fetishized detail) produces a "counter-narrative," see "The Third Meaning," in *The Responsibility of Forms*, trans. Richard Howard (New York: Hill and Wang, 1985), p. 57. For Bazin on *Boudu*, see André Bazin, *Jean Renoir*, trans. W. W. Halsey II and William H. Simon (New York: Delta, 1973), p. 86. Noël Burch's comments on chance appear in his *Theory of Film Practice*, trans. Helen R. Lane (Princeton, N.J.: Princeton University Press, 1981), pp. 105–121, especially pp. 109–115.

5. Noël Burch, "Carl Theodor Dreyer: The Major Phase," in *Cinema: A Critical Dictionary: The Major Filmmakers*, vol. 1, ed. Richard Roud (New York: Viking, 1980), pp. 301–302. Daniel Dayan, "The Tutor-Code of Classical Cinema," in *Movies and Methods*, ed. Bill Nichols (Berkeley: University of California Press, 1976), pp. 446–447.

6. Roland Barthes, *S/Z*, trans. Richard Miller (New York: Hill and Wang, 1974), pp. 156, 105.

7. The information on Arthur Edeson comes from Aljean Harmetz, *Round Up the Usual Suspects: The Making of Casablanca* (New York: Hyperion, 1992), pp. 133–136. Roland Barthes, "The Third Meaning," in *The Responsibility of Forms*, trans. Richard Howard (New York: Hill and Wang, 1985), pp. 55, 58.

8. The Flitcraft story appears in *The Maltese Falcon* (New York: Vintage, 1992), pp. 62–64. The other anecdotes appear in Hammett's "From the Memoirs of a Private Detective," in *Dashiell Hammett: Crime Stories and Other Writings*, ed. Steven Marcus (New York: Library of America, 2001), pp. 905–909. For the Godard story from *Une Femme est Une Femme*, I have used the translation by Jan Dawson appearing in *Godard: Three Films* (New York: Harper and Row, 1975), pp. 45–46.

9. Roland Barthes, *S/Z*, trans. Richard Miller (New York: Hill and Wang, 1974), p. 79. On the myth of the engineer and modernity,

see Cecilia Tichi, *Shifting Gears* (Chapel Hill: University of North
Carolina Press, 1987); and Peter Wollen, *Raiding the Icebox: Reflections
on Twentieth-Century Culture* (Bloomington: Indiana University Press,
1993), especially pp. 1–71. On the Golden Gate Bridge, see John
McGloin, *San Francisco: The Story of a City* (San Rafael, Calif.: Presidio,
1978); and M. M. O'Shaughnessy, "Hetch Hetchy: Its Origin and
History," http://www.sfmuseum.org/bio/mmo.html.

10. On the Honolulu move, see John M. Desmond and Peter Hawkes,
    Adaptation: Studying Film and Literature (New York: McGraw-Hill,
    2006), pp. 70–71.

11. Pauline Kael, "Circles and Squares," in *I Lost It at the Movies* (New York:
    Little, Brown, 1965), p. 302. Kael is quoting Andrew Sarris's essay
    "Notes on the *Auteur* Theory in 1962," reprinted in his book, *The Primal
    Screen: Essays on Film and Related Subjects* (New York: Simon and Schuster,
    1973), pp. 38–53. The quoted passages appear on pp. 50–51.

12. Roland Barthes, *S/Z*, trans. Richard Miller (New York: Hill and
    Wang, 1974), p. 38. Henri Bergson, *An Introduction to Metaphysics*,
    trans. T. E. Hulme (New York: Putnam's, 1912), p. 7. Dudley
    Andrew, "The Neglected Tradition of Phenomenology in Film
    Theory," in *Movies and Methods*, vol. 2, ed. Bill Nichols (Berkeley:
    University of California Press, 1985), pp. 627–628, 632.

13. Ford's remarks appear in John A. Meixner's *Ford Madox Ford's Novels*,
    excerpted in Martin Stannard, ed., *The Good Soldier* (New York:
    Norton, 1995), p. 248.

14. For the story about Thalberg, see Samuel Marx, *Mayer and Thalberg:
    The Make-Believe Saints* (Hollywood, Calif.: Samuel French, 1975),
    pp. 82–83. A useful reference to radio shows is John Dunning, *On
    the Air: The Encyclopedia of Old-Time Radio* (New York: Oxford
    University Press, 1998). Noël Burch's remarks appear in his essay
    "Porter; or, Ambivalence," reprinted in his book *In and Out of Synch:
    The Awakening of a Cine-Dreamer* (Aldershot, England: Scolar, 1991),
    p. 143. For Hawks's various remarks, see the following: Gerald
    Mast, *Howard Hawks, Storyteller* (New York: Oxford University Press,
    1982), p. 37; Peter Bogdanovich, *Who the Devil Made It* (New York:
    Knopf, 1997), p. 334; Joseph McBride, ed., *Hawks on Hawks*
    (Berkeley: University of California Press, 1982), p. 82.

15. Eisenstein's remark about editing appears in David Bordwell and
    Kristin Thompson, *Film Art: An Introduction* (New York: McGraw-Hill,

2004), p. 480. For Dyer's comment, see Richard Dyer, *Stars* (London: British Film Institute, 1979), p. 162.

16. Dashiell Hammett, *The Maltese Falcon* (New York: Vintage, 1992), pp. 155, 160. Roland Barthes, *S/Z*, trans. Richard Miller (New York: Hill and Wang, 1974), pp. 80–81.

17. For information on the Maltese-cross system, see David Cook, *A History of Narrative Film* (New York: Norton, 2004), p. 9.

18. Chatman's distinction between literary assertion and cinematic presentation appears in his famous article "What Novels Can Do That Films Can't (and Vice Versa)," in *Film Theory and Criticism*, ed. Leo Braudy and Marshall Cohen (New York: Oxford University Press, 1999), pp. 438–443. Dashiell Hammett, *The Maltese Falcon* (New York: Vintage, 1992), p. 7.

19. Dai Vaughan, *For Documentary* (Berkeley: University of California Press, 1999), p. 119. Benjamin's remark comes from his essay "The Work of Art in the Age of Mechanical Reproduction," in *Illuminations*, trans. Harry Zohn (New York: Schocken, 1969), p. 247. Eric Rohmer, "The Land of Miracles," in *Cahiers du Cinéma: The 1950s*, ed. Jim Hillier (Cambridge, Mass.: Harvard University Press, 1985), p. 206.

20. *The Arabian Nights*, trans. Husain Haddawy (New York: Norton, 1990), p. 11. For a useful commentary on *The Arabian Nights*, see Robert Irwin, *The Arabian Nights: A Companion* (London: Allen Lane/Penguin, 1994). Roland Barthes, *S/Z*, trans. Richard Miller (New York: Hill and Wang, 1974), pp. 75–76, 62. Geoffrey O'Brien's short essay is the best thing I have read on *The Thousand and One Nights*: "Djinn Mill: Hussain [*sic*] Haddawy Chases His Tales," *Voice Literary Supplement*, May 1990, p. 31. Joan Fontaine's remark about fear appears in Ronald L. Davis, *The Glamour Factory: Inside Hollywood's Big Studio System* (Dallas, Tex.: Southern Methodist University Press, 1993), pp. 115–116.

21. For a discussion of O'Hara's blown veil, see Joseph McBride, *Searching for John Ford* (New York: St. Martin's, 2001), p. 332; and Aljean Harmetz, *Round Up the Usual Suspects: The Making of Casablanca* (New York: Hyperion, 1992), p. 6. James Gleick, *Chaos: Making a New Science* (New York: Penguin, 1987), pp. 19, 21. I discovered Gleick's remarks in Kent Gramm's "The Chances of War: Lee, Longstreet, Sickles, and the First Minnesota Volunteers," in *The Gettysburg Nobody Knows*, ed. Gabor S. Borritt (New York: Oxford University Press, 1997), p. 99; see also pp. 84, 86. Turkle's remark appears in

"Dynasty," *London Review of Books*, 6 December 1990, p. 8, where she calls for "a sociology of superficial knowledge."

De Vany's remarks appear in John Cassidy, "Chaos in Hollywood," *New Yorker*, 31 March 1997, pp. 36–37. For a brief summary of Hollywood's Taylorist/Fordist attempts to rationalize production, see my "How a Film Theory Got Lost," in Ray, *How a Film Theory Got Lost and Other Mysteries in Cultural Studies* (Bloomington: Indiana University Press, 2001), pp. 1–3. Godard's proposition appears in his "Introduction à une véritable histoire du cinéma," trans. Jean Andrews, *Camera Obscura* 8–10 (Fall 1982): 77–78.

22. Jean Negulesco, *Things I Did . . . and Things I Think I Did* (New York: Linden, 1984), p. 116. Eric Ambler, *A Coffin for Dimitrios* (New York: Vintage, 2001), p. 24.

23. Roland Barthes, *S/Z*, trans. Richard Miller (New York: Hill and Wang, 1974), pp. 101–102.

24. James Naremore, "John Huston and *The Maltese Falcon*," in *The Maltese Falcon*, ed. William Luhr (New Brunswick, N.J.: Rutgers University Press, 1995), p. 154.

25. Roland Barthes, "The Reality Effect," in *The Rustle of Language*, trans. Richard Howard (New York: Hill and Wang, 1986), pp. 141–148. Rossellini's remark appears in an interview with *Cahiers du Cinéma* reprinted in James Hillier, ed., *Cahiers du Cinéma: The 1950s* (Cambridge, Mass.: Harvard University Press, 1985), p. 212. Friedrich Nietzsche, *The Gay Science*, trans. Walter Kaufmann (New York: Vintage, 1974), p. 131.

26. For a description of the "paranoiac-critical activity" at work, see Salvador Dali, *The Tragic Myth of Millet's Angelus: Paranoiac-Critical Interpretation* (St. Petersburg, Fla.: Salvador Dali Museum, 1986). Roland Barthes, "The Third Meaning," in *The Responsibility of Forms*, trans. Richard Howard (New York: Hill and Wang, 1985), pp. 41–44, 47–48, 58–60.

27. *The Maltese Falcon* budget and costs come from Thomas Schatz, *The Genius of the System: Hollywood Filmmaking in the Studio Era* (New York: Pantheon, 1988), pp. 308, 310. Walter Benjamin, "The Work of Art in the Age of Mechanical Reproduction," in *Illuminations*, trans. Harry Zohn (New York: Schocken, 1969), pp. 220–225.

28. On the Webley-Fosbery, see Peter P. Gillis, "An Anomaly in *The Maltese Falcon*," *ANQ* 8, no. 3 (Summer 1995): 29–31. Hammond's

remark appears in his *The Shadow and Its Shadow: Surrealist Writings on the Cinema* (London: British Film Institute, 1978), p. 19.

29. For Thucydides' opening, see M. I. Finley, ed., *The Portable Greek Historians* (New York: Viking, 1959), p. 219. The quotations expressing the new historicists' approach to writing history come from Catherine Gallagher and Stephen Greenblatt, *Practicing New Historicism* (Chicago: University of Chicago Press, 2000), pp. 6, 15, 23, 22. For Chatman's distinction between verbal and cinematic description, see his essay "What Novels Can Do That Films Can't (and Vice Versa)," in *Film Theory and Criticism*, ed. Leo Braudy and Marshall Cohen (New York: Oxford University Press, 1999), p. 438.

30. Seymour Chatman, "What Novels Can Do That Films Can't (and Vice Versa)," in *Film Theory and Criticism*, ed. Leo Braudy and Marshall Cohen (New York: Oxford University Press, 1999), p. 438. William Luhr, ed., *The Maltese Falcon* (New Brunswick, N.J.: Rutgers University Press, 1995), p. 11. Edward Said, *Orientalism* (New York: Vintage, 1979). Stanley Cavell, *The World Viewed* (Cambridge, Mass.: Harvard University Press, 1979), pp. 55–57. For Baudelaire's pioneering discussion of dandyism, see Charles Baudelaire, *The Painter of Modern Life and Other Essays*, trans. Jonathan Mayne (London: Phaidon, 1965), pp. 26–28. For Barthes on dandyism and the pleasures of perversity, see *Roland Barthes*, trans. Richard Howard (New York: Hill and Wang, 1977), pp. 63–64, 106; and also Barthes, *The Grain of the Voice*, trans. Linda Coverdale (New York: Hill and Wang, 1985), p. 335.

31. Noël Burch, *Theory of Film Practice*, trans. Helen R. Lane (Princeton, N.J.: Princeton University Press, 1981), pp. 26, 19–22. For Burch's remarks about Hollywood cinema's "thrift," see his *To the Distant Observer: Form and Meaning in the Japanese Cinema* (Berkeley: University of California Press, 1979), p. 114.

32. On Hammett's pseudonym, see Peter Tuska, *The Detective in Hollywood* (Garden City, N.Y.: Doubleday, 1978), p. 164.

33. Dashiell Hammett, "Zigzags of Treachery," in *Crime Stories and Other Writings* (New York: Library of America, 2001), p. 92. The dictionary definitions of *to shadow* come from the *Shorter Oxford English Dictionary*, 5th ed., vol. 2 (Oxford: Oxford University Press, 2002), p. 2783. For Gorky's famous remark, see his "The Kingdom of Shadows," in Gilbert Adair, *Movies* (London: Penguin, 1999), p. 10. Benjamin's descriptions of the *flâneur* and the detective come from

his book *Charles Baudelaire: A Lyric Poet in the Era of High Capitalism*, trans. Harry Zohn (London: Verso, 1983), pp. 38, 41–42.

Meet Me in St. Louis

1. For a useful summary of Minnelli's background, see Stephen Harvey, *Directed by Vincente Minnelli* (New York: Museum of Modern Art/ Harper and Row, 1989), pp. 25–35. Disagreement exists about Minnelli's role in sabotaging *Very Warm for May*. See, for example, Gerald Bordman, *Jerome Kern: His Life and Music* (New York: Oxford University Press, 1980), pp. 380–383, which blames producer Max Gordon. On the other hand, Hugh Fordin's *Getting to Know Him: A Biography of Oscar Hammerstein II* (New York: Random House, 1977), pp. 166–169, makes Minnelli the principal culprit.

    François Truffaut, "A Certain Tendency of the French Cinema," in *Movies and Methods*, ed. Bill Nichols (Berkeley: University of California Press, 1976), p. 233. For Wilder's comments about Mitchell Leisen, see Andrew Sarris, *"You Ain't Heard Nothin' Yet": The American Talking Film: History and Memory, 1927–1949* (New York: Oxford University Press, 1998), p. 332. Gerald Kaufman, *Meet Me in St. Louis* (London: British Film Institute, 1994), p. 40. Richard Dyer, "Entertainment and Utopia," in *Movies and Methods*, vol. 2, ed. Bill Nichols (Berkeley: University of California Press, 1985), pp. 222–223 (emphasis added).

2. Bertrand Russell, *The Problems of Philosophy* (Oxford: Oxford University Press, 1971), no page number.

3. The list of fair attractions comes from Marshall Everett, *The Book of the Fair* (Philadelphia: Ziegler, 1904). The Bad Lands story comes from Elana V. Fox, *Inside the World's Fair of 1904*, vol. 2 (n.p.: 1st Books, 2003), pp. 216–217.

4. Kael's remark appears in her book *5001 Nights at the Movies* (New York: Holt, 1985), p. 257.

5. Barthes uses the phrase "a vast 'dissolve'" to refer to his idea of "the text"; see *S/Z*, trans. Richard Miller (New York: Hill and Wang, 1974), p. 20. Walter Benjamin's remarks appear in his book *Charles Baudelaire: A Lyric Poet in the Era of High Capitalism*, trans. Harry Zohn

(London: Verso, 1973), pp. 51, 131–132. William R. Everdell, *The First Moderns* (Chicago: University of Chicago Press, 1997), p. 209.

6. See Minnelli's own account of his interest in the scene and Freed's initial eagerness to cut it in Vincente Minnelli, with Hector Arce, *I Remember It Well* (Hollywood, Calif.: Samuel French, 1990), pp. 129, 140. For Ulmer's remarks on mood, see Gregory L. Ulmer, *Internet Invention: From Literacy to Electracy* (New York: Longman, 2003), pp. 49, 59–61. Holmes's protosurrealist formulation appears not in the actual novel, *The Hound of the Baskervilles*, but in the BBC television series with Jeremy Brett.

7. Burch's analysis of *Tom, Tom, the Piper's Son* appears in his essay "Film's Institutional Mode of Representation and the Soviet Response," in *In and Out of Synch: The Awakening of a Cine-Dreamer*, trans. Ben Brewster (Aldershot, England: Scolar, 1991), pp. 118–119.

8. On the fair's racism, see William R. Everdell, *The First Moderns* (Chicago: University of Chicago Press, 1997), pp. 215–217. Roland Barthes, *S/Z*, trans. Richard Miller (New York: Hill and Wang, 1974), pp. 38, 172.

9. Andy Warhol, *The Philosophy of Andy Warhol* (New York: Harvest/HBJ, 1975), pp. 100–101. Anne Mendelson, *Stand Facing the Stove: The Story of the Women Who Gave America "The Joy of Cooking"* (New York: Holt, 1996).

10. Roland Barthes, "The Third Meaning," in *The Responsibility of Forms*, trans. Richard Howard (New York: Hill and Wang, 1985), pp. 41–62. André Bazin, *Jean Renoir*, ed. W. W. Halsey II and William H. Simon (New York: Delta, 1974), p. 86.

11. See Walter Benjamin's observation:

> A clock that is working will always be a disturbance on the stage. There it cannot be permitted its function of measuring time. Even in a naturalistic play, astronomical time would clash with theatrical time. Under these circumstances it is highly revealing that the film can, whenever appropriate, use time as measured by a clock. ("The Work of Art in the Age of Mechanical Reproduction," in *Illuminations*, trans. Harry Zohn [New York: Schocken, 1969], p. 247)

Cavell's remark comes from *The World Viewed* (Cambridge, Mass.: Harvard University Press, 1979), p. 23 (emphasis added).

12. Astor's remark comes from her book *A Life on Film* (New York: Delacorte, 1971), p. 126.

13. For Robert Desnos's remark, see Paul Hammond, ed., *The Shadow and Its Shadow: Surrealist Writings on the Cinema* (London: British Film Institute, 1978), p. 4.

14. Barthes's discussion of "hermeneutic enigmas" appears in *S/Z*, trans. Richard Miller (New York: Hill and Wang, 1974), p. 19. For discussions of MGM's problems with *Meet Me in St. Louis*'s initial lack of plot, see Thomas Schatz, *The Genius of the System: Hollywood Filmmaking in the Studio Era* (New York: Pantheon, 1988), pp. 372–374; Stephen Harvey, *Directed by Vincente Minnelli* (New York: Museum of Modern Art/Harper and Row, 1989), pp. 46–50; Hugh Fordin, *The World of Entertainment: Hollywood's Greatest Musicals* (Garden City, N.Y.: Doubleday, 1975), pp. 91–94. Charles Eckert, "The Anatomy of a Proletarian Film: Warner's *Marked Woman*," in *Movies and Methods*, vol. 2 (Berkeley: University of California Press, 1985), pp. 407–425. Eckert's essay contains a useful discussion of Lévi-Straussian structuralism. The George Jessel story appears in David Shipman, *Judy Garland: The Secret Life of an American Legend* (New York: Hyperion, 1993), p. 39. Shipman also speculates that "Garland" may have derived from the theater's movie *Twentieth Century*, whose heroine (played by Carole Lombard) changes her name from Lilly Plotka to Lily Garland. The movie's title, of course, refers to the train that connected New York with the West Coast.

15. The Benson passage appears in *Meet Me in St. Louis* (New York: Bantam, 1963), p. 13. For the Godard passage, I have used the translations provided by Alfred Guzzetti, *Two or Three Things I Know about Her: An Analysis of a Film by Godard* (Cambridge, Mass.: Harvard University Press, 1981), pp. 194–202 (the more literal rendering); and by Marianne Alexander, in *Godard: Three Films* (New York: Harper and Row, 1975), pp. 153–154 (the more idiomatic version).

16. Vincente Minnelli, *I Remember It Well* (Hollywood, Calif.: Samuel French, 1990), p. 134.

17. Roland Barthes, "The Reality Effect," in *The Rustle of Language*, trans. Richard Howard (New York: Hill and Wang, 1986), p. 141. The

quote from Benson appears in her *Meet Me in St. Louis* (New York: Bantam, 1963), p. 142.

18. Flaubert's remark about railways from his *Dictionnaire des idées reçues* (*Dictionary of Received Ideas*) appears in *Bouvard and Pécuchet*, trans. A. J. Krailsheimer (New York: Penguin, 1976), p. 323.

19. Nietzsche's remark comes from *The Gay Science*, trans. Walter Kaufmann (New York: Vintage, 1974), p. 343. Barthes's remarks appear in *Roland Barthes*, trans. Richard Howard (New York: Hill and Wang, 1977), pp. 94, 148.

20. Richard Dyer, "Entertainment and Utopia," in *Movies and Methods*, vol. 2, ed. Bill Nichols (Berkeley: University of California Press), p. 231. The information about Garland's MGM audition comes from Hugh Fordin, *The World of Entertainment: Hollywood's Greatest Musicals* (Garden City, N.Y.: Doubleday, 1975), p. 5.

21. For an account of Paul Poiret's fashion revolution, extended in the 1920s by Coco Chanel, see Peter Wollen, *Raiding the Icebox: Reflections on Twentieth Century Culture* (Bloomington: Indiana University Press, 1993), pp. 2–3, 20–21. One account of Margaret Sullavan's influence on Jimmy Stewart appears in Gary Fishgall, *Pieces of Time: The Life of James Stewart* (New York: Scribner's, 1997), p. 83. Patrick McGilligan's biography of Cukor maintains that the director "preferred the problem of toning down excesses to turning everything up a notch. 'Less' was one of his favorite directions." *George Cukor: A Double Life* (New York: St. Martin's, 1991), p. 163. Barry King's theory of "hyper-semioticisation" appears in his essay "Articulating Stardom," in *Stardom: Industry of Desire*, ed. Christine Gledhill (London: Routledge, 1991), p. 175. John Ellis's discussion of movie stars' need to underact comes from his essay "Stars as a Cinematic Phenomenon," in *Film Theory and Criticism*, ed. Leo Braudy and Marshall Cohen (New York: Oxford University Press, 1999), p. 546. For Cukor's anecdote about Lewis Milestone and Gary Cooper, see Gavin Lambert, *On Cukor* (New York: Rizzoli, 2000), p. 57.

22. Engels's remark comes from his famous April 1888 letter to Margaret Harkness, reprinted in *Marxist Literary Theory*, ed. Terry Eagleton and Drew Milne (Oxford: Blackwell, 1996), p. 40.

23. The information on the Parisian department stores comes from Stephen Bayley, ed., *Commerce and Culture* (London: Design Museum/Fourth Estate, 1989), pp. 46–49. The Zola quotation from *Au*

Bonheur des Dames is the April Fitzlyon translation, appearing in *Commerce and Culture*, p. 54; for a slightly different translation, see *Au Bonheur des Dames*, trans. Robin Buss (London: Penguin, 2001), p. 85. On "the chaotic-exotic," see Rosalind H. Williams, *Dream Worlds: Mass Consumption in Late Nineteenth-Century France* (Berkeley: University of California Press, 1982), p. 69. For Schickel's remarks about Minnelli and the director's about his preparation for *Meet Me in St. Louis*, see Richard Schickel, *The Men Who Made the Movies* (New York: Atheneum, 1975), pp. 243–244, 257. I have taken the idea of Cornell's order as "spiritual" from Lindsay Blair, *Joseph Cornell's Vision of Spiritual Order* (London: Reaktion, 1998). For Cornell's description of his boxes as "forgotten games" and his belief in the mystical correctness of certain arrangements, see Charles Simic, "Forgotten Games," *New York Review of Books*, 27 April 2000, pp. 4, 6. For a discussion of Cornell's valise, *The Crystal Cage: Portrait of Berenice*, and its connections to *Meet Me in St. Louis*, see Jodi Hauptman, *Joseph Cornell: Stargazing in the Cinema* (New Haven, Conn.: Yale University Press, 1999), pp. 174–175. Thoreau's "Why do precisely these objects which we behold make a world?" comes from the "Brute Neighbors" chapter of *Walden*. It also appears as the epigraph to Stanley Cavell's *The World Viewed* (Cambridge, Mass.: Harvard University Press, 1979).

24. Seymour Chatman, "What Novels Can Do That Films Can't (and Vice Versa)," in *Film Theory and Criticism*, ed. Leo Braudy and Marshall Cohen (New York: Oxford University Press, 1999), p. 438. On Fermat's theorem, see Amir D. Aczel, *Fermat's Last Theorem: Unlocking the Secret of an Ancient Mathematical Problem* (New York: Four Walls Eight Windows, 1996), p. 9.

25. On timbre and our inability to retain it, see Theodore Gracyk, *Rhythm and Noise: An Aesthetic of Rock* (Durham, N.C.: Duke University Press, 1996), pp. 59–61.

26. "I felt that the whole picture should have the look of Thomas Eakins's paintings, though not to the point of imitation." Vincente Minnelli, *I Remember It Well* (Hollywood, Calif.: Samuel French, 1990), p. 131. James Naremore's discussion of this point appears in his book *The Films of Vincente Minnelli* (Cambridge: Cambridge University Press, 1993), p. 75. The second Eakins painting referred to is *Max Schmitt in a Single Scull* (1871), which is in the Metropolitan Museum of Art.

Index

la politique des auteurs, xx, 19–20, 91–
    92, 160–61, 180–81
polycentricism, 14, 306
Pope Leo XII, 291
pornography, 151, 287
Porter, Cole, 285
Porter, Edwin S., 159–60, 199
poster, 221–22, *221*, 236
Potemkin, 25, 230, 292
Powell, William, 114, 163, 206, 237
Power, Tyrone, 154
Preminger, Otto, 20–21, 91, 160
Presley, Elvis, 46, 80
Pretty Lady (play), 247
Pretty Woman, 77
Preysing (in *Grand Hotel*)
    and *Blue Danube Waltz*, 10
    and Flaemmchen, 49, 51, 67, *67*,
        75–76
    German accent of, 82
    hotel room of, 65–66, 69
    as hypocritical capitalist, 71
    irrational enlargement questions
        about, 64
    and Kringelein, 76
    and "Manchester," 52–54, 67, 75
    murder of the Baron, 30, 71, 76
    and Saxonia negotiations, 27–28
Price of Possession, The, 264
Pride and Prejudice (Austen), 54–55,
    109, 123
primitive cinema, 14, 29, 170, 270–
    71
Principles of Scientific Management, The
    (Taylor), 31–33, 57
Problems of Philosophy, The (Russell),
    250
Production Code, 67, 73
product promotion, 76–77, 225
Prohibition Act, 87
prologue, 159, 195

prostitutes, 74, 75, 81
Public Enemy, 107
publicity, 76, 111–12, 136–37, 260

Quaker Girl, The (1911), 130
Quaker spirit, 130, 156
Quaker State Coal, 130, 131
Les Quatre Cents Coups, 137
quay, 222–23, *222*
Queen Christina (1933), 18, 34, *34*,
    35, 38
queer theory, 103
Quentin (in *Meet Me in St. Louis*), 319
questions, 62–64, 223, 300–301
quick swim, 131–32

racial purity, 17
racism, 278–79
Racket Busters (1938), 164
radio, 198–200, *198*, 235
Radio City Music Hall, 246
Raft, George, 229
Raiding the Icebox (Wollen), 8–9
rationality, 53–54, 187, 269
Rauschenberg, Robert, 321
Ray, Nicholas, 91, 160
RCA Victor, 76–77, *77*
realism
    Barthes on, 193
    Bazin on, 81, 175
    and characterization, 78–79
    and coffin scene, 14
    and curtains, 175
    and drunken man, 22–23
    and empty rooms, 66
    and Garland, 299
    and Germanness, 82–83
    and Honolulu, 191
    and irrational enlargement
        questions, 62–63
    and MGM's stylistic realm, 14